BEFORE
BRITTNEY

A Legacy of Champions

Dr. Nancy R. Goodloe

Sic 'Em, Lady Bears!

Nancy Goodloe

Produced by:

FriesenPress

Suite 300 – 852 Fort Street
Victoria, BC, Canada V8W 1H8

www.friesenpress.com

Distributed to the trade by The Ingram Book Company

Image of Suzie Snider-Eppers, Baylor Bearettes, 1973-1977 compliments of The Olga Fallen Collection, Box 38, Folder 9, The Texas Collection, Baylor University. Image of Brittney Griner, Lady Bear, 2009-2013, Compliments of the Baylor University Athletic Department, 2013.

CONTENTS

This book is dedicated to:

Mary E. Tindle, for 48 years,
Teacher,
Mentor,
Colleague
and
Friend

And to:

E.E. "Dutch" Schroeder,
#1 Fan,
Supporter,
and
Advocate
For Bearettes Everywhere!

Thanks to both of you...

ACKNOWLEDGEMENTS

I'm grateful to so many people for making this book happen. It truly has been a team effort to get the stories, to do the research and to put it all together. Kudos to Olga Fallen for collecting and storing hundreds of documents during her twenty-three year career as Women's Athletic Coordinator at Baylor. Much of the credit for the content of this book goes to the information found in these documents. Thanks to Dutch Schroeder, retired Baylor faculty member, these materials were submitted to John Wilson, Director of the Texas Collection, on the Baylor University campus.

To John Wilson, I tip my hat to you and your wonderful staff. I don't think I have ever worked on a project where I felt more supported for the work I was doing and where people genuinely were happy to address my every request. I know the front desk staff got tired of going down to the stacks to get different editions of the *Baylor Roundup* or another box from the Fallen Collection because I had forgotten to get that information the day before (or sometimes it was earlier in the same day) and needed the resource again. They retrieved the materials with smiles and a sense of humor, and we all got a good laugh about my memory challenges. Special thanks to Amanda Norman who guided my project and who searched on her own when I was trying to tie up some loose ends on those last few citations that I had to have. I'm also grateful to Geoff Hunt who got me started and taught me how to scan documents from the Collection, who worked with me collecting pictures from so many different sources, who showed me how to access the archival materials from the *Baylor Lariats* and *Roundups*.

I spent several days in the Blagg-Huey Library at Texas Woman's University in Denton, Texas. I owe a debt of gratitude to the staff in the Women's Collection. They were of great assistance reviewing the records of the Texas Commission for Intercollegiate Athletics for Women and the Texas Association for Intercollegiate Athletics for Women. These two organizations governed women's intercollegiate athletics in Texas during the sixties and seventies. The records in this collection provided information on the governing board meetings, the rules of competition, and the annual results of intercollegiate competition in each sport being played by the women's teams.

I interviewed over twenty people to get different parts of this story, some in person, some by phone. I taped the conversations and had their comments transcribed so I could get their details with accuracy. Their names are in Appendix II of the book. Every person willingly talked with me and spent hours sharing their part of this story. Every one of these folks is a champion in my mind, and I am thankful for the legacies they left.

I owe a special debt to Dutch Schroeder who helped me in a number of ways to bring this book to fruition. For one, he provided me with stories of athletes and teams during the decade of the seventies, in particular, stories that caused me to do more research and find the details, stories that enriched the content immeasurably. He introduced me to Betty Rogers who played on the first intercollegiate tennis team in the 1950s and to LaRuth Kendrick Gates, a member of the first women's basketball team at Baylor University. Betty shared a great story about the four women who played tennis for Baylor in the 1950s. The pictures LaRuth sent me are included in Chapter 3 of the book. And, finally, Dutch helped find the financial support to get this book published. Financial contributions from Mary Tindle, Sara Lou Bracken, Jeanne Nowlin, Debbie Bradley Mann, Bearette Letterwinner, and anonymous contributions in honor of Bearette Letterwinners, Karen Aulenbacher and Debra Routh were greatly appreciated.

I am indebted to Marisa Humphrey for the incredible editing job she did on my manuscript. Your insights and suggestions were fantastic and amazing, given that you knew nothing about the story and very little about women's athletics. This book is better because of your work.

I would like to acknowledge the support I received from the Baylor University Athletic department. They gave permission for me to use and helped locate most of the photos in Chapters 10 and 12 and on the front cover.

To the former Baylor athletes who contributed your stories to this book, I thank you for taking the time to write down those memories. They added the personal touch I was looking for in many of the chapters. To the many friends and colleagues who helped in so many ways, thank you.

To my Texas family, particularly my brother, David, thanks for all the rides to and from DFW airport and for the use of the family car. What an incredible gift you gave me.

Finally, to Dr. Melody Madlem, thank you for your support on this project. You have encouraged me and supported me in the many hours, days and weekends required to do the writing and travel. I couldn't begin to tell you how much I appreciate you.

INTRODUCTION

November 2012: Two minutes left in the game. Baylor Lady Bears, #1 in the nation, vs. the U Conn Huskies, #3 in the nation….whose idea was it to play this game in November anyway? This looks more like the NCAA Final Four tournament!

Baylor up by two. Brittney Griner, pre-season All American, and 2012 Naismith Award winner, has come alive in this second half, scoring 21 points. Griner only needs four points to go over 3000 career points in her Baylor career. Pass into Griner on the left side, she turns she shoots, she scores! Baylor by four. Two minutes to go. Griner needs two points. Pass to Griner, feeds off to Williams. Shoots scores. Baylor leads 71–67. 1:05 on the clock. Feed to Brittney. She is fouled. Her chance at the 3000-point record will come at the foul line. She bounces the ball, focuses and lets it fly. It's good! The second shot goes right through the bottom of the net as well, and Brittney Griner has reached another career milestone for her—3000 career points. A few minutes later, Baylor wins the game, 76–70. Fans exalt over the potential preview of things to come at the NCAA Tournament in April.

So, who is this Brittney Griner? Kim Mulkey had a pretty good idea of Griner's potential when she recruited her in 2009, but even Mulkey may have been surprised at exactly how much Brittney would mature and develop as a player in her four-year career at Baylor University. One could say that Griner is the greatest female basketball player that ever played the game, and many people would agree. She is certainly the most decorated female basketball player in the history of Baylor University. In April 2012, with Griner's help, the Baylor University Lady Bears won the NCAA Division I National Basketball

Championship. This championship was the second title since the beginning of the twenty-first century for Kim Mulkey's Lady Bears. The 2012 team went undefeated and won forty games in the 2011-12 season. This feat had never been accomplished by any other National Collegiate Athletic Association (NCAA) basketball team (men or women's). Ironically, both of these accomplishments occurred in the 40th anniversary year of Title IX, the 1972 legislation that required equal opportunity for women in sport at the high school and collegiate levels. What a perfect way to celebrate the passage of this legislation!

Brittney Griner finished her Baylor basketball career in 2013 having scored 3,283 points, 1,305 rebounds and 748 blocked shots. Her record for blocked shots is the highest for any woman ever to play the game. The list of additional honors she received and records she broke is exhaustive. She brought incredible prestige and success to Baylor women's athletics. She was the number one draft pick in the 2012 Women's National Basketball Association draft. She currently plays for the Phoenix Mercury.

In contrast, few basketball fans ever heard of Suzie Snider-Eppers. Snider-Eppers also played basketball for Baylor University and was also the most decorated Baylor female basketball player in her time. That time period, however, was the mid-1970s. The Association for Intercollegiate Athletics for Women (AIAW) governed women's intercollegiate competition during this time, not the NCAA. This Association also was not well known. Snider-Eppers was Baylor University's first female athlete to be awarded an athletic scholarship. She still holds the career scoring and rebounding record for women's basketball at Baylor University. Snider-Eppers scored 3,861 points, and snagged 2,176 rebounds in her career. She was the first female All-American at Baylor, being named to the 1977 State Farm/WCBA All-American first team. Snider received little prominence because she played under the auspices of the AIAW, with little prestige at this time. However, she recently was honored at the 2013 NCAA Division I Women's Basketball Championship game for being the highest scoring basketball player in the history of women's intercollegiate basketball.

When Brittney Griner arrived on the Baylor campus in 2009, she represented a recruiting milestone for Coach Kim Mulkey. In 1973, Suzie Snider-Eppers represented an unprecedented milestone for Coach Olga Fallen. Brittney Griner led her team to a national championship in basketball. Suzie Snider led her team to two national basketball tournament appearances and a fifth place finish in 1977. Brittney Griner was the national player of the year in 2012 and 2013. Suzie Snider was the AIAW National Shot Put champion in 1975. Brittney Griner was a Lady Bear. Suzie Snider was a Baylor Bearette.

Both Brittney and Suzie were champions; both took Baylor programs to championship levels. Both created peer champions, both were led and supported throughout their college careers by champions. Both stories make it clear that it takes champions to make champions. This is what this book is all about—Baylor University has always had champions—athletes, coaches, decision-makers, and alumni. Their stories are told in the following pages.

In developing this book, I wanted to do two things: First, it was important to me to document the team members and accomplishments of the Baylor Bearettes through the sixties and seventies. These women provided the shoulders on which the women's programs of today stand. Having been a Bearette and having coached Bearettes, I played a role in those accomplishments. I wanted to honor those who played the games, who coached the teams and who advocated in Baylor's halls of ivy for women to have the same opportunities in athletics as the men did. These persons, men and women, were all champions. They all left a legacy. This is their story.

For the female intercollegiate athletes in this country who played prior to 1982 (when the National Collegiate Athletic Association took control of women's intercollegiate athletics), the records of their accomplishments may or may not be filed away in libraries across this country. There are no websites or media guides with information from that era. Some of these records may be gathering dust stashed away in storage rooms and closets, in private homes or university archives. These names and their team accomplishments are not easy to find. It was important to me that the names that belong to Baylor be organized and captured as part of this book. Those names, the personal stories of former Baylor athletes, and the won-loss records of those teams are found in Chapters 3, 4, and 6. Pictures of these teams and/or individuals are included as they were available. Those who played for the Bearettes will read these chapters with great anticipation. The intent of these chapters was to capture in perpetuity as much information on the players and teams of the sixties and seventies that was available.

Secondly, the story of how Baylor University's women's athletic program came from humble beginnings in the early twentieth century to its current position of national prominence plays out against the larger national struggle within the leadership of women's athletics for the recognition women leaders believed should come to women athletes. This struggle began as a philosophical issue but ultimately became a struggle against the cultural, political and socio-economic ideas and realities of American society. It was the late 1980s before these forces abated. The reader will discover that it took nearly seventy years for the leadership of women's athletics in this country to gain the recognition and respect they wanted. When the Association for Intercollegiate Athletics for Women (AIAW) was born in 1972, the leadership believed they had "arrived". However, these women soon realized that putting this organization in place was only the first step in a new struggle for recognition.

Two things lurked in the background and challenged the very core of these pioneering women: the Title IX legislation in 1972 and the quest for control of AIAW by the NCAA. Chapter 1 provides an overview of how the AIAW was created, the philosophical underpinnings that separated it from the NCAA, and how the leadership battled with the NCAA for almost ten years before the NCAA took control of women's intercollegiate athletics forever. Chapter 2 covers the Title IX legislation, explaining the mandates it established for colleges and university athletic programs and the legal challenges it faced. Included in this chapter is a discussion of how Title IX challenged the very existence of the AIAW.

In Chapter 4, 5 and 6, the reader will follow Baylor's struggle with Title IX, noting that Baylor's administrative leaders opposed the legislation on three fronts. First, there was a religious struggle for the leadership. Baylor University was a private, Southern Baptist school. Abner McCall, Baylor University President in 1972, believed strongly that Title IX violated some of the basic tenets of the Southern Baptist faith, i.e. Southern Baptists did not ordain female pastors. Secondly, the Baylor leadership believed the law only pertained to college programs that received federal financial aid. In their minds, since the athletic department did not receive this aid, the University should not be subjected to the requirements of the law. Finally, the Baylor administration knew that there was little to no funding for a women's athletic program. Like many university administrators, Abner McCall, President, was convinced the legislation was going to ruin collegiate athletics.

Baylor University was only one of many universities that responded negatively to the Title IX legislation and its implementation. These universities were helped in the eighties by the politics of the Reagan administration, its efforts to weaken the civil rights legislation of the sixties and seventies, and several Appellate and Supreme Court rulings that muddled the national landscape on Title IX. It took a bipartisan act of Congress in 1988 before Title IX became the law of the land and all universities with athletic programs were forced to comply with the regulations.

The reader will see how the Baylor leadership's stall tactics through the seventies, eighties, and to some extent the nineties impacted the growth and success of the women's athletic program. If not for the people who coached the teams during these years, Baylor's legacy of champions could not be written. Credit must be given to these individuals, the players and the coaches. They wrote a story of struggle, dedication and perseverance for the love of the game and a commitment to equity for women in athletics. The coaches had no other incentives to work with the women athletes, to give the time and energy it took to coach these teams, to travel, to plan, to motivate. Salaries were poor, athletic facilities for the women were worse. There was limited financial support for team travel, equipment, and supplies. These individuals dealt with all of these barriers in the face of an administration and athletic leadership that provided no advocacy and no recognition for their work. They were champions. These stories are told in Chapters 4, 6, 8, and 10.

Baylor's turnaround in terms of support for women's athletics began in the nineties. Several events lined up during this decade to make things happen, and many faculty and staff on the campus served in significant positions to effect this change. Taken alone, none of these events or the work of these people would have changed the tide of women's athletics, but working in sequence everything came together to cause the perfect storm. Across the board, funding for all of the programs, men and women's, increased. By the end of the decade Baylor was very close to being in compliance with Title IX. The losing culture that had so dominated Baylor sports for years was gone. Now, Baylor alums, faculty, staff and students expected victory from each team, each year. The athletic department had become a highly functioning business, producing the funding needed for this cultural turnaround. The traditional philosophy of allocating revenues was changed to a philosophy of equity for all programs, especially for the women. Traditional revenue avenues were expanded. Fundraising for specific programs was the name of the game. Marketing strategies were strengthened. A sustainable system for funding Baylor athletics emerged. This system grew and strengthened and remains today. Numerous champions for Baylor athletics emerged during this time. Their story is told in Chapter 9.

As a result of these changes in funding for athletics, alumni willing to provide financial support to Baylor athletics emerged. They were the Financial Champions. They gave the money to fund the tremendous athletic facilities on the Baylor campus today. An explosion of facility construction began in the mid-nineties and continues into 2012. Chapters 10 and 11 describe this building campaign and include pictures of some of the facilities. By 2012 Baylor University had built some of the finest athletic facilities in the country. That building campaign continues on the campus in 2013.

In 2000 the Office of Civil Rights declared that Baylor University was in compliance with the mandates of Title IX. Chapter 11 chronicles how this level of financial and public relations support has impacted the Baylor women's athletic program growth in the number of teams available for women as well as the steady progression of each team toward the national prominence these women have in 2012. How Baylor officials made the decision to increase their women's opportunities and what these opportunities would be are discussed. The reader will relive key accomplishments of women's teams and individuals since 2000. In 2011, the Year of the Bear, all eleven women's teams qualified for postseason NCAA play. In 2012 the women won national championships in basketball and Hunter Seat.

It took a team of champions to build what Baylor University experiences today in the successes of its women's athletic programs. The legacy of these former champions laid the foundation for the national recognition and prestige Baylor University women's athletics enjoys in 2012. The great athletes, the great coaches, the great leaders and advocates, and the generous Baylor alumni deserve recognition for their contributions. This book chronicles their story through the 2011-2012 academic year.

CHAPTER 1

WOMEN'S SPORT IN AMERICA: THE BACKDROP, 1900–1972

OVERVIEW

The story of how women's athletics at Baylor University developed and grew in the twentieth century has its own nuances, but it is essentially the story of every woman's intercollegiate athletic program in America. Until the late fifties and early sixties, there were no formal intercollegiate athletic programs for women at any university in America. Several things had to happen for women to have the same kind of opportunities to compete against each other as their male counterparts had had for decades. Among those were (1) the female leadership had to have the national conversations about women's athletics, (2) traditional and stereotypical views of women in our society had to change, and (3) legislative action mandating equal opportunities for women in the workplace and on the athletic fields had to happen. It took the first seventy-two years of the twentieth century before all of these events happened. In the course of those years, a great national story emerged, and hundreds of smaller stories played out on college campuses across this country. This book is Baylor's story.

This chapter describes the cultural and political events that provided a dramatic backdrop for the development of women's intercollegiate athletics in this country. Along the way there were many champions for women's athletics that participated in the myriad of conversations, meetings, discussions, and committees that led to the development of the first national structure for governing women's intercollegiate athletic, the Association for Intercollegiate Athletics for Women (AIAW). These champions were particularly notable in the sixties and seventies as women began to develop this structure, at the same time fighting off attempts by the National Collegiate Athletic Association (NCAA) to take control of this organization. Beyond these events was the passage of Title IX of the Education Amendments of 1972. This piece of legislation and its influence on women's athletics is discussed against the backdrop of these events in Chapter 2.

EARLY CULTURAL INFLUENCES—1880-1900

Victorian culture prevailed during the nineteenth century in America. Men dominated society and were expected to be aggressive and independent with the capacity for reason and action. Men's ideas of culture, politics, science and religion strongly influenced society's thinking, and people in American lived as a patriarchal society. Because they were in the power positions, men made all the decisions that ultimately influenced women's worth, their health, and their civil rights. Deciding that women were irrational, sensitive and dutiful, men enacted laws that prevented women from working, owning property and making a living wage. Thus, the only place for women in this society was as a wife and mother in the home. In most instances a woman married because it was literally her only way to survive.[1]

As the era progressed, these strict societal norms began to ease, and women found more opportunities to step out of the homemaker role and into a wage-earning occupation. The expansion of travel and leisure opportunities served to broaden horizons for both men and women, but the predominant role for women continued to be in the home.

The first opportunities to attend college/university in America were given to men beginning in the early 1600s. From that time until the 1860s, the sight of a woman on a college campus was rare indeed. All of this changed in the last half of the nineteenth century, however, as women moved out of the house and onto the campus. A woman who went to college was considered a crusader, one who challenged the traditional view of women in society and one who wanted to prove that women had equal mental and physical ability to men. These women believe in their right to have these opportunities and many of the schools they attended were private schools developed specifically for women. Among these were the Hartford Female Seminary, the Rockford Female Seminary, the

Chicago Normal School and the Cincinnati Female Seminary. School like these trained the first female physical educators in this country and infused into these women two very important values about women's sport: (1) women should train women and (2) women's physical activity programs should be separate and autonomous from the men's. This idea of autonomy was a significant value that female physical educators carried into the twentieth century and passed on to those who took the leadership in the development of women's intercollegiate athletic programs. There continues to be pockets of women who espouse this belief in modern society. It was certainly a basic tenet of the female leaders that fought for equity in women's intercollegiate athletics.

By the late 1800s women also found an outlet for expansion of their experiences through the volunteer movement. Bringing them out of their home and providing additional opportunities to meet other women, volunteerism enabled women to find challenging and rewarding experiences. In the volunteer movement were the roots of social reform resulting in legislative and educational efforts to improve the welfare of women in America. By 1890 a New Woman had emerged in this country, a woman with a college education and job skills, and one with a choice to become a wage earner and/or a household caretaker.[2]

The Victorian notion that women were the weaker sex was based on the knowledge that, anatomically, the female body had less muscular strength than men, less lung capacity, and smaller hearts. The conservation of energy theory espoused the notion that each human had a set amount of energy dispersed throughout the body. This energy was allocated as needed based on the way one lived and worked during the day. Women's reproductive processes dominated her energy needs and limited energy for anything else. Sport and play were not viewed as legitimate activities for women because of this scientific theory. Women were viewed as easily prone to emotional breakdowns and physical exhaustion. By this reasoning if women did anything beyond their homemaker duties, they would break down and not be able to provide the nurture and support needed for their families.[3] Added to this thinking was the cultural value of sport espoused by Theodore Roosevelt—that sport existed for men, to make men more masculine and aggressive.

Catherine Beecher, 1800–1878, the first female leader in physical education for women rebuked these prevailing beliefs and embraced the notion that women were stronger physically, mentally and morally when they were active with their bodies. While Beecher believed women could do more to develop their bodies physically, she coined the word calisthenics from the Greek words for beautiful and strength and put her exercise routines to music. Beecher's system of exercise was the first system designed by an American for residents of this country.[4] It was widely popular on university campuses.

By the late twentieth century most colleges and universities in America had an intramural sport program for women students along with a formal intercollegiate athletic program for their male students. Within the intramural structure the sport that caught on the quickest and was played the most consistently was women's basketball.

Following Catherine Beecher, one of the early female physical educators at the turn of the century was Senda Berenson. A member of the faculty at Smith College, Berenson is credited with starting women's basketball in the United States in 1892. She had learned the game from James Naismith at the YMCA Training School in Springfield, Massachusetts and had adapted the men's rules so that women students could play. Not only did Berenson invent the women's game of basketball, she was a strong supporter of the value of autonomy for women in sport learned through her training. Berenson rose to a national leadership role in women's sport because of the popularity of the game of basketball with female students across the country. She influenced the values that would drive the development of women's sports for almost seventy years.

Berenson disliked the "male" model of athletics at the time, the win-at-all-cost philosophy prevalent in men's athletics, particularly football, and so designed her game to emphasize sportsmanship and teamwork. In 1900 she cautioned:

> Unless we guard our athletics carefully
> in the beginning, many objectionable
> elements will quickly come in...
> {and} the great desire to win and the
> excitement of the game will make our
> women do sadly unwomanly things [5]

The rules of Berenson's game differed considerably from those of today but women played the game with great enthusiasm and a desire to win.

The game caught on quickly and by 1895, hundreds of women had played the game at many of the teacher training schools on the east coast. Its popularity easily spread to the west coast. Two of the first women's intercollegiate basketball games that garnered the most publicity during this time period occurred within a week of each other in April 1896. These games featured California-Berkeley against Stanford and the University of Washington (UW) against the Ellensburg Normal School. Stanford won their game, 2-1, and Washington beat the Ellensburg Normal School 6-3.[6] While these scores may seem odd by today's standards, it must be remembered that the rules of the game were very different in its formative years. For example, the teams had nine players, each player assigned to a specific section of the court. There were no set plays to run such as we have today, and only certain players were able to shoot the ball. As well, the skills of the women, the lack of practice regimens, the length of the games, all impacted the scoring.

GOVERNANCE BEGINS WITH RULES

In its early beginnings there were no standardized rules for women's basketball. Women relied on the men's rules as a starting point but Berenson modified them considerably for women's competition. Depending on where the game was played, the rules could be modified further by the host school, e.g. the size of the game ball. By 1899 it was obvious to those involved in the sport that a standard set of rules for women was needed. Toward this end, the American Physical Education Association (APEA), the national governing body for physical education professionals, formed the Women's Basketball Rules Committee. This group met in Springfield, Massachusetts to formulate these rules that became the first governance structure for women's athletics in this country. It was decided that Spalding's Athletic Library, the publisher of the men's rules, would also publish the women's. Furthermore, it was recommended that Senda Berenson be the editor for the publication. Berenson's appointment, while surprising in athletic circles of the day, made perfect sense by APEA standards. After all she was a physical educator, a member of APEA, and had gained notoriety within the group from her publications and speeches on women's basketball. Spalding published the first set of rules for women in 1901. Senda Berenson remained as editor of this publication until 1917.[7] It was widely popular on university campuses.

For the next fifty years, the leadership and efforts toward the governance of women's athletics would remain among the ranks of the female physical education professionals in the colleges and universities in America. The Women's Basketball Rules Committee and the APEA morphed several times in that time span, becoming the Division of Girls and Women's Sport (DGWS) and the American Association for Health, Physical Education and Recreation (AAHPER) in 1957. By this time DGWS was a powerful organization, standardizing rules and regulations for every woman's sport and producing an annual rules manual for each sport. These rules guided women's sports through the play days and sports days of the thirties, forties and fifties, and became the standard for the extramural competition of the sixties. The authors of these rulebooks continued to espouse the early philosophical underpinnings of women's sports started by Beecher and affirmed by Berenson, and the rules reflected these values.[1]

PLAY DAYS AND SPORTS DAYS

The early programs for women in colleges and universities were dominated by intramural competitions among the women. However, as physical education courses for women became a standard on college and university campuses, a more highly skilled female athlete emerged. These athletes wanted more competition and opportunities to utilize their skill training. By the late twenties and early thirties, the play days concept for women on college campuses had emerged. With play days, teams of women from universities (primarily women physical education majors and minors) would gather on a designated campus for a day, choose up sides, and compete in a variety of contests, i.e. team sports such as basketball, volleyball, field hockey, and individual sports such as tennis, bowling, and archery.

While these venues provided outlets for skilled women to display their talent, the real value behind these play day competitions was the socialization of the athletes. The slogan for these events was: A Sport for Every Girl and Every Girl in a Sport. Winning was not the objective. These play days did, however, represent the first opportunities for women to travel to other schools, meet

---

1 For a more detailed timeline of the metamorphosis of women's athletic governance structures in the United States, see Appendix I.

other women, and participate in a variety of sport competitions. By 1930 and into the forties most colleges and universities in America were participating in play days.

Sports days followed on the heels of plays, during the 1950s, ushering in the first significant opportunities for intercollegiate competition for women. With sports days, university women formed a team, traveled to another university, and competed as a team in several individual and teams sports against athletes from one or more universities. At these competitions, points were given for first, second and third place teams/individual placements in each event. The team whose collective victories in individual and teams sports garnered more points than the other participating teams was the overall winner. The hallmark of these sports days was that the teams were not coached, at least not in the sense that we think of coaching today. Prior to the sports day, there were no formal team practices, no strategy sessions, and no planned plays for specific situations. Coaching during a sports day event consisted primarily of game management types of activities, i.e. calling timeouts and making substitutions. Sports days extended well into the 1950's on many campuses and eventually morphed into extramural (outside of school) athletics for the women in the early 1960s.

INTERCOLLEGIATE ATHLETICS FOR WOMEN—1917-1941

As women's sport opportunties grew in number and popularity, the notion of women competing intercollegiately like the men began to emerge. The first effort to have a national conversation about women's college athletics began in 1917 at the University of Wisconsin. Blanche M. Trilling, Director of Physical Education for Women, and student members of the Women's Athletic Association (WAA), organized a meeting of representatives from colleges and universities in the Midwest to come together and discuss common sports aims, objectives and problems. Labeled the Athletic Conference of American College Women (ACACW), this meeting was so popular that WAA student leaders and their faculty physical education directors continued these meetings for the next twenty years. Members of this group became the national spokespersons for what women's college sports should be -- intramurals, NOT intercollegiate programs. They espoused the philosophy of the early pioneers and provided members with the tools and ideas to build strong women's intramural programs at their universities.

Membership in the Women's Athletic Associations (WAA) on college campuses was composed of physical education majors and minors. The groups actively solicited intramural participation for women on their campuses, providing instruction to the female students on the rules of various sports and teaching the skills of the game.[8]

By 1933 the conversation about women's competitive athletics for colleges and universities had gained momentum. Trilling's organization, the ACACW, had changed its name to the Athletic and Recreation Federation of College Women (ARFCW). This organization continued ACACW's original stand against varsity athletics for women. Their purpose was to uphold the standard of athletics for girls and women as set forth originally by the original Women's Basketball Committee and Senda Berenson. Intercollegiate athletic programs for women were not encouraged. Strong intramural programs for women were the focus.

In spite of the fact that these two national groups did not support intercollegiate competition for women, not all physical education leaders in the country agreed with this position. In 1941 Gladys Palmer from the Ohio State University approached two national organizations, the National Section on Women's Sports (NSWA)[2] and the National Association of Physical Education for College Women (NADPECW), and asked them to create a national governing body to regulate competitive intercollegiate athletics for women. The NSWA, evolved from the 1899 Women's Basketball Committee, represented the rules-making body for women's sport. The NADPECW, formed in 1924, consisted of the female leaders charged with the administration of the women's physical education programs on college campuses.[3] Palmer and her associates wanted the support of both of these groups to host a national collegiate

2   See Appendix 1 Timeline

3   Author's note: I am confident that the membership of NADPECW and ARFCW overlapped. I believe Palmer was hoping that the NADPECW would take a different position on intercollegiate competition for women since this group represented the academic programs where most highly skilled athletes were trained to teach and coach.

8

golf tournament. Neither organization agreed to the request. The NADPECW issued the following position statement:

> Since one institution has sent a letter to members, stating the belief that a need exists for opportunities in competition for college women of superior skill, and recommends the formation of a Women's Collegiate Athletic Association, the NADPECW has considered the matter and states its position as follows:
>
> We believe that the needs of competition can be met in more advantageous ways than in competition on a national basis and therefore consider national tournaments inadvisable.
>
> We do not approve the formation of a national organization which would tend to increase the number of varsity competitions.[9]

In spite of the resistance from both national organizations, Palmer and her colleagues at Ohio State decided to move forward with their idea and launched the first National Collegiate Golf Tournament in 1941. Thirty college women from across the country participated in the event. So successful was the event that Palmer and her colleagues at Ohio State were commended by the NSWA, but neither the NSWA nor the NADPECW reversed their positions on intercollegiate competition for women. The National Collegiate Golf Tournament was not held from 1942–1945, in deference to World War II. It returned in 1946 and continued as the only national intercollegiate event for women until 1967. It's presence forced the conversation in the early sixties about a national governing body for women's intercollegiate sport, leading to the establishment of the Commission on Intercollegiate Athletics for Women in 1966.

CULTURAL AND LEGAL CHANGES IMPACT WOMEN'S SPORT

With the advent of World War II and the draft, the American workforce needed replacements to continue manufacturing and production efforts. For the first time in history, women went to work with the blessing of society. "Rosie the Riveter" became the icon for women in the workplace as women held down men's jobs and became independent and strong-willed. Women embraced their roles as the breadwinners and heads of the household but also relished in their new freedom to make independent decisions and be successful. A cultural shift had happened as a new day for women in this country began. In spite of cultural pressure to return to the home after the war, many women continued in the workplace even though the best and highest paying jobs went to the men who had returned from the war.[10]

Several events and movements reinforced the new roles of women in our society during the sixties and seventies. The Women's liberation movement was born and grew up during the this time period. Legislation such as the Equal Protection Clause of the Fourteenth Amendment broadened its protection provisions to include gender. Legal tools provided by The Equal Pay Act of 1963 and the 1964 Civil Rights Act helped women combat race and sex discrimination in the workplace.

The Vietnam War birthed a generation of young people who questioned authority, who sought a better way to live in peace and harmony. Organizations such as the National Organization for Women (NOW) and the Women's Equity Action League (WEAL) helped catalyze the feminist movement and strengthen women's roles in our society.

Correspondingly, during this time the American Medical Association reversed an earlier stand on women and physical activity. Instead of cautioning women about the dangers of vigorous activity and competition, they heartily endorsed the benefits of this type of activity for health and well-being. In college physical education programs, instructional focus was on developing fitness, strength and conditioning for productive living. Programs emphasizing fitness for peace, vigorous activity, and competitive values were common.

Title IX of the Education Amendments Act of 1972 provided equal access to employment and promotional opportunities for women on the college campuses. This legislation complemented the Civil Rights Act of 1964, providing equal access to jobs and opportunities for women in educational settings. Reforms in the job market, education, and family life followed. Women were out of their traditional roles and actively seeking opportunities in every area of life. Resultantly, women athletes redefined themselves, and women's intercollegiate athletic programs sprung up all over the country.

WOMEN'S INTERCOLLEGIATE ATHLETICS—1946-1982

When the National Collegiate Golf Tournament resumed in 1946 and became an annual event, a more supportive environment for women's competitive sports in this country existed. Women had more of a 'bring it on' attitude. In the meantime a younger generation of women physical educators had come on the scene and were driving a different agenda for the NWSA/DGWS.[4] These women had lived through the play days of the past. They taught highly skilled female athletes and they wanted competitive opportunities for these women. Sports days became the venue for this competition, followed by extramural programs in the early sixties.

The success of the National Collegiate Golf tournament and the evolution of women's extramural programs led to the need for a more formal structure to continue the tournament and govern this extramural competition. In response, the National Association of Physical Education for College Women (NAPECW), the National Section for Girls and Women's Sport (NSGWS), and the American Federation of College Women (AFCW),[5][6] formed the Tripartite Committee in 1956. This group became the National Joint Committee for Extramural Sports for Women (NJCESW) in 1957. The purpose of this body was to guide and administer the women's extramural athletic programs that had begun in earnest. However, the NJCESW, only able to function in a limited capacity, disbanded in

4 The NSWA became the Division of Girls and Women's Sport (DGWS) in 1957.

5 The National Section for Women's Athletics became the National Section for Girls and Women's Sport (NSGWS) in 1953. NSGWS becomes the Division of Girls and Women's Sport (DGWS) in 1957.

6 The American Federation of College Women was formerly the American Recreation Federation of College Women.

1965 and delegated its functions to the DGWS. These leaders quickly realized they were not prepared to provide a governing structure for women's intercollegiate athletics either. They asked their parent body, the American Association for Health, Physical Education, and Recreation (AAHPER) to step in and solve this problem. Although the DGWS leadership now supported athletic competition for intercollegiate women, they adopted a position in 1965 against providing athletic scholarships for college women.

THE STRUGGLE FOR RECOGNITION: NATIONAL CHAMPIONSHIPS

Responding to the pressure from the NJCESW and the DGWS, the AAHPER established the Commission on Intercollegiate Athletics for Women (CIAW) in 1966 the first national governing body for women's intercollegiate sport. The Commission became an arm of DGWS in the AAHPER governing structure. The Commission had three Commissioners with three additional members of an executive board. All were women and all had come from the ranks of the American Association for Health, Physical Education, and Recreation (AAHPER). All were educators and coaches. Their task was to create a national championship structure for women's intercollegiate athletics. The Commission became operational in 1967.[11]

Moving quickly, the CIAW announced a schedule for new national intercollegiate championships in December 1967 to include the National Collegiate Golf Tournament. Finally, college women had a path to national championships as the CIAW implemented a sanctioned structure for women at the local, state, regional and national levels. By 1968 the CIAW sponsored its first national championship – tennis—and by 1970-71, the CIAW was sponsoring national championships in seven sports – gymnastics, track and field, volleyball, speedball, swimming, badminton, golf, and basketball.

In addition to developing a structure for national championships, the Commission had multiple purposes:

1. To provide a framework and organizational pattern for intercollegiate athletics for women at the state, regional and national levels;

2. To develop and publish guidelines and standards for the conduct of these sports;

3. To sanction tournaments;

4. To conduct national championships for college and university women.[12]

Additionally, the Commission established policies and procedures for conducting national championships, established a committee to select the sites for the championships, established a mechanism allowing technical advisory committees to be used at the various championships, and established regional qualifying events for the national championships.

Part of the discussions in developing national championships included extensive consideration of the notion of having athletic scholarships for women. In 1966, it was common knowledge that some colleges and universities were awarding these scholarships to women, albeit under questionable circumstances, so there was some support for making this a CIAW policy. The question for CIAW leaders was do we allow these schools to participate in our national championship events? Because of their 1965 position against women's athletic scholarships, the DGWS pressured the CIAW not to allow schools that awarded athletic scholarships to compete in CIAW sanctioned events. The CIAW conceded this point and in its 1968 Procedures for Women's Intercollegiate Athletic Events, the CIAW stated that scholarships based solely on a woman's athletic ability were not allowed and that any woman receiving an athletic scholarship was not allowed to participate in CIAW events.[13]

Other eligibility rules under the CIAW were:

a. Student must be an amateur;

b. Student must be a fulltime undergraduate who maintains the academic average required for participation in all other major campus activities at her institution;

c. Transfer students are immediately eligible for participation following enrollment;

d. Student cannot participate more than four times in the same national championship.

e. No scholarship or financial assistance specifically designated for women athletes.[14]

Because of these strong efforts against awarding scholarships to women, the CIAW did not address recruiting. Their rationale was simple. If there were no scholarships, there would be no recruiting issues.

Within two years, the leadership of the CIAW realized that a six member Board of Directors could not possibly develop the structure, power and financial resources needed to govern women's intercollegiate athletics on a national scale. A membership-based organization was needed to make the important policy decisions necessary for this structure. The CIAW members approached the DGWS and AAHPER leadership and began discussions about how to evolve to this next level of governance. The CIAW Board of Directors had done valuable work and had laid the groundwork for a national governing organization for women's intercollegiate athletics going forward. Perhaps their greatest contribution was realizing a different, more powerful structure was needed if women's intercollegiate sport was going to get the national recognition it deserved.

ASSOCIATION OF INTERCOLLEGIATE ATHLETICS FOR WOMEN – 1972–1982

Following a series of meetings and discussions with AAHPERD and DGWS leaders, the CIAW became the Association for Intercollegiate Athletics for Women (AIAW) in 1971. AIAW became operational in June 1972.

During the 1971-72 academic year, AIAW solicited charter memberships. A school or university could elect to be an active member or could opt for an associate membership. Only active members could participate in championship events, however, and vote on policy matters at the annual meetings. Two hundred and seventy-six institutions obtained charter memberships during the first year.[15] Baylor University was not a charter member of AIAW but did join quickly and sent representatives to all annual Delegate Assemblies beginning with the inaugural Assembly in 1973.

The AIAW model for women's intercollegiate athletics maintained the philosophical positions of the CIAW and the DGWS, tracing its origins back to Senda Berenson in 1892. AIAW members wanted a student-centered, 'sport for all' model for college athletics and denounced the more commercial, win-at-all cost, model of the men's governing organization, the NCAA. They also wanted women to control this intercollegiate athletic structure.

Student athletes in AIAW institutions were expected to be students first, and athletes second. Their participation in collegiate athletics was viewed as a privilege. The educational benefits of this participation came not only from the athlete's ability to earn a college degree but also from the value placed on her participation and the personal and social satisfaction gained from excellence in sport performance.

Structurally, AIAW divided the country into the nine regions. Each region was divided into states, each state into districts or zones. Teams played through the district/zone structure to the state to the regional tournament to qualify for the national tournament in each sport. The winner of the state tournament advanced to the regional; the winner here advanced to the national tournament.[16] More information on this state and regional structure follows in later pages.

Operationally, the AIAW had four standing committees—Finance, Constitution and By-Laws, Nominating, and Protest. The AIAW leadership adopted the CIAW structure and eligibility rules for national championships. Schools awarding scholarships for athletic ability were ineligible for membership in AIAW. AIAW defined an athletic scholarship as a sum of money or fee waiver designated specifically for a female sports performer who at any time competed on an intercollegiate team. This definition meant that women who received athletic scholarships competed for these awards only with other women athletes, not the general student population.[17] AIAW was clear that women athletes could have scholarships, just not athletic scholarships. Scholarships that did meet their eligibility criteria were academic scholarships based on the high school or college grade point average, university economic need scholarships, economic need programs offered by city, state or federal government in the form of grant-in-aid or work-study programs, and talent scholarships when the talent was not athletics.[18]

AIAW's scholarship policy was immensely controversial. In Texas, Wayland Baptist College was a nationally recognized powerhouse in women's basketball in the sixties and seventies. They provided scholarships for their athletes. In 1972, AIAW's scholarship policy prohibited the Wayland Flying Queens from participating in a sanctioned tournament. This meant that one of the best women's basketball teams in the country could not compete for a national championship. Closer to home, Temple Junior College (TJC) provided athletic scholarships for its female basketball players. An archrival of Baylor's during the seventies, TJC easily and consistently beat Baylor's teams in the sixties and early seventies. Coaches from schools such as these two consistently lobbied the AIAW to change this policy. Little did members realize this change would come sooner rather than later.

Throughout its short 10-year history, AIAW was constantly challenged by two forces: (1) the passage and implementation of Title IX of the Education Amendments Act in 1972 and (2) the NCAA efforts to take control of women's intercollegiate athletics. For the AIAW, Title IX represented a conundrum. On the one hand, Title IX strengthened AIAW's advocacy position for women in sport; on the other hand, the law represented an immediate assault on its (AIAW) scholarship policy. Within seven months after the formation of the AIAW, their policy against awarding athletic scholarships to women faced a legal challenge.

THE KELLMEYER LAWSUIT

In January 1973 the Kellmeyer lawsuit was filed in U. S. District Court for the Southern District of Florida. Plaintiffs in the lawsuit were Fran Kellmeyer, director of physical education at Marymount College, eleven scholarship athletes from Marymount and Broward Community College, and women's tennis coaches from both schools. The purpose of the lawsuit was to invalidate DGWS/ AIAW rules that prevented women recipients of athletic scholarships from participating in AIAW-sponsored intercollegiate competitions.[19] The plaintiffs wanted to compete under the AIAW structure, but their athletic scholarships were preventing their participation. Title IX of the Education Amendments Act was one of several statutes cited in the lawsuit. AIAW was being accused of discriminating against women! Named as defendants in the lawsuit were the National Education Association, the Association of Intercollegiate Athletics for Women, the American Association for Health, Physical Education, and Recreation, the Division of Girls' and Women's Sport, the National Association of Physical Education for College Women, the Florida Association for Physical Education of College Women, the Florida Commission on Intercollegiate Athletics for Women, and the Southern Association for Physical Education for College Women. All of these organizations represented different facets of the leadership of women's intercollegiate athletics on college and university campuses at the time. Plaintiffs were certainly covering their bases and playing it smart. The more organizations that were threatened with this lawsuit, the greater the chances the AIAW policy would be overturned.

CHANGE IN SCHOLARSHIP POLICY

Defendants in the lawsuit immediately began to put pressure on AIAW to reverse their position. AIAW leaders were faced with a complex decision. For one, if they stuck to their scholarship policy, they risked losing the support of the AAHPER/DGWS alliance. These groups represented their financial purse strings and their financial stability for now. Secondly, the AIAW leaders had to face the fact that awarding athletic scholarships was an attractive idea among many college and university coaches. Afterall, the NCAA allowed this practice. Since the NCAA had begun to make noises about offering national championships for women, AIAW feared a mass exodus from their ranks to the NCAA if they did not change their scholarship policy. On the other hand, if AIAW gave up their policy on scholarships for women, there was concern that relinquishing this policy would undermine their focus on an educational model for women's athletics.

Nevertheless, the issue was on the agenda at the first Delegate Assembly in November 1973 only seventeen months after AIAW began operations. Delegates to this meeting overwhelmingly voted to reverse the scholarship policy, signaling a new beginning in intercollegiate athletics for women. The Kellmeyer lawsuit was dropped after this vote.

Sonja Hogg, women's basketball coach at Louisiana Tech and a delegate to this AIAW Assembly, echoed the sentiments of many female coaches at the time:

> I certainly supported the AIAW. I was on committees. [However] I did not agree with us [women] not being able to give scholarships. I could understand why they [AIAW leaders] didn't want the women's game to get muddled and bad like the men's with (sic) all the corruption and whatever. But at the same

time I knew that my ladies practiced
as long and as hard as the men did.[20]

Women's athletic scholarships were now legal. In an effort to minimize the impact of the policy change on the educational model for women's sport, AIAW leaders implemented maximum financial aid limits on scholarships per sport. The chart below provides the structure that was in place in 1978. This was unlike the NCAA structure at the time where no scholarship limits for male athletes existed.

Sport	Maximum/year	Sport	Maximum/year
Badminton	8	Softball	13
Basketball	12	Swimming	15
Cross Country	8*	Synch. Swim	12
Field Hockey	14	Tennis	8
Golf	8	Track & Field	20*
Gymnastics	10	Volleyball	12
Skiing	12		

Table I. AIAW Scholarship Limits 1978-82
*Students receiving a scholarship in one are counted as participants in the other.[21]

On a positive note, the scholarship reversal opened up AIAW membership to those colleges and universities already providing athletic scholarships to women. Resultantly, membership in AIAW immediately jumped from 278 at the beginning of 1973 to 379 and then to 757 institutions in 1976.[22]

Over the next five years, the AIAW leaders would play an incredible balancing act in an effort to remain true to their philosophical underpinnings of an educational model for women's athletics. They also supported Title IX implementation as they learned to deal with the realities of big time college athletics. Women leaders believed that limiting scholarships per sport and then strengthening their policies around eligibility and recruiting would emphasize that an educational model for women's sport was still possible. They adopted three policies that formed the foundation for this strategy. One policy addressed recruiting requirements for women, and two policies addressed the woman athlete's eligibility to compete.

STRICT RECRUITING REQUIREMENTS

Unlike the NCAA, the AIAW did not allow active recruiting. Leaders held a strong belief that protecting the woman student-athlete from the recruiting pressures often faced by their male counterparts was critical. These women did not want their athletes to be bought or to be put in in a position where two or more schools were competing for the athlete's talents. Ideally they wanted the athlete to choose the school first and then receive the athletic scholarship.

Resultantly, coaches could not visit prospective athletes in their homes or at their schools. Coaches could only assess talent when attending high school athletic events, and they were not allowed to talk to the athletes during these visits. Coaches could not solicit contact with prospective athletes before, during or after speaking to public groups or making other public appearances that were not intended to assess talent. Coaches' expenses for trips to assess talent were not reimbursable, and coaches were not allowed to use their normal business hours to assess talent. Athletes could initiate contact with the coach while visiting the campus and during normal business hours for the coach. Prospective athletes paid their own way for these visits.

College and university coaches could host tryouts or auditions for women athletes but had to invite all interested females, not just a select few, to attend these events. Individual auditions were not allowed and athletes had to pay their own way to these tryouts. During these events, players and coaches could talk with prospects and answer questions prospects might have. Coaches could verbally offer a scholarship to an athlete during the tryout period, but athletes could not sign any contract while on the campus. Over the years, the AIAW recruiting regulations slackened somewhat. Eventually coaches could be reimbursed for recruiting expenses and letters of intent were instituted to help coaches secure athletes in a timely fashion.

STRONG ELIGIBILITY RULES
AND REGULATIONS

Under AIAW rules, athletes had to be academically eligible for every game they played during the year including any post-season play. Academic eligibility was determined by the university and was the standard grade point average that was required of all students who participated in extraclass activities, i.e. intramurals, debate club, etc. Additionally, AIAW required athletes to participate in a majority of practices, to be academically eligible for a majority of the team's total competitions, and academically eligible to participate in all qualifying events leading to a national championship. Failure to meet all of these eligibility requirements resulted in the athlete not being eligible to play in a national championship. The paperwork to track these records was extensive, but the coaches were responsible for keeping these eligibility records.

Secondly, athletes on scholarship that transferred from one school to another during their academic career were <u>immediately</u> eligible to play for their new school. There was no redshirt concept requiring athletes to sit out a season before they could participate. AIAW leaders believed that if athletes wanted to transfer from one institution to another to get a better education, they should not be punished as athletes for this decision. AIAW leaders felt strongly that their recruiting and eligibility policies put the athlete at the center of the conversation, not the school and not the team. They maintained these policies throughout their history.

Although they had an Ethics and Eligibility committee at the national level, the AIAW lacked the resources to investigate infractions by the member schools and assess appropriate penalties. As such, the AIAW initially implemented a self-policing structure for rules violations. Members policed each other and reported infractions to the national committee. This committee then followed up with the appropriate rulings. As one might imagine this self-policing approach presented numerous problems and issues. Ultimately the AIAW asked their state affiliates to develop their own Ethics and Eligibility committees and provide state-level oversight for these infractions. After this, only issues that could not be decided at the state or regional level were referred to the national committee for resolution.

Throughout its history the AIAW members evaluated and strengthened all of their policies, but the leadership never waivered in their intent or interpretation where an athlete's eligibility was concerned. Athletes were students first and athletes second.

The contrast between AIAW's approach to the student-athlete compared to the NCAA's policies and procedures was stark. At the time of the birth of the AIAW, the NCAA had no scholarship limits, members engaged in active recruiting, and their eligibility rules for competition were lax. The organization was awash in punishments for college after college because of recruiting violations. The organization dealt with charges where university officials were bribing players. Furthermore, drug use by male athletes tended to be overlooked, and the violent behavior of some male athletes rippled through the NCAA structure. Many athletes who were not meeting their eligibility requirements continued to compete. Some of these athletes ultimately received degrees from their universities. The NCAA invested a lot of time and money enforcing its academic eligibility regulations but university faculty struggled constantly with male athletes with poor class attendance and poor efforts on exams. AIAW leaders were determined not to fall into these traps.

In 1978 AIAW adopted a divisional structure for its membership, offering participation in Division I, II, or III, depending on the amount of scholarship support the university could provide. To compete in Division I, a school could offer up to 100 percent of the AIAW allowable scholarships in the sport. Division II schools offered up to 50 percent of the allowable scholarships per sport, and Division III schools offered up to 10 percent of the allowable scholarships per sport. A school could choose what sport went into each division thus establishing an appropriate financial pace for full Title IX implementation of their women's athletic program. This ruling enabled Baylor University to make the decision to keep basketball at the Division I level and move volleyball, softball, and track and field to Division II in 1979.

FINANCIAL VIABILITY

AIAW leaders realized that controlling women's athletics meant controlling the finances for their organization. Accordingly they began in earnest to seek out the financial resources they needed to become viable and ultimately independent. Initially AIAW entered into a 1975 agreement with the Public Broadcasting System to broadcast the Swimming and Diving and Basketball National Championships that year. The ABC network had also purchased the rights to the national basketball championship to rebroadcast in a special program. The 1976 Delegate Assembly established the AIAW as the sole proprietor for the TV rights for women's college sports and effected a more formal TV arrangement through Marv Sugarman Productions. Sugarman guaranteed an annual payment and equal profit participation to AIAW in exchange for Sugarman's serving as the exclusive agent for the AIAW media efforts. A promotions committee, established by the AIAW Board in 1977, sought to identify endorsement opportunities and promote the Association. Their initial work created a partnership with the Eastman Kodak Company as the first major sponsor of an AIAW National Basketball Championship and the Women's Kodak All-American team in 1976. The Kodak All-American team announced at the 1977 national basketball championship included Suzie Snider-Eppers, a member of the Bearette Basketball team. The Kodak arrangement sealed the deal on the value of endorsements for the AIAW. In subsequent years other deals were reached with the Hanes Corporation, the Tea Council of the USA, the Coca-Cola Corporation, and the Broderick Corporation. In 1978 the AIAW Delegate Assembly decided to allow beer and malt beverages to be advertised at AIAW events.

AIAW's leap toward financial security moved forward substantially, culminating in a multi-year contract in 1979 with NBC for the television rights to all AIAW Division I national championships. Additionally, AIAW had an agreement with ESPN for carrying Division II and III events. In 1980-81 AIAW received record high revenues for its national television exposure, a total of $223,000 for twelve of its national championships.[23] The NBC contract would bring in an additional $400,000 per year.

At its high point in 1980-81, the AIAW offered a program of 39 national championships in 17 different sports to more than 6000 women's teams in over 900 member institutions. That same year over $30 million in financial aid was awarded to women in educational institutions in this country. Over 99,000 female athletes played under the leadership of the AIAW.[24] AIAW was the largest Association of its kind in the United States, and it was set to become legally and financially separated from its parent organizations, American Alliance for Health, Physical Education, Recreation and Dance (AAHPERD) and the DGWS. However, dark days for the AIAW lay ahead.

THE NCAA TAKEOVER OF WOMEN'S ATHLETICS

The National Collegiate Athletic Association (NCAA) formed in 1906 after a series of meetings called by President Theodore Roosevelt to get control of college football. Because of repeated injuries and deaths from participating in the sport, many colleges and universities had dropped football from their athletic programs. So was born the organization that would govern men's athletics in the United States. Over the years the Association grew in numbers and in power and today controls both men and women's athletics.

In the earliest decades of the NCAA, a struggle for control of all amateur sports ensued with the Amateur Athletic Association. Long before the 1920 Olympics where the American Olympic Committee, controlled by the AAU, was accused of mismanaging the U. S. Olympic Team, the NCAA had sought to gain control of all amateur athletics in the United States. Adoption by both groups of the Articles of Alliance in 1946 ushered in a period of mutual respect between the two organizations until the late 1950s.

The Soviet's domination of U.S. athletes in the Olympic games during the Cold War years prompted the NCAA to cancel the Articles of Alliance in 1960 and launch its federation movement, an effort to create sports federation separate from AAU control. Initial efforts in this arena resulted in individual federations being formed for basketball, gymnastics, baseball, and track and field in 1962. These federations were the brainchild of Walter Byers, the NCAA Executive Director. Byers believed that by having strong NCAA representations on these federations boards, the NCAA could begin to move the their agenda for control from within these federations. This move only served to further the hostility between the NCAA and the AAU.

The DGWS quickly was sucked into the NCAA-AAU controversy and became virtually a pawn for each of these organizations in their efforts to gain control of amateur sport in this country. The DGWS leadership was constantly in communication with both the NCAA and the AAU, as these two organizations came a courting for the favor of the DGWS. With the AAU's position weakened through the formation of the sport federations, it was no secret that Walter Byers was interested in gaining control of the women's programs. However, the official position of the NCAA was that it was organized for male students and had no interest in including women in its structure. Women leaders would soon realize that the official NCAA position was not Walter Byers' position.

In 1965 before forming the Commission on Intercollegiate Athletics for Women (CIAW), the leadership of the Division of Girls and Women's Sports (DGWS) contacted the NCAA officials to verify their stated position that they did not want to govern women's intercollegiate athletics. NCAA leaders, in fact, wished the DGWS well in forming their new organization. With this understanding, DGWS moved forward and formed the CIAW.

Over the next several years, the NCAA response reflected above became the party line when officials were asked about having women's competition. However, behind the scenes, several things were happening that confused the conversation for a long time. For one, there was increasing interest among NCAA schools to have their women's athletic programs under the NCAA. Secondly, Walter Byers manipulation of the powerful NCAA Council resulted in actions that continuously sent a different message to the female leadership of DGWS, CIAW, and eventually the AIAW. Byers wanted control of the women, and he was determined to get it. His first move from came in 1967 when he influenced the NCAA Council to establish an NCAA committee to study the feasibility of providing for the development and supervision of women's inter-collegiate athletic programs. This happened just as the CIAW was beginning to organize itself. Needless to say, the women leaders were surprised and shocked when they heard of this move. It seemed to them that the NCAA was talking out of both sides of its mouth. In retrospect it is clear that the NCAA leadership and Walter Byers were at odds with each other over the control of women's athletics. Byers' ace in the hole was his understanding of the politics of the NCAA. He used his influence with the Council to go over the heads of the NCAA leadership on this issue.

Three DGWS members were invited to be a part of an NCAA joint committee to study a women's athletic structure in 1967. Betty McCue, Katherine Ley and Lucille Magnusson attended the meetings of the committee known as the McCoy Committee. Going into these meetings, the CIAW/AIAW was open to moving the women's programs under the NCAA umbrella, but they wanted a structure that would allow women to maintain control of their programs as part of the NCAA structure. Prior to meeting with the McCoy committee, the three women representatives tried very hard to get the NCAA to commit to a stance on the control of women's athletics. They believed it would help clarify the issue if the NCAA would come clean on this issue. Correspondence ensued, and the NCAA leaders never changed their official position. In effect the NCAA was still maintaining their position that they were not set up for and were not interested in including women in their structure. However, the very existence of the McCoy Committee sent a different message to the CIAW leadership. In their minds the NCAA was effectively announcing that it might be interested in folding the women under their structure if the time ever came for that move. As well, Walter Byers was always lurking in the background, dropping little tidbits and opinions about women's athletics and keeping the CIAW/AIAW leadership off-balance. The CIAW and then the AIAW dealt with these two contrasting positions from the NCAA until 1982.

At the first meeting of the McCoy Committee, January 1968, the NCAA position began to emerge. On the surface the conversations seemed supportive of the women's ideas and structure, but the unspoken messages were clear to the women in the room. Betty McCue reflected:

> ...My impression was that the NCAA simply wanted to take over completely. One of the problems was with women setting the policies. They [NCAA officials] wouldn't guarantee that women could set the policies.
>
> "We had the impression that they were offering and wanting to take over women's sports within their structure. We couldn't see how they were offering us the opportunity to fit within their structure. It sounded just like a takeover.[25]

Rachel Bryant added:

> The McCoy committee was established primarily as a move by the NCAA to establish itself as a governing body in women's sports to gain further recognition from the International Olympic Committee. It was a part of the battle against the AAU....The NCAA wanted in on the women's program because this was a wedge for international recognition...[26]

In spite of these perspectives the NCAA never officially changed its position during this time. The McCoy Committee disbanded, producing no documents and no records of its meetings. When discussions to form the AIAW began in the early seventies, leaders from the CIAW, the AAHPER, and DGWS were not concerned about the NCAA's position on women's athletics. After all, nothing of substance had been heard from the NCAA in almost four years. Granted the McCoy committee had been meeting, but nothing had come out of these meetings. With no meeting minutes or other documentation from the Committee, why would anyone have been concerned?

In 1971 the proposal to form the AIAW was developed and sent to colleges and universities nationwide for review. When Walter Byers received this document, he immediately informed the DGWS that he had asked the NCAA legal council to draft a legal opinion on the implications for the NCAA of not offering women opportunities to participate in its national tournaments. Byers further informed the group that the preliminary report from his legal counsel indicated that the NCAA was indeed in a difficult legal position. He further stated that, if this were the final assessment, the NCAA would likely take action to provide opportunities for women. While this announcement provided only more shock and surprise for the women leaders, they persevered, forming the AIAW in 1972. The NCAA legal opinion was finalized and released, but no immediate consequences were seen. However, in 1973 the NCAA rescinded its rule preventing women from participating in NCAA events. This was the first shot taken at the AIAW and began a series of NCAA-instigated events that would last for nine more years and provide a continuous assault on the viability of the AIAW. The irony of all this was the amount of money the NCAA spent during the 1970s fighting the implementation of Title IX legislation. Indeed, the NCAA wanted to control women's athletics but they did not want the women's program to have equity with the men's. One wonders what women's athletics would have looked like under the NCAA structure if Title IX had not been implemented and the AIAW had not persevered as long as they did.

From 1973–1975, the NCAA and AIAW played cat and mouse, appointing Joint Committees and special committees, all to study the issue of the governance of women's athletics. In all of these negotiations the NCAA leadership was saying one thing but behind the scenes, Walter Byers and the NCAA Council were moving forward to takeover the women.

At the 1976 NCAA Convention in January, the Executive Council placed three issues on the ballot for discussion and vote of the membership: (1) a resolution to apply NCAA rules to women athletes, (2) a resolution to initiate championships for women, and (3) a resolution to establish a standing committee on women's athletics. By vote of the membership, the resolution to apply NCAA rules to women athletes was referred to committee. The resolution to initiate women's championships was tabled. The resolution to form a standing committee on women's athletics within the NCAA was passed.[27] For the time being, the AIAW had dodged an important bullet.

In 1978 AIAW tried once again to have conversation with the NCAA about the governance of women's athletics. They extended an invitation to representatives from the National Association for Intercollegiate Athletics (NAIA)[7] and the NCAA to discuss possible governance structures for the future. The NAIA accepted the invitation, but the NCAA did not. The NCAA leadership did not want to continue these joint meetings or any discussions that might develop a governing structure that was anything less than their complete control of both collegiate men and women's programs. Following closely on the heels of the NCAA's refusal to attend this meeting was an invitation from the NCAA to the AIAW to meet and discuss "Women's Participation in the Governance of Athletics." Considering this invitation as a slap in the face to any kind of proposed negotiation they had proposed, the AIAW leadership did not accept this invitation. They did, however, issue a statement expressing their displeasure with the NCAA leadership.

In 1979 the NCAA Council continued its efforts to move forward with plans to takeover the AIAW proposing at its annual Convention that championships for women be initiated at the Division III level. The AIAW strongly opposed this measure sending a resolution to the NCAA Convention. The NCAA membership defeated this measure. Clearly the membership of the NCAA was not inclined to include women in its structure at this point in time. The AIAW leadership had a bit of a reprieve, but they were growing weary of Walter Byers' persistence regarding their Association.

Only one year later at the 1980 NCAA Convention, a motion to initiate women's championships in five sports for Division II and Division III schools passed the vote of the membership. Needless to say, the AIAW leadership

---

7   NAIA membership includes medium-sized colleges and universities in the United States that do not embrace the philosophy of big-time athletics.[28]

became very alarmed at this development. History would show that this vote was the beginning of the end for AIAW. With Division II and III national championships for women offered by the NCAA, the universities in these divisions began a mass exodus to the NCAA from the AIAW. The handwriting was on the wall. It was only a matter of time before NCAA Division I championships for women would follow.

The NCAA received a boost in their efforts at a takeover when several prominent women leaders in the AIAW "defected" to the NCAA, embracing the male model of sport for women. These defections tipped the balance of opinion and support in favor of the NCAA. The AIAW launched one last effort to convince college and university presidents to support the AIAW's alternative model for women's athletics. The power of the NCAA was too much to overcome, however, and the membership of the NCAA voted to host national championships for Division I schools beginning in 1982.

AN ABRUPT END

While it took ten years to establish the AIAW as the national governing body for women's intercollegiate sports, it took less than a year to bring its success to an abrupt halt. Since its inception in 1972, the Association had successfully warded off efforts by the NCAA to takeover the governance of women's athletics. Once the Division II and III defections began in 1980, NBC and ESPN immediately cancelled their contracts with the women's organization. None of the AIAW national championships in 1981-82 received the television coverage that had been negotiated. AIAW was losing its viability as a governing body. Several reasons stand out as to why AIAW was so vulnerable in 1982.

First, AIAW was only ten years old. It was just really getting its feet under it, so to speak, in terms of the strength of its structure. It was in a fight with an organization that had been in existence for decades. AIAW was the David in a battle with Goliath.

Secondly, for all of its work and effort to achieve recognition for women's intercollegiate athletics, the philosophical foundation of the AIAW was not well-known. Furthermore, it had been compromised with the change in the scholarship policy and its move to endorsements and contracts toward a more commercial model for sport. College and university administrators saw the AIAW and the NCAA as essentially the same organizations.

Thirdly, one of the fallouts from Title IX was that most universities merged their men and women's athletic programs under one governing structure during the seventies, and that structure was the existing male athletic department structure. When these mergers occurred, hundreds of women, formerly known on their campuses as the Women's Athletic Coordinators or Women's Athletic Directors, lost their authority over their programs and their autonomy as administrators. The AIAW model, the educational model for sport, lost its advocates. It became relatively unknown and very undervalued.

Lastly, when the NCAA announced its championships in 1982, college and university presidents were forced to choose between the NCAA or AIAW structure for their women's programs. AIAW represented an additional governing structure for athletics, a structure where the rules were different, another membership fee was required, rules and eligibility were stricter, and representation in the organization would require additional funds to support. Most university presidents and athletic directors wanted only one structure for both programs. Moving the women under the NCAA structure was the simplest and easiest solution for these leaders. They were more comfortable with and more familiar with the NCAA model. That was the choice that Baylor made.

Pat Summitt, head women's basketball coach at the University of Tennessee, offered a perspective on the women's move to the NCAA.

> It's different when it's the NCAA. I've been around the game a long time, and I'm appreciative of all the pioneers, the women who fought for women's championships under the AIAW, but I also recognize that what really gave our sport the boost in the eyes of the country was the NCAA. That gave us some clout, and eventually brought about the television package that otherwise we never would have gotten.
>
> I definitely saw the [the AIAW model of governance and recruiting] as restrictive. Players had to come to you...[Recruiting

> in the NCAA] has really brought about
> an opportunity for student-athletes
> to have choices, because they can,
> regardless of financial background,
> select colleges of the greatest interest,
> visit, and have their way paid. It just
> opened up the door of opportunity.[29]

Summitt's perspective echoed that of many women in a leadership role for women's athletics at the time. While they appreciated the work of the AIAW, they were ready to move on to bigger and better things for their athletic programs.

The defection of schools from the AIAW to the NCAA was swift and extensive. By 1981 the organization was financially strapped. In October 1981, AIAW leaders filed a lawsuit against the NCAA, claiming they (NCAA) were trying to monopolize women's intercollegiate athletics. On March 2, 1982 in the U.S. District Court in the District of Columbia, the judge in the lawsuit ruled the AIAW had failed to make its case. The organization was finished. On August 3, 1982 the AIAW closed its doors, and women's intercollegiate athletic formally came under the control of the NCAA. In reflection the AIAW leaders felt they had done everything they could do to save the organization.

THE LEGACY OF AIAW

Even though the AIAW leaders had made some ideological sacrifices in an effort to maintain control of women's intercollegiate athletics, they continued to operate from a position based on idealistic principles and practices, principles that embodied the best that sport had to offer to both men and women. The beauty of the early structure for women was that participation was based on geographical parameters. School size was not an issue. Beginning with no scholarships and no recruiting created a level playing field for everyone. That's how Baylor University competed against McLennan Community College as well as the University of Texas and Texas Lutheran College. It's also how tiny Immaculata College won the first three AIAW National Basketball Tournaments, 1972–74.

In 1982 there were actually two women's national basketball champion-ships held in this country. The AIAW tournament was held in Philadelphia, Pennsylvania and featured the University of Texas, Rutgers University, Villanova and Wayland Baptist College in the final four. Rutgers defeated the Lady Longhorns to win this last AIAW National Championship.

The inaugural NCAA Women's Basketball Championship was held in Norfolk, Virginia and featured Tennessee, Louisiana Tech, Maryland, and Cheyney State in the Final Four. Louisiana Tech, led by star guard Kim Mulkey, defeated Cheyney State to win that championship.

Reflecting on this period of time, Jody Conradt, then coach of the University of the Texas Lady Longhorns, shared:

> I wanted to [play in the NCAA tournament] because our team was good and that's where the best competition is, and you want to have a chance to do that. Donna [Lopiano, Women's Athletic Director at Texas] and I locked heads over that. But, obviously, she won out and as I look back now, I'm really happy it worked out that way because I think it was a statement that I am very proud that [the University of] Texas made. You knew it was gonna be the one year thing only. We did go to the national tournament in Philadelphia. We lost in the finals to Rutgers. But to give you a contrast, that final four was us, Rutgers, Wayland Baptist and Villanova. I think that was the epitome of what the AIAW was. It didn't matter about the size of the school, the conference affiliation. It had more to do with geographic [location] in terms of how the structure was.[30]

After women's athletics moved under the auspices of the NCAA, the AIAW leadership wanted to be involved with women's intercollegiate athletics under this structure. The NCAA passed a resolution to have eighteen percent female representation on its committees and in its governing structures. Joan Hult, one of the AIAW leaders at the time felt this percentage could have been larger if AIAW could have held out for a couple more years.[31] However, many of the values and changes in rules and regulations within the NCAA can be attributed to the influence of the AIAW leaders. According to Willey in 1996, the basic premise of striving towards an `educational' model of athletics in the NCAA was still very much alive. There is no question that the AIAW was a positive force for good in women's athletics. Willey suggested the following:

1. The AIAW served a special purpose – that of the governance of women's intercollegiate athletics – when no other alternative was available.

2. The AIAW model for athletics catered to the student-athlete through its rules and regulations and emphasized an "educational" model for athletics.

3. The state, regional, and national structure for women's intercollegiate athletics established a strong network for women leaders in athletics and provided many leadership opportunities for women.

4. Competent AIAW leaders governed women's athletics during an historical decade for female athletes.[33]

Women's intercollegiate athletics had gained the recognition it so wanted. The AIAW did such an effective job of bringing structure, recognition, and credibility to women's intercollegiate athletics that they won the battle but ultimately lost the war to a financially and politically stronger entity, the NCAA.

STATE AFFILIATES OF THE NATIONAL STRUCTURES

Beginning with the American Recreation Federation of College Women (ARFCW), the first national body to form around women's intercollegiate athletics in 1933, the states began to form affiliates of these national bodies so that women would have a framework for functioning at a district and state level. Texas women were front runners in organizing themselves, having three governing organizations: the Texas Recreation Federation for College Women (TRFCW), the Women's Recreation Association (WRA) on college campuses, and the Texas affiliate of the DGWS. The WRA was involved in organizing competitions between colleges on an unofficial basis, providing an informal structure for extramural competitions through the 1950s and early sixties. Prior to 1963 there was a very inconsistent application of rules and regulations to the competitions.

With growing concern over the lack of a unified structure for women athletes in Texas, the Texas affiliate of the WRA approached the TRFCW at its 1963 state convention in Belton, Texas, asking this group to sponsor district and state competitions for female intercollegiate athletes in Texas. With the assistance of the Texas affiliate of the Division of Girls' and Women's Sport (DGWS) to provide consistency in the rules and a structure for competition between the colleges and universities at the local and state levels, the new TRFCW structure was operational by the end of 1963.

TRFCW divided itself into seven districts and sponsored intercollegiate competitions through the state level. Beginning with tennis in 1964, TRFCW quickly added sports to include badminton, basketball, volleyball, tan and field, golf, and bowling over the next five years. Labeled as "extramural" programs, the popularity of these sports grew rapidly.

When the Commission on Intercollegiate Athletics for Women was created in 1967, the leadership of the TRFCW had begun to realize that they could no longer manage these extramural programs in the colleges and universities. At its spring planning conference, March 22-23, 1968, an advisory group of the TRFCW proposed the following: "That a Texas commission on intercollegiate athletics be formed under the sponsorship of the Texas unit of the Division of Girl's and Women's Sports."[34] This recommendation came as a result of the creation of the Commission for Intercollegiate Athletics for Women (CIAW) as the first national governing body for women's intercollegiate athletics that included state affiliates.

The Texas Commission for Intercollegiate Athletics for Women (TCIAW) officially formed on October 5, 1968 as a non-profit organization to provide educational and competitive experiences for college women in Texas. With its inception, TCIAW became one of the first state affiliates of the CIAW to develop a state structure that promoted and sponsored intercollegiate athletics for women.

The TRFCW officially endorsed the new organization at its state convention October 25-27, 1968 with the passage of the following proposal:

> "In light of the recent forming of the TCIAW, TRFCW desires to relinquish sponsorship of district and state organized tournaments in Basketball, Volleyball, Tennis, Badminton, Golf, and Bowling, and Track and Field as of September 1969. All tournaments will proceed as planned for the 1968-69 season under the TRFCW supervision but will be called TCIAW approved tournaments. All tournament fees, as of October 1968, will be paid to the Texas Commission for Intercollegiate Athletics for Women. TRFCW desires to financially support the cost of all tournaments previously sponsored for the 1968-69 season, to insure a sound financial backing for the beginning [sic] of the Texas Commission for Intercollegiate Athletics for Women."[35]

The TCIAW sponsored district and state tournaments in badminton, basketball, bowling, golf, tennis, track and field, and volleyball in 1968. Swimming and gymnastics were added to the list of sports for the 1969-70 academic year.[36]

The organization utilized the tools and rules provided by the Division of Girl's and Women's Sports to develop its own handbook for how competitions in every sport would be organized and structured, the rules of competition, and the schedule and sites of district and state tournaments for the year. One excerpt from the 1972 Handbook, pg. 43, Rule #10 illustrated these rules:

> No basketball team shall play no more than three games per day and there

**shall be a minimum of 3 hours rest
for a team between the close of one
contest and the beginning of another.**[37]

While this policy may seem humorous by today's standards, it was not uncommon at the time for women's basketball teams to play three games in a day, especially when participating in a one day tournament. Illustrative of this idea is an announcement in the March 18, 1967 *Lariat* stating that the Bearettes were leaving at 5:00 am on Saturday morning to participate in the North Texas State University basketball tournament. The team was returning home at the conclusion of the tournament that same day. The real significance of this rule was the designated length of at least three hours between games. With this time frame, the number of games played in a day would automatically be limited. Prior to this policy, the length of time between games was set by the individual schools and/or tournament organizers. Sometimes players were able to rest and sometimes they had to play immediately following a game.

TCIAW maintained the district model of the TRFCW but added one representative from each district to its governing body. Baylor University was a member of District IV of the TCIAW. Other schools represented in District IV were: Huston-Tillotson, Incarnate Word College, Paul Quinn College, Our Lady of the Lake, Southwest Texas State, Southwestern, St. Francis, St. Mary's, Texas Lutheran, University of Texas, and Trinity University. Junior college representatives included Central Texas College, Concordia College, McLennan Community College, San Antonio Junior College, Southwest Texas Junior College, St. Phillips, and Temple Junior College.[38] Each district had its own officers and conducted its own business per the state handbook. An Executive Committee of the TCIAW was the ultimate decision-maker for all of the districts in the state. There are extensive records of TCIAW Executive Committee minutes in the Woman's Collection, Blagg-Huey Library, Texas Woman's University.

TCIAW became the Texas Association for Intercollegiate Athletics for Women (TAIAW) at its March Delegate Assembly meeting, 1974. Realizing the need for a more decentralized structure, the leaders of the TCIAW began the process in 1973 of restructuring itself to align with the membership structure created by the Association for Intercollegiate Athletics for Women (AIAW) at the national level. Many of the changes incorporated by the leaders mimicked those of the national organization, particularly the incorporation of voting members to a delegate assembly. This structure enabled the membership of TAIAW to govern itself instead of that responsibility falling on one centralized Board such as the TCIAW had provided. Other significant structural changes for TAIAW included a new constitution and bylaws creating new offices for the organization as well as an Executive Board to carry out the governance of the Association. Athletic communities were organized initially into seven zones, instead of six districts.

Within two years, the structure changed to four zones, North, East, South and West and then morphed again into a structure for large and small colleges. These changes were driven by changes in the national governing body, the AIAW. In 1979, TAIAW adopted the same three-division structure as that of the AIAW and decided to restructure itself again in 1981 into a conference structure. This structure was set to go into effect in the 1982-83 academic year. However, the NCAA announced the implementation of a women's governance structure with national championships beginning in 1982-83. This announcement sealed the fate of the AIAW as universities jumped from the AIAW as well as its state and regional affiliates. The final Delegate Assembly for TAIAW occurred in April 1982 with the adoption of an article of dissolution to be added to the bylaws.[39]

With the dissolution of the TAIAW and the move to the NCAA, women moved under the traditional conference structure already in place for men's intercollegiate athletics. The Baylor women's teams competed in the Southwest Conference until the move to the Big 12 in 1996. Baylor continues to be a member of the Big 12 conference in 2012.

NOTES ON CHAPTER 1

WOMEN'S SPORT IN AMERICA: THE BACKDROP, 1900–1972

1. "Victorian Women: The Gender of Oppression." *Historical Analysis: Women as "The Sex" During the Victorian Era.* http://webpage.pace.edu/nreagin/tempmotherhood/fall2003/3/HisPage.html. Accessed July 16, 2013.

2. Joan S. Hult, "Introduction to Part I," in *A Century of Women's Basketball: From Frailty to Final Four*, eds. Joan S. Hult and Marianna Trekell (Reston, VA: American Alliance for Health, Physical Education, Recreation and Dance, 1991), 6.

3. Nancy Cole Dosch, "'The Sacrifice of Maidens' or Healthy Sportswomen? The Medical Debate Over Women's Basketball," in *A Century of Women's Basketball: From Frailty to Final Four*, eds. Joan S. Hult and Marianna Trekell (Reston, VA: American Alliance for Health, Physical Education, Recreation and Dance, 1991), 126.

4. Mabel Lee, *A History of Physical Education and Sports in the U.S.A.* (Reston, VA: American Alliance for Health, Physical Education, Recreation and Dance, 1991).

5. Ying Wushanley, *Playing Nice and Losing: The Struggle for Control of Women's Intercollegiate Athletics, 1960–2000.* (Syracuse: Syracuse University Press, 2004), 6.

6. Lynne F. Emery and Margaret Toohey, "Hoops and Skirts: Women's Basketball on the West Coast, 1892–1930s," in *A Century of Women's Basketball: From Frailty to Final Four*, eds. Joan S. Hult and Marianna Trekell, (Reston, VA: American Alliance

for Health, Physical Education, Recreation and Dance, 1991), 138–139.

7. Betty Spears, "Senda Berenson Abbott: New Woman, New Sport," in *A Century of Women's Basketball: From Frailty to Final Four*, eds. Joan S. Hult and Marianna Trekell (Reston, VA: American Alliance for Health, Physical Education, Recreation and Dance, 1991), 32.

8. Mabel Lee, *A History of Physical Education and Sports in the U.S.* (New York: John Wiley and Sons, 1983), 27.

9. Virginia Hunt, "Governance of Women's Intercollegiate Athletics: An Historical Perspective." (PhD diss., University of North Carolina, 1976), 19-20.

10. Wushanley, *Playing Nice*, 15.

11. Suzanne Willey, "The Governance of Women's Intercollegiate Athletics: Association for Intercollegiate Athletics for Women (AIAW), 1976-1982," PhD diss., Indiana University, 1996, 7.

12. Phebe M. Scott and Celeste Ulrich, "Commission on Intercollegiate Sports for Women," *Journal of Health, Physical Education and Recreation,* October 1964: 10, 76.

13. Commission on Intercollegiate Sports for Women. Report to the Division for Girls and Women's Sports, November, 1968, quoted in Virginia Hunt, "Governance Of Women's Intercollegiate Athletics: An Historical Perspective" PhD diss, University of North Carolina Greensboro, 1976, pg. 126.

14. Joan S. Hult, "The Legacy of AIAW," in *A Century of Women's Basketball: From Frailty to Final Four,* eds. Joan S. Hult and Marianna Trekell, (Reston, VA: American Alliance for Health, Physical Education, Recreation, and Dance, 1991), 283.

15. Virginia Hunt, "Governance of Women's Intercollegiate Athletics: An Historical Perspective." (PhD diss., University of North Carolina, 1976), 89.

16. Hunt, 91.

17. "Minutes of the Executive Board Meeting," Texas Commission on Intercollegiate Athletics for Women, June 19, 1972, 16.

18. Texas Commission, 15.

19. Wushanley, *Playing Nice*, 63.

20. Hogg, Sonja, interview by author, Waco, Texas, July 2, 2012.

21. Part One: Future Regulations—Academic Year 1978–79, *AIAW Ethics and Eligibility Newsletter*, 6. The Women's Collection, MSS 77, Blagg-Huey Library, Texas Woman's University, Denton, Texas.

22. Wushanley, *Playing Nice*, 70.

23. Wushanley, *Playing Nice*, 140.

24. Joan Hult, "The Saga of Competition: Basketball Battles and Governance Wars," in *A Century of Women's Basketball: From Frailty to Final Four*, eds. Joan S. Hult and Marianna Trekell, (Reston, VA: American Alliance for Health, Physical Education, Recreation and Dance, 1991), 238.

25. McCue, Betty, interview by Virginia Hunt, Eugene, Oregon, October 9, 1975, quoted in Virginia Hunt, "Governance of Women's Intercollegiate Athletics: An Historical Perspective," PhD diss., University of North Carolina, 1976), 193.

26. Bryant, Rachel, interview by Virginia Hunt, Manassas, Virginia, September 5-7, 1975, quoted in Virginia Hunt, "Governance of Women's Intercollegiate Athletics: An Historical Perspective," PhD diss., University of North Carolina, 1976, 194.

27. Wushanley, *Playing Nice,* 103.

28. Phyllis Holmes, "National Association of Intercollegiate Athletics," in *A Century of Women's Basketball: From Frailty to Final Four,* eds. Joan S. Hult and Marianna Trekell (Reston, VA: American Alliance for Health, Physical Education, Recreation and Dance, 1991), 385.

29. Welch Suggs, *A Place on The Team: The Triumph and Tragedy of Title IX,* (Princeton, NJ: Princeton University Press, 2005), 65.

30. Conradt, Jody, interview by the author, Austin, Texas, June 22, 2012.

31. Hult Joan, interview by the author, Lake Chelan, Washington, September 22, 2012.

32. Ibid.

33. Suzanne Willey, "The Governance of Women's Intercollegiate Athletics: Association for Intercollegiate Athletics for Women (AIAW), 1976-1982," (PhD diss., Indiana University, 1996), 231-232.

34. Sue Beall, "TRFCW 1967–68 Spring Planning Conference, Central Office Secretary Report." Texas Recreation Federation of College Women, 1968. The Women's Collection, MSS 77, Box 7, Blagg-Huey Library, Texas Woman's University, Denton, Texas, p. 5.

35. Sue Beall, Personal Correspondence to TCIAW Membership, October 15, 1968. The Women's Collection, MSS 77, Box 7, Blagg-Huey Library, Texas Woman's University, Denton, Texas.

36. Sue Gunter, Commissioner of TCIAW District III, "Texas Association for Intercollegiate Athletics for Women, 1968–1981." The Women's Collection, MSS 77, Box 7, Blagg-Huey Library, Texas Woman's University, Denton, Texas.

37. The Olga Fallen Collection, Accession 3747, Box 7, Folder 5, The Texas Collection, Baylor University.

38. The Olga Fallen Collection, Box 7, Folder 8.

39. See note 36 above, 11.

CHAPTER 2

TITLE IX: THE LEGISLATION THAT CHANGED THE PLAYING FIELD

"No person in the United States shall,
on the basis of sex, be excluded from
participation in, be denied the benefits
of, or be subjected to discrimination
under any education program or activity
receiving Federal financial assistance"[1]

On June 23, 1972 President Richard Nixon signed Title IX of the Education Amendment Act into law. The Act focused on eliminating discrimination on the basis of sex in academic institutions and complemented a long list of civil rights legislation from the 1960s. Institutions that did not comply with Title IX risked losing their federal funding. Its implications for intercollegiate athletics were not on anyone's radar screen at the time of its passage, but the direct result of Title IX was an immediate boost to women's intercollegiate and interscholastic athletics.

The passage of the Title IX legislation in 1972 was simple and uneventful, but its implementation was complex and controversial. Between 1972 and 1974 challenges that would have altered its application to college and university programs were contested in the U.S. Senate. Congress finally approved the implementation regulations in 1975, having dealt with four resolutions before the guidelines could be approved. Congress rejected efforts by additional individuals to amend the bill in 1977. It took seven years before the implementation regulations were finalized in 1979. The bill continued to face legal challenges into the eighties.

This chapter tells the story of the passage and implementation of the legislation and how it increased participation rates for girls and women in interscholastic and intercollegiate sports. It also explains the mandates of the law for university athletic programs and provides an overview of why it was such a controversial piece of legislation.

GENERAL OVERVIEW

Ware referred to Title IX as the "thirty-seven words that changed American sports."[2] While Title IX was given many descriptions over the years, some good, some not so good, there is no question that it was the most significant piece of legislation to impact equity in athletics for girls and women in the twentieth century. While hardly mentioning athletics in its language, Title IX addressed discrimination in educational institutions at the student, administrative, and professorial levels where there were widespread problems at the time.

In the minds of legislators the law would fill in a gap created by Title VII of the Civil Rights Act of 1964. That law prohibited discrimination based on race, sex, national origin, and religion in employment but it did not apply to educational institutions. Patsy Mink from Hawaii explained:

> When it was proposed, we had no idea that its most visible impact would be in athletics. I had been paying attention to the academic issue. I had been excluded from medical school because I was female.[3]

The legislation represented a bi-partisan effort to address the discrimination issues in education. Representative Edith Green from Oregon sponsored the bill in the House and Senator Birch Bayh of Indiana authored the Senate version. A Joint House-Senate Conference Committee reconciled the two bills. There was hardly any debate about the final bill, and it seemingly was not a controversial issue for the Congress. In addressing the importance of the legislation, Bayh stated that Title IX represented an important first step in the effort to provide for the women of America something that is rightfully theirs.[4]

PRE-TITLE IX WORLD OF WOMEN'S SPORTS

Prior to the passage of Title IX, inequities in women's sport at both the high school and college levels were easily found. With little to no financial support, girls and women used hand-me-down equipment and scrambled to piece together uniforms for competition.

Participation rates further emphasized the inequality for women. In 1971, only seven percent of the total number of high school athletes in the United States were females. This figure represented approximately 250,000 individuals. At the college and university level, there were fewer than 30,000 women competing in intercollegiate athletics, and less than two percent of overall athletic budgets were being spent on women's sports.[5] Ware made several comparisons between the level of support for men and women prior to the legislation.

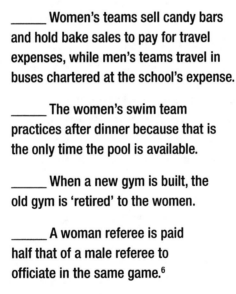

_____ Women's teams sell candy bars and hold bake sales to pay for travel expenses, while men's teams travel in buses chartered at the school's expense.

_____ The women's swim team practices after dinner because that is the only time the pool is available.

_____ When a new gym is built, the old gym is 'retired' to the women.

_____ A woman referee is paid half that of a male referee to officiate in the same game.[6]

Vivian Stringer, women's basketball coach at Cheyney State College, 1971–1983, indicated that she used her own money to recruit and drove her team to games in an old, highly unreliable prison bus. According to Stringer, intersections were a real challenge because if she stopped the bus, she wasn't real sure it would start again. She stated: "I'd slow down but not enough to stop….so my assistant would crane her neck out the window and yell: 'Vivian, keep going, no one's coming.'"[7]

At Baylor University, coaches and athletes used their own cars to get to competitions. Players often bought their own meals. The only time a Baylor team stayed in a motel was when we traveled to Canyon, Texas for the State TCIAW Track and Field meet, a distance of about five hundred miles. We stayed overnight because it was too far to drive this distance in a timely manner and compete in the track meet. The team would leave on Friday morning early and spend that night at a motel in Canyon. Early on Saturday morning the qualifying heats were held. The final heats usually started right after lunch and ended in the late afternoon. The team would then drive the entire five hundred miles back to Waco.

This was the same scenario for all of Baylor's women's teams. If we were in a tournament in Denton, for example, we would leave the Baylor campus early on Saturday morning, drive to the tournament, play several games, and then drive home that night. The farther we were going, the earlier we left. Keep in mind that most tournaments or track meets started by 9:00 am. If Baylor played in the first game, our departure time could be very early. Coaches as well as athletes used their private cars and did their own driving. The University reimbursed drivers for their gas. As an athlete in the sixties, I remember driving in the early morning hours on many occasions to get to tournaments. For the most part our driving time varied from two to four hours depending on the destination. We traveled north and south from Denton, Texas to Houston, Texas. From east to west we went as far west as Brownwood, Texas and as far east as Nacogdoches, Texas. On rare occasions when we had a very early starting game, we would stay in the houses of players' or coaches' families, in the basements of Baptists churches, and any other place we could find where we didn't have to pay to stay.

Kay Yow, head coach Women's Athletics Coordinator at Elon College, 1971–1975, indicated that her players and coaches paid for their own food and gas. Additionally, they bought their own uniforms and ironed the numerals on. Coach Chris Weller, Maryland, recalled how she and her players pinched pennies on every travel meal. "The players said I could smell a Denny's a hundred miles away."[8]

Cheryl Reeve, former player at Tennessee, shared the story of how head coach, Pat Summit, 1974–2012, would drive the van to carry her team to a game, coach the game and then sleep overnight alongside her players on a gym floor. Speaking to a group of high school female athletes, Reeve stated: "That's what that generation of women athletes did to be in the game."[9]

Sue Gunter, women's basketball coach at Stephen F. Austin University, 1964–1980, recalled asking her department chair, a woman, for money to buy uniforms for her team. In response, the chair took her to meetings beginning with the dean and extending to the President's office and allowed Gunter to make her case for the financial allocation for new uniforms. Unfortunately, it became clear to both women that none of the administrators (all males) had any interest in spending money on the team. Reflecting on this experience Gunter recalled: "I left that building and there were tears running down my cheeks I was so angry."[10]

Gunter's experience was that of many women athletic leaders on college and university campuses across this country. In their efforts to advocate for women they were repeatedly met by a power structure that was very entrenched in traditional views of women's roles in society and in sport. Gunter's chair, a woman, had provided her with the opportunity to see firsthand what the battles looked like.

TITLE IX IMPLEMENTATION

While the law was signed into law in 1972, the guidelines for implementation were not due out until 1975-76. Colleges and universities were expected to be in compliance with the law by 1979. The Office of Civil Rights (OCR) in the Department of Health, Education and Welfare was tasked with writing and implementing the guidelines, and then with investigation and enforcement of the legislation. OCR staff had a daunting task, and they were not prepared for the number of complaints they received. They were sorely understaffed to handle the investigation and enforcement part of their responsibilities. Controversy resulted.

The three-year period waiting for the guidelines was full of speculation and controversy about the language in the law and how it would be interpreted. Numerous Congressional hearings occurred, hundreds of phone calls, and dozens of letters were sent to President Gerald Ford and to Casper Weinberger, Secretary of Health, Education and Welfare in an effort to influence the guidelines. What does equal opportunity mean? Does it mean financial equality? Are all sports included in the legislation? What about football? It's a revenue-generating sport. Is it included in the equality formula? College presidents and athletic directors alike were convinced that Title IX was going to ruin intercollegiate athletics. Supporters of women's athletics maintained that there was enough fluff in intercollegiate budgets, particularly the football budgets, that the purse strings could be tightened in order to equalize opportunity for women. Senator John Tower of Texas put forth the Tower Amendment in 1974 that would exclude revenue-producing sports from the equality calculation mandated by Title IX. The amendment was defeated and replaced by the Javits Amendment. Authored by Senator Jacob Javits from New York the amendment proposed that the Office of Health, Education and Welfare must include "reasonable provisions" considering the nature of particular sports when developing the implementation guidelines.[11]

After the regulations were signed by President Gerald Ford in July 1975, there continued to be controversy because the language in the regulations still failed to delineate clearly the specifics of the guidelines. College and university administrators continued to contest the legislation as numerous hearings with the House Subcommittee on Equal Opportunities were held. There is abundant documentation of the testimony in those hearings. Other legislative efforts were made in 1975 and 1977 to curtail Title IX enforcement, but the Senate refused to act on these new bills.

The first Title IX investigation ever mounted against an athletics program involved the University of Georgia and occurred in 1978. Complaints against the university had been filed both in 1972 and 1975. In 1978 OCR decided it was time to launch an investigation. According to Lamar Daniel, the OCR investigator, the university was out of compliance on everything. He recalled some of the controversy surrounding these hearings.

> I went over there and looked at the program and oh, it was enormously controversial. Attorneys were in on all the interviews. It was no surprise that Georgia was in violation of the law "up one side and down the other". I remember in one of the interviews they had, five women basketball players came in to talk. They might have been the starting five, and

they brought their game ball. It was a used ball from the men's team. The entire women's coaching and administrative staff was crammed into cubicles in the trophy room in the university's basketball arena. There were far fewer female athletes than men, and hardly any of them were receiving scholarships.[12]

Daniels was instructed to hold off on his report until OCR finalized its policy interpretations. That process took until late 1979. When Daniel returned to campus in 1979, the University of Georgia had made significant strides toward compliance with Title IX and had a plan in place to come into full compliance with its women's office space and scholarship issues.

While the University of Georgia case represented a win for OCR, the office was chronically understaffed and was not able to address many Title IX complaints in a timely manner. Resultantly, OCR came under attack from numerous civil rights groups, namely the National Organization for Women's Project on Equal Education Rights and the U. S. Commission on Civil Rights. A 1980 report from the Civil Rights Commission revealed that most colleges had not complied with the 1975 Title IX regulations, noting that ninety-two complaints had been filed with the OCR against colleges and universities. The report however was not able to quantify how many complaints had been resolved.[13]

In 1979 President Jimmy Carter elevated the Department of Education to a cabinet position and appointed a Secretary of Education. His plan was to transfer all of the education-related functions of the Department of Health, Education and Welfare as well as the education-related functions of the Department of Justice and the Department of Housing and Urban Development and Agriculture to the Department of Education. The significance of this decision and the centralization of these programs of the government could not be overstated. The Republicans opposed the move maintaining that the department was unconstitutional since it was not mentioned in the constitution, but the move did put Title IX and its enforcement under the auspices of the Department of Education. Many people thought some real progress in terms of Title IX investigation and enforcement was poised to happen.

TITLE IX, THE AIAW, AND THE NCAA

As mentioned earlier, Title IX became a conundrum for the Association of Intercollegiate Athletics for Women (AIAW). The legislation was passed into law in the same time period that AIAW became a legal entity and started functioning as the national governing body for women's intercollegiate athletics. While the AIAW leaders knew that Title IX would force the issue of athletic scholarships for women, something the organization opposed in its philosophical underpinnings, they also knew that the equity Title IX mandated would not end with scholarships for women. It would permeate every area of the athletic programs for women, including salary equity, enhanced budgets, recruiting, etc. In the end leaders made the decision to fight hard for Title IX because they realized that having the force of legislative mandates behind the move toward equity was the only way equity was going to be achieved. The leaders understood that if changing the structure on college campuses to guarantee equity in athletics for women was left up to the good will of those in the power positions, those changes would come very slowly. Jody Conradt, head coach for women's basketball at the University of Texas, 1976–2007, summed up this thinking: "... it takes big things to get people's attention. People wait until they are pushed."[14]

The National Collegiate Athletic Association (NCAA), on the other hand, opposed the Title IX legislation. The organization allocated $1 million dollars to fight it. At the time, the NCAA was beginning to show interest in women's athletics, but their staunch opposition to the legislation synched with the outcry being heard from their membership. College and university presidents and athletic directors were convinced that Title IX was going to ruin college sports, that intercollegiate athletics could not grow if Title IX became law. They further emphasized that in order to implement the law, many men's sports would have to be dropped. Their voice was heard at all levels of government, initially lobbying Richard Nixon not to sign the legislation. When the law was enacted, their opposition became an effort to influence the guidelines and regulations and to stall the implementation of the law. History would show that the implementation of Title IX did not threaten men's programs. It did not cause reductions in men's programs as feared, and it ultimately resulted in a huge growth in intercollegiate athletic programs.

LANDMARK LEGAL CASES IMPACTING TITLE IX

The Department of Health, Education and Welfare issued the final policy interpretation on Title IX and intercollegiate athletics in December 1979. There followed numerous lawsuits across this country. There were so many different interpretations of the law that where you lived in this country became an important factor in how the law was interpreted. Appellate courts issued a wide variety of rulings and contributed little to a clearer understanding of the law.

In an effort to establish some consistency in interpretations of the law the Supreme Court agreed to hear the Title IX case of Grove City College v. Bell in 1983. In its landmark ruling in that case, the Court held that only programs receiving federal funds were subject to Title IX requirements. Since athletic departments did not receive federal funding, they would be exempt from Title IX. Members of the NCAA rejoiced and for a time colleges and universities had a reprieve from the mandates. However, the Grove City case was only one in a series of targets of the Reagan administration's desire to downsize governmental regulations and civil rights laws. Civil rights groups were up in arms about Reagan's efforts and took their protest to lawmakers. In 1988 Congress passed the Civil Rights Restoration Act of 1987. This bill restored the civil rights mandates from the 1960s legislation and nullified the Supreme Court ruling in the Grove City case. The Act mandated Title IX coverage for every educational institution that received federal funding, directly or indirectly.[16] President Ronald Reagan vetoed this bill, but the bipartisan Congress overrode his veto.

In Franklin vs. Gwinnett County Public Schools, 1992, the Supreme Court ruled that plaintiffs filing Title IX lawsuits were entitled to monetary damages when intentional action to avoid Title IX compliance was established. The ruling was unanimous and substantially reinforced the importance of Title IX compliance.[17]

Finally, the Equity in Athletics Disclosure Act (EADA) was passed by Congress in September 1993. This law required institutions with intercollegiate athletic programs to disclose the following information for both men and women's sports annually: roster size, budget for recruiting, scholarships, coaches' salaries, and other expenses. The first EADA reports were due in 1996. These reports are public information and can be acquired from every university.[18]

Numerous other hearings, Supreme Court decisions, and OCR updates generated by Title IX occurred steadily from the seventies into the twenty-first century. As late as 2011, the Department of Education issued policy guidelines related to Title IX.[19] However, the original intent of the law has not changed since its creation.

TITLE IX MANDATES FOR COLLEGES AND UNIVERSITIES

Once the regulations for Title IX were implemented, it was very clear that equal opportunity did not mean equal funding for women's athletics. The language of the law was clear on this issue. The regulations identified three primary areas that were judged in the determination of whether an institution was or was not in compliance with Title IX -- financial aid, participation, and program components, such as facilities, equipment, etc. Universities had only to meet one of these standards to be judged in compliance with Title IX.

Essentially, the law required proportionality in the awarding of financial aid. In considering the student body at a university, the proportion of undergraduate male and female students would determine the amount of financial aid offered to male and female athletes in the intercollegiate athletic program. For example, if a university had a fifty-five percent male population then fifty-five percent of the financial aid for athletics would be allocated to the men's programs. Forty-five percent of the aid would go to the women's programs. Universities were allowed to be within five percent of this proportionality rate to be judged in compliance.

Participation rates were addressed by the three-prong test. Programs were considered in compliance with Title IX if they could document evidence to support one of three areas. The proportionality rule continues to be the criteria most often used to document compliance in universities in 2012. Curtis and Grant explained the criteria like this:

> Substantial proportionality in rates of
> participation between men and women.
> Structured like proportionality for financial
> aid, universities can be in compliance
> if the total number of male and total

number of female athletes is the same
proportion as the total number of males
and females in the student body.

Universities can document a history
of and continuation of program
expansion opportunities for the sex
that is underrepresented in athletics.

Universities can document that the
interests and abilities of underrepresented
athletes have been accommodated.[21]

Program components were measured by documentation of equivalent benefits, treatment and opportunities in the following:

Equipment and Supplies;

Facilities;

Scheduling of games and practice time;

Travel and per diem allowance

Opportunity to receive academic tutoring

Opportunity to receive coaching, assignment and compensation;

Locker rooms, practice, and competitive facilities;

Medical and training facilities and services;

Housing and dining facilities and services;

Publicity;

Support services;

Recruitment of student-athletes.[22]

Universities found it particularly challenging to comply with the proportionality rule. On many college campuses during the seventies, the number of women undergraduates was greater than the number of men. However, the greatest challenges came with the need to document equivalency in the items listed above. Most universities could show some support in many of the categories, but few could document equivalency for their women's programs.

AFTERMATH OF TITLE IX

There is no question that Title IX was a positive force for women, particularly for women athletes. According to the Women's Sport Foundation, the ratio of female high school athletes in sport has increased from one in twenty-seven girls in 1972 to two out of five in 2011. The National Federation of State High Schools reported the number of high school girls participating in 1972 was less than 205,000. By 2011 that number jumped to nearly 3.2 million.[23]

Beginning in 1977, Acosta and Carpenter, Professor Emerita, Brooklyn College, began a longitudinal study of the impact of Title IX on women's intercollegiate athletics. In their thirty-five year update, the found significant growth in women's intercollegiate athletics as a result of Title IX. In 2012 the number of college women participating in athletics had grown from approximately 16,000 to 200,000, the highest number in history. Additionally, women were participating in an average of 8.73 sports per school in 2012 compared 2.5 sports in 1972. Finally, they found the total number of sports opportunities available for women intercollegiate athletes in 2012 was 9274. Acosta and Carpenter noted this number indicated not only an increase in the total number of women's teams but also an increase in the number of schools offering collegiate athletic opportunities for women from 1972-2012.[24] Division I schools averaged 9.44 sports per institution for women in 2012, the highest of all NCAA divisions.[25]

One of the biggest arguments against Title IX offered by male athletic directors and college administrators throughout the seventies was the notion that the money for women's athletics would result in hardships for men's athletic programs. There was a fear that some of the men's sports would have to be dropped in order to provide funding for the women. In 2012 Acosta and Carpenter found no information suggesting that was what had happened on college campuses. On the contrary, the researchers found that these increases in female participation rates (i.e. adding programs for the women) had not adversely affected male participation rates. In fact male participation rates had grown steadily (though not as exponentially as women) over the years.[26]

Basketball is the most popular women's sport, reported in 98.8% of the schools in all three divisions of the NCAA. Soccer and cross-country have shown the most growth since Title IX was implemented.[27]

Acosta and Carpenter speculated there were several reasons for the high participation rates reported in 2012.

Perhaps it is due to society's ability to embrace females as athletes. Perhaps it is encouraged by a long line of successful Title IX lawsuits urging non-discriminatory treatment. Perhaps it is another generation of post Title IX men and women who know that the benefits available from sport participation enrich the lives of both females and males, their daughters and sons. Perhaps it is increased media coverage of women's sports, and perhaps it is due to the long term efforts of energetic advocacy efforts by organizations such as the National Organization for Girls and Women in Sport and coalitions of a variety of organizations such as found under the umbrella of the National Coalition for Girls and Women in Education. Whatever the cause, female athletes are being afforded opportunities in greater numbers than ever before.[28]

Athletic opportunities for girls and women boomed after Title IX and the decade of the seventies will go down in history as an unprecedented decade for growth in the number of colleges and universities offering intercollegiate athletic programs as well as the number of college and university women participating in an intercollegiate athletic program. Indeed, women sport leaders eagerly awaited a continued explosion of growth in the 1980s. However, the political climate in the United States changed significantly, and the eighties would ultimately be viewed as a decade of "hanging on to what we got" with little additional growth in programs.

The second great growth spurt occurred during the nineties. Once this decade got underway, there was no turning back in the development of intercollegiate athletics for women in this country.

The growth of women's athletic programs at Baylor followed the same growth curve as is told in the broader story of women's intercollegiate athletics, from its early intercollegiate opportunities in the thirties and forties to its play days and sports days of the fifties to its extramural sports in the 1960s and formal intercollegiate programs beginning in the seventies. While national politics and cultural trends influenced the Baylor campus and its women, Baylor's evolution of its women's athletic program is its own. Baylor's leadership in the sixties and seventies was challenged by civil rights legislation and Title IX and influenced by national conservative politics in the eighties. Ultimately, it took a change in leadership and a "perfect storm" to realize the treasure that is Baylor women's athletic programs in 2012.

TITLE IX WAS NOT A PANACEA

There were downsides to the implementation of Title IX and fallout from its requirements. Title IX is often viewed as the undoing of the AIAW because the legislation opened the door and forced AIAW to allow athletic scholarships for women. When this happened, the floodgates opened and AIAW's commitment to an educational model for women's sport was challenged. This model was further weakened as the AIAW developed its financial underpinnings and relied more and more on the commercialism of television contracts and company endorsements.

When Title IX became law and the issue of equality was under debate, the norm for a national structure for college athletics was that of the NCAA. Consequently, a prevalent thought was that the easiest way to achieve equality of opportunity was to utilize the NCAA model. The NCAA wanted control of the women's programs, and the college and university administrators wanted one structure for all of its programs.

The issue with the NCAA structure was that it represented a male model of collegiate athletics, a model built by men on the perceptions and experiences of men. At the core of its values were competition, achievement, commercialization, aggressiveness, domination and conformity. These values were a far cry from the AIAW model that emphasized, sportsmanship, education, student-centered, cooperation, comradery, and respect. Forty plus years after Title IX, women's programs and women athletes have been assimilated into this male model, developing highly competitive athletic programs with aggressive recruitment practices, a focus on handing out honors and awards, and winning,

winning, winning. Is this system inherently discriminatory? Research in this area is ongoing.

One effect of Title IX on college campuses was the merging of the men and women's programs on university campuses. These mergers immediately resulted in a decrease in the number of women in athletic leadership positions. One cannot find an example of a university where the men and women's programs were merged and the woman became the athletic director. Women played second fiddle to the men, often relegated to a less influential leadership role. Frequently, the women's voices were not heard and their opinions were not valued.

Title IX forced the women's athletic coaching positions into fulltime status with a competitive salary structure. This resulted in the knowledge that men could support their families if they coached women's sports. A mass migration of men to the coaching ranks for women's teams followed. Frequently, both a man and a woman applied for the head coaching position. Because the persons hiring these coaches were male athletic directors, male applicants generally were hired more often than their female counterparts. This phenomenon occurred in both the high school and intercollegiate ranks. As an example, in 2012, men coached 57.1 percent of women's intercollegiate teams. Prior to Title IX, over 90 percent of women's athletic teams were coached by women.[29]

Other losses from Title IX, however, were in the leadership role models for today's women athletes. Prior to Title IX, women filled almost one hundred percent of these roles. In 2012, slightly over twenty percent of these administrative positions were held by women. Additionally, sixty-nine percent of head athletic trainers were men and over ninety percent of sports information directors were men. At Division I universities, only thirty-four percent of schools had a female strength and conditioning staff person to work with the women. These numbers were even lower in Division II and III schools.[30]

These facts illustrate the discriminatory nature of intercollegiate athletic programs in today's society. There is an inherent incompatibility between men and women's sport cultures and value for sport. Yet, this incompatibility continues to be overlooked and ignored, marginalizing women in the sport system. Everhart and Pemberton, in their review of literature in 2001, spoke to the consequences of this continued marginalization:

Historically and traditionally sport has evolved as a male domain, and it is clear that women and girls, as well as men and boys, have different sport participation roots. The evidence presented supports the notion that gender bias in sport is a product of not only different sport histories and traditions, but also an inherent incompatibility between female and male sport cultures and values. The dominant male sport value system has defined and delimited the parameters of sport for women and girls, especially and ironically since the passage of Title IX. Further, evidence has been presented to show that gender bias and gender discrimination are manifest in sport through differences in both the quantity and quality of the sport experiences/ programs available, as well as the virtual elimination of female sport administrative leadership and dramatically reduced numbers of female sport coaches.[31]

Hult likened what happened to women in athletics after Title IX to what happened to Black Americans after the Civil Rights legislation in the sixties.[32] While the laws mandated equality of opportunity for both women and minorities, frequently the social and political structures these individuals had to navigate to achieve this equality were so dominated by a male system that change was slow and difficult. Forty years after Title IX Everhart and Pemberton's review of the research indicated there was still inequality in women's athletic programs in this country. How many generations will have to pass before it ends?

NOTES ON CHAPTER 2
TITLE IX: THE LEGISLATION THAT
CHANGED THE PLAYING FIELD

1. Susan Ware, *Title IX: A Brief History with Documents*, (Boston: MA: Bedford/St. Martin's Press, 2007), 3.

2. Ware, *Title IX*, 1.

3. See note 1 above.

4. Ware, *Title IX*, 4.

5. See note 2 above.

6. Ibid.

7. Pamela Grundy and Susan Shackelford, *Shattering the Glass: The Remarkable History of Women's Basketball*, (Chapel Hill, NC: The University of North Carolina Press, 2005), 139.

8. Ibid.

9. Marcus Fuller, *In 40 years, Title IX revolutionized women's sports, but there's still a ways to go*, Twin Cities.com Pioneer Press, June 23, 2012. http://www.twincities.com/sports/ci_20926231/40-years-title-ix-revolutionized-womens-sports-but.

10. See note 7 above.

11. Mary Curtis and Christine Grant, "Landmark Title IX Cases in History," *History*, accessed October 3, 2012. http://bailiwick.lib.uiowa.edu/ge/aboutRE.html, 1.

12. Welch Suggs, *A Place on The Team: The Triumph and Tragedy of Title IX*, (Princeton, NJ: Princeton University Press, 2005), 83.

13. Ibid.

14. Grundy and Shackelford, *Shattering the Glass,* 108.

15. Title IX at 35, *Beyond the Headlines: A Report of the National Coalition for Girls and Women in Education, 2008. Accessed December 10. 2013. http://www.ncwge.org/PDF/TitleIXat35.pdf,* 5.

16. Ibid

17. Mary Curtis and Christine Grant, 3.

18. Ibid

19. Women's Sports Foundation, "Get Your Game On, Girls! Celebrating the 40th Anniversary of Title IX," *Women's Sports Foundation,* accessed March 17, 2013. http://www.womenssportsfoundation.org/home/media-center-2/press-releases/june-23-2011-press-release.

20. Grundy and Shackelford, 147.

21. Mary Curtis and Christine Grant, 2.

22. Mary Curtis and Christine Grant, 2–3.

23. Maya Dusenbery and Jaeah Lee, *Charts: The State of Women's Athletics, 40 Years After Title IX,* Mother Jones, June 22, 2012, accessed March 17, 2013. http://www.motherjones.com/politics/2012/06/charts-womens-athletics-title-nine-ncaa.

24. R. Vivian Acosta and Linda Jean Carpenter, *Women in Intercollegiate Sport: A Longitudinal, National Study Thirty-Five Year Update,* Participation Commentary, 1, January 28, 2012. Accessed November 2012. www.acostacarpenter.ORG.

25. Ibid.

26. Acosta and Carpenter, 2.

27. See note 24 above.

28. See note 26 above.

29. Acosta and Carpenter, 17.

30. Acosta and Carpenter, 32, 38.

31. Robert B. Everhart and Cynthia Lee A. Pemberton, *The Institutionalization of a Gender-Biased Sport System,* Advancing Women: International Business and Career Community News, Networking & Strategy for Women, Winter 2001, accessed July 18, 2013. http://www.advancingwomen.com/awl/winter2001/everhart_pemberton.html

32. Joan Hult, personal interview by the author, Lake Chelan, WA., September 22, 2012.

CHAPTER 3

BEARETTES ARE BORN

THE FIRST FEMALE ATHLETES AT BAYLOR

Baylor University's history of providing athletic opportunities for women began in 1904 under the leadership of Mrs. J. W. Erps. This leadership passed to Miss Anne Corey Maxwell, a former student of Erps, in 1908 and extended for several years. Under this leadership, Baylor women had cutting-edge instruction in gymnastics and physical activity utilizing Indian clubs, wands, mats, dumb bells, flying rings and other apparatus. Maxwell received her training from the McFadden Physical Culture School and the Chicago Normal School of Physical Education, two strong preparatory programs for female physical educators. Under her leadership, Baylor women's competitive opportunities came from their strong intramural programs. Basketball was the main sport, organizing into teams such as the Goblins, the Lone Stars, the Yellow Jackets, the Ku Klux Klan. Competitive opportunities were also available in volleyball, indoor baseball, and tennis.

1909 Goblins

Motto: If At First You Don't Succeed, Keep-a-Tryin!

Baylor University, Round Up 1909 Yearbook, (Waco, TX: [Baylor University], 1909), The Texas Collection, Baylor University, p. 217.

1909 Ku Klux Klan

Motto: Do It or Die! (So, We'll Do It!)

Baylor University, Round Up 1909 Yearbook, (Waco, TX: [Baylor University], 1909), The Texas Collection, Baylor University, p. 219.

Baylor women had their own gymnasium, utilizing the old chapel that was converted to a women's gym in 1905.[1] Between 1909 and 1914 the best athletic performers were recognized by the University Athletic Council and awarded the coveted "B", the same recognition given to their male peers who participated in varsity athletics and became letter winners in their sports. These women were Jane Freeman, Ette Hutton, Ruby Johnson, Myrtle Tarrant, Jennie Whitman, Zou Steele Daniel, Ruth Glass, Tressa Scholars, Emily Dixon, Willie D. Farrington, Vesta Heath, Alice Mansell, Autie Marrs, Lera Brown, Georgia Buck, Willie Mae Henry, Myra Kilpatrick, Sallye Tidwell, Winnie Warren, and Willis (no first name given).[2] Their names appear in the annals of the Baylor Letterman's Association. The University did not award varsity letters to women athletes again until 1976.

1912 Tennis Players – The Fighting Four

Lois Kelley, Emma Winfrey, Euphemia Ritchey, Bess Whitehead

Baylor University, Round Up 1912 Yearbook, (Waco, TX: [Baylor University], 1912), The Texas Collection, Baylor University, p. 223.

The Baylor "B" was awarded to women for several years beyond 1914, but the women who won these awards were not given varsity status by the University.

In 1928 the Women's Athletic Association (WAA) formed on campus to generate an interest in intramural participation for all Baylor women. Consisting of physical education majors and minors and organized by Dorothy Sparkman, Women's Athletics Director, the club's motto was "Play for Play's Sake". The

WAA that awarded intramural letters to women members of the basketball, football, and track teams.[3] Yes, the women played football during this time!

Baylor's legacy of strong leadership from women physical education faculty continued with individuals such as Sparkman and Lucille Douglass through the decades of the thirties and forties. In 1938 the WAA had over 100 members. Although there are gaps in the research, it would seem that the WAA group morphed into Upsilon Delta Gamma sometime in the late thirties or early forties. Club members met regularly, planning activities for the fall, winter, and spring quarters for Baylor women, and organizing practices for teams in basketball, volleyball, tennis, softball, deck tennis, badminton, shuffleboard, and ping pong. Since Monday morning chapel was required for all students at the University, the WAA frequently utilized this venue. These letters, in Baylor green, were described as being 3" x 2.25".[4, 5]

On November 6, 1948, Upsilon Delta Gamma became Delta Psi Kappa, a professional physical education fraternity for women. The focus of Delta Psi Kappa changed more from promoting strong intramural programs for women to mentoring and fundraising activities to promote the club. Dr. Evelyn Kappes, women's physical education director, led this group for many years. Because of the work of WAA and Upsilon Delta Gamma through the decade of the 30s and 40s, Baylor has a tradition of strong and popular women's intramural programs still in existence on the campus. Additionally, Baylor has always had a strong professional preparation program for women students because of the leadership of Evelyn E. Kappes and the legacy she built through her work with Delta Psi Kappa.

WOMEN'S INTERCOLLEGIATE ATHLETICS AT BAYLOR, 1939-1970
BADMINTON

In 1939 the Baylor-Waco Badminton and Fencing club formed to provide intercollegiate opportunities for men and women as well as competition for interested citizens of Waco.[6] Historical documents about this organization indicate that both fencing and badminton were popular sports with the Baylor coeds at this time. Badminton, however, afforded the most opportunities for intercollegiate competition for the women. The Baylor-Waco Badminton team traveled and played numerous matches in San Antonio, Dallas, Temple, and Waco. If the event was an "open" tournament, then team members from both the university and the community entered and competed; but if the event was a collegiate tournament, only the college players attended. At the 1940 Collegiate State Tournament, Baylor's Mary McCormick won the singles championship and paired with Cal Newton to win the mixed doubles championship.[7]

The first Baylor University Invitational Badminton Tournament occurred in Marrs McLean Gymnasium on the Baylor campus in February 1940. Billed as the largest badminton event ever held in Texas, teams from Baylor, Texas A&M, Texas, Rice and Abilene Christian College entered the College/University tournament while additional teams from cities such as Houston, Austin, Dallas, Temple, Waco, Hillsboro, and Corsicana were added in the Open tournament.[8] During World War II, the proceeds from this event went to Army relief.

The Baylor Invitational, as it became known, continued well into the 1990's. As a member of the Baylor Badminton team, 1965–69, I played on both the collegiate and open divisions of this tournament every year. Once I graduated, I played in the Open tournament for several years. This event featured the best badminton players from all over Texas and the Southwest. It lasted two full days. The college tournament played on Friday and the Open tournament occurred on Saturday. Individuals could compete in singles or doubles. A man and women could also team together and enter the mixed doubles competition. Within each tournament there were five separate tournaments occurring at the same time—men and women's singles, men and women's doubles and mixed doubles. Play would begin at 8:00 in the morning and continue until the tournament finished. Because of the popularity of the sport and the number of male and female entries in both the collegiate and open tournaments, there were many college tournaments decided in the wee hours of a Saturday and many Open tournaments finished in the early hours on a Sunday morning. It was not uncommon for over 300 contestants to play in these two tournaments. Both of these tournaments continued play well into the 1990s, and history will document that Baylor was a strong badminton school and a hub for badminton activity in the state. However, badminton was never recognized as a varsity sport by the University Athletic Department.

FENCING

Lariat articles from May 13, 1939 indicated a Fencing Club was started on campus in the Fall of 1936 and it appeared to be a men and women's club. Men generally competed in foil, epee and sabre events while the women competed only in foil. By all accounts, fencing was a popular sport at Baylor with evidence of the team traveling to numerous meets and hosting intercollegiate events in Waco, Texas. The April 30, 1937 *Baylor Lariat* reported that the Baylor Fencing Club was hosting an official Southwest Fencing League sanctioned meet at Cameron Park in Waco. The event was expected to draw teams, men and women's, from SMU, Baylor, Texas, Texas A&M, Dallas, Shreveport, and Ft. Worth and include fifty contestants. Later editions of the *Lariat* reported that the competition at this meet lasted until 10:00 at night. References to fencing opportunities for Baylor men and women were scant throughout the decade of the 1940's.

However, as reported in the *Baylor Lariat*, December 7, 1955, Dr. H.F. Hollien announced a revival of the Fencing club with plans to have men's team competing in foil, epee, and sabre. Women were invited to join the club as well. The effort was met with great enthusiasm by students, and George Sauer, then Athletic Director at Baylor, indicated he would make "full provisions in Baylor's sports program for the muskateers." No record was found indicating fencing was ever a varsity sport at Baylor, however. Fencing as a club sport continued with varying degrees of success as late as 2011.

TENNIS

The Baylor Tennis Association formed in 1941 under the direction of Cal Newton, the varsity tennis coach. Newton stated, "Its aims are to promote interest in tennis by sponsoring club tournaments and home matches of the Baylor net teams and by bringing players of national reputation to the campus for exhibition matches."[9] Tennis was a club sport. The teams scheduled matches with Texas State College for Women, Mary Hardin-Baylor, and Texas University. No information about the women's competition on this team was available, and it could not be confirmed just how long this team stayed in existence.

Though not officially sponsored by the University or recognized as a varsity sport, six Baylor women represented the University playing against other Texas schools in the years 1955-58. Having played tennis in high school, these women were accomplished tennis players, several competing at the state level for their respective high schools—Betty Rogers, Pat Gregory, Barbara Cox, Carolyn Savage, Billie Eck, and Virginia Brown. Undaunted in their desire to compete with other schools and utilizing Roger's 1952 Chevrolet, the women traveled to tennis meets in Dallas at Southern Methodist University, in Austin and at San Antonio College. Although they were given permission to represent the University by Lloyd O. Russell, chair of the Health, Physical Education and Recreation Department, these women received no financial support. Roger's best memory was that Baylor did pay their entry fees at a San Antonio tournament in the mid-fifties. While the Physical Education Department furnished the tennis balls, the women furnished their own equipment, even stringing their own rackets. B and B Sporting Goods, a local sporting goods store, sometimes provided discounts on equipment and clothing for the women. The team competed well but never won a tournament. They had no coach.[10]

BAYLOR OLYMPICS

In the early 1950s, Baylor women physical educators began inviting teams from other universities to compete in an annual sports day event. In 1954 this event became known as the Baylor Olympics and occurred annually until the last event in 1960. Under the early leadership of Kay Mitchell and Mary Tindle, the Baylor Olympics were visionary, providing a structure of intercollegiate competition for women that was unique in Texas.[11] True to their historical roots, these competitions emphasized the values and philosophy of women's sport up to that point: skill development, wholesome competition and strong social relations between the universities.

Baylor physical education majors helped organize and also participated in the Baylor Olympics. The event was modeled after the International Olympics and featured an opening and closing ceremony. An elaborate point system was devised so that awards to the winning team and the high point individual were presented at the end of the day.

In 1959, teams from Baylor, Howard Payne University, the University of Texas (UT), Stephen F. Austin State College, Southwest Texas State Teachers College, and Southern Methodist University participated in the Baylor Olympics. Events included volleyball, basketball, softball, badminton, court tennis and table tennis, bowling, and archery. Participants also entered a modified swim meet and track meet at the end of the day.[12]

The May 6, 1959 *Baylor Lariat* indicated that Baylor would be represented in the upcoming Baylor Olympics by Carolyn Fuller, Kay Smith, June Reynolds, Cindy Hull, Jamie Shanan, Jody Autry, Virginia Brown, Virginia Shannon, Barbara Goar, Sue Carpenter, Dot Swogetinsky, Carrie Palmer, Jeanie Eikenloff, Barbara Goley, Billie Eck, and Sue Sorrell. According to the *Baylor Lariat*, May 12, 1959, the University of Texas won the team event with Baylor finishing second. Colleen O'Connor from UT was the high point individual.

In 1961 the Baylor Olympics became an event for local high schools and offered the same structure for competition as the collegiate program had. Six high school teams were invited to participate each year. These Olympics for high schools continued into the 1970s, providing valuable leadership opportunities for women physical education majors at Baylor.

EXTRAMURAL ATHLETICS AT BAYLOR
1959-69

Under the leadership of Olga Fallen, faculty member in the women's physical education program, a focused effort began in 1959-60 to identify highly skilled physical education majors/minors for participation in "extramural" competitions between universities. Baylor's move in this direction coincided with a similar national movement, as well as the organization of the National Joint Committee on Extramural Sports for Women in 1958[8]. Per documents obtained from the Fallen Collection, this effort had four major objectives:

To provide competitive opportunities above and beyond the realm of intramurals.

To furnish more advanced training opportunities for student officials.

To challenge and motivate students toward the development of a more skilled performance in as many activities as possible.

---

8 See Chapter 1 for more detail on this organization.

To broaden the range of social
contacts allowing the major students
to view other physical education
programs and departments.[13]

Initially, Fallen created teams from the freshman, sophomore, junior and senior physical education major classes and organized tournaments among these teams in volleyball, basketball, speedball, softball and individual sports such as badminton and tennis. The women physical education faculty coached the various teams. Shirley Rushing Poteet, faculty member at the time, recalled that while she knew nothing about coaching basketball, she did have Jody Conradt on her team. Her strategy was get the ball to Jody![14]

Jody Conradt, from Goldthwaite, Texas, had been an outstanding high school basketball player. Growing up, she had learned to shoot a jump shot, something women athletes were not doing at the time. Like many, she thought her playing days were over when she went to college. By chance she found out about the women's basketball team as a freshman at Baylor, but there was a hitch to her playing. She had to be a physical education major. Conradt was getting a teaching degree, but at the time could see no future teaching physical education so she was reluctant for a while to change her major. Like so many young women during that time, myself included, Olga Fallen decided Jody needed to major in physical education and began a campaign to try and persuade her in that direction. Olga Fallen had an eye for talent, and when she found someone that she believed would help further the profession of women's physical education, she was somewhat relentless in her efforts to persuade the young woman to change her major to physical education. Jody finally gave in, becoming a major and a member of the Bearette basketball team, averaging twenty points per game in her collegiate career. Obviously, the decision to change her major study was a good one for Jody as she went on to use her physical education training to coach at Midway High School, Sam Houston State University, and the University of Texas-Arlington, before moving to coach the women's basketball team at the University of Texas in 1976. At UT, she became the all-time winningest coach in collegiate women's basketball history with a career won-loss record of 900–306. Her 1986 NCAA Championship team was the first team in history to go undefeated and win the national championship and is the only women's national championship basketball team from the University of Texas. Condradt was enshrined in the Naismith Memorial Basketball Hall of Fame in 1998 and was a member of the first women's class to be inducted into the Women's Basketball Hall of Fame, June 1999. Jody Conradt retired in 2007, leaving a huge legacy for women's sports.[15]

Fallen's strategy to recruit highly skilled athletes worked well. In November 1959, Baylor fielded a team and accepted an invitation to a tennis meet and supper at Mary-Hardin Baylor College in Belton. Subsequent to that, Baylor hosted three volleyball teams from Mary-Hardin Baylor in December for a "Christmas Party-Volleyball Jamboree". Fallen also scheduled matches with local high school teams, and in February 1960, a Baylor women's volleyball team participated in the Texas Wesleyan College tournament in Ft. Worth, Texas.[16]

Somewhere along the line, the women's intercollegiate athletic teams at Baylor University adopted the name, the Baylor Bearettes. No information could be found indicating how or when this happened. However, it was common practice in both high schools and colleges during this era for the women's teams to add an 'ettes` to the end of the name of the school mascot when adopting a name. Baylor's mascot was the Bears, hence Bearettes.

In Spring 1960 the first women's extramural basketball team, coached by Fallen, was formed and played four games against other schools and independent groups. The women's badminton team, coached by Mary Tindle, traveled to Austin for the University of Texas Intercollegiate Badminton Tournament and made additional trips to Houston and Texas Woman's University in Denton.[17]

In 1961 women's competition began in earnest for women's basketball teams across Texas. Organized under the auspices of the Division of Girls and Women's Sports (DGWS) and the Texas Recreation Federation for College Women (TRFCW), Baylor found itself competing in Region IV against the likes of Mary-Hardin Baylor, Southwest Texas State Teacher's College, Texas Lutheran College, Southwestern, Del Mar College, Incarnate Word, and the University of Texas. The Bearettes competed favorably, compiling a won-loss record of 9-0 in 1961 and winning the DGWS/TRFCW District IV Tournament.[18]

1961 Bearettes

*Back row: Donna Cleland, Jo Flint, Rachael Colson, Coach Olga Fallen, Karen Stephenson, Dorothy Swogetinsky, Ann Roscoe, Manager, Sharon Lester
Front row: Gloria Pruitt, Loyce Volcik, Joyce Volcik, LaRuth Kendrick*

Used by Permission: LaRuth Kendrick Gates, 2012

Bearettes Strategize

Jody Conradt (glasses), Olga Fallen, LaRuth Kendrick
Used by Permission: LaRuth Kendrick Gates, 2012

According to the *Baylor Lariat*, March 2 1962, the Bearettes won the North Texas State University tournament defeating Sam Houston State, North Texas State University, and Abilene Christian College in the championship game. Jody Conradt, the team's leading scorer, scored 40 of 60 points in the semifinal game against North Texas State. Their trophy for this tournament win can be found in the Texas Collection Library on the Baylor campus. The 1962 team also placed third in a tournament at Southwest Texas State University. By the time the District IV Tournament rolled around in 1962, the Bearettes were 7-0 and highly favored to repeat as champions. No record could be found of the results of this tournament.

According to Donna Cleland, one of the original Bearettes, the team, consisting of ten to twelve girls, practiced several times a week, and participated in three to four games and a couple of tournaments each season. Cleland noted:

> Our uniforms were whatever shoes we had – low cut Converse or Keds – whatever white shorts we had, and some hand-me-down white cotton camp shirts with green and gold trim. I recall the shirts weren't all exactly alike. The shirt supply was short by one, so Jody Conradt used green shiny tape to make a number on the back of a plain white shirt. That was her uniform. I don't know how or where Coach Fallen came up with those shirts but we were Baylor Proud of them.[19]

Members of the 1961-62 Bearette Basketball team were: Jamie Shahan, Ruth Kendrick, Jody Conradt, Barbara Goar, Karen Stephenson, Ardith Hartung, Joyce Volcik, Loyce Volcik, Jo Flint, Gloria Pruitt, Virginia Shannon, Carol Noel, Rachel Colson, Ann Roscoe, Cynthia Pillsbury, Tulisha Shahan, Dorothy Swogetinsky, and Donna Cleland. Managers were Brenda Clause, Ethel Blackman, and Sharon Lester.[20, 21]

Bearettes Warm Up

Rachael Colson (back to picture), Jody Conradt, Joyce (or Loyce) Volcik

Used by Permission LaRuth Kendrick Gates, 2012

In March 1962, Baylor hosted Ouachita Baptist College in a game to demonstrate the new DGWS rules for women's basketball. Coaches from high schools in the area were invited to attend in an effort to see how the game would change if these new rules were adopted by the Texas Interscholastic League (TIL). At the time the women's rules divided the court into two halves and put three team members from each team on each half. Defensive players for one team were on the same half of the court as offensive players from the other team. No player was allowed to cross the center line.

The new rules introduced an era of what became known as the "Rover" era in women's basketball. These rules maintained six players per team but allowed two of the players from each team to rove and play on both ends of the court. Two offensive players remained on one end of the court and two defensive players were in place on the other end of the court. The rovers ran the full length of the court, creating a 4-person offensive and defensive strategy. The new rules were not met with excitement by the TIL coaches, according to Olga Fallen, Bearette coach. As reported in the *Waco Tribune Herald* March 25, 1962, Fallen said that "Most of the coaches thought that the game was too fast. They hate the drastic change in the rules because it will involve the redoing of many years of work." Although Baylor lost this exhibition game 48-46 in overtime, Fallen indicated the new rules were well-received by the Bearette players. She further stated: "The new rules will make the game much more interesting and challenging and the players themselves love it." These rules were utilized in colleges and universities until 1970 when the current five-person game was adopted for women.

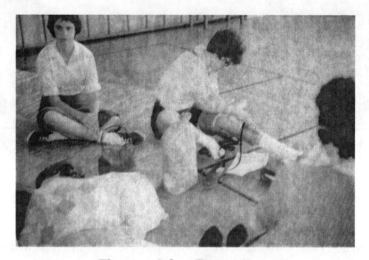

Time out for Bearettes

Rachael Colson, Donna Cleland adjusts her knee brace

Used by Permission LaRuth Kendrick Gates, 2012

The March 12, 1964 *Baylor Lariat* reported that Baylor teams would be competing against Sam Houston State College, Mary-Hardin Baylor College, and Temple Junior College in volleyball, badminton and tennis. No information on how these teams fared in competition was available. Donna Cleland, who played on the basketball, volleyball and tennis teams for Baylor during the early sixties, offered this insight.

As an eighteen year old, I would have
been happy to play a game every day.
Fifty years later, I realize the program's
scale left time for other interests,
including other sports. In a way, it was
the best of both worlds. I'm also mindful
that if participation in the 60's era

program had required today's skill and
commitment levels, most of us would not
have had an opportunity to play at all.[22]

INTERCOLLEGIATE ATHLETICS, 1965-69

Although records were sketchy, Baylor fielded women's teams in basketball, volleyball, tennis, badminton, swimming, golf, bowling, track and field, and fencing
by the end of the 1960s. Fallen coached basketball, volleyball, tennis, and track
and field while Mary Tindle coached badminton, TeDe Lifland coached golf
and fencing, and Elizabeth Bianchi coached swimming. These women were
dedicated and passionate about their sport and supported athletic competition
for women. In addition to their teaching responsibilities, they conducted practices and traveled consistently with their teams, providing the opportunities for
Baylor's women to be involved in collegiate athletics.

There were hundreds of similarly dedicated women across the state of
Texas during the 1960s and 1970, teaching and coaching and making the same
sacrifices to provide athletic opportunities for their female students. In addition, many of these committed additional time and energy assuming leadership roles in the governing organizations in Texas. Some were involved at the
national level. Because of the dedication of these women, Texas had one of
the most organized and effective state associations for women's athletics in the
country, TCIAW.[9]

At Baylor, Olga Fallen and Mary Tindle were very involved with these
state organizations. Fallen was elected and served as Vice-Chair of the Texas
Commission for Intercollegiate Athletics for Women (TCIAW) in 1972. After
her term of office, she remained active in the Commission, attending the annual
meetings of the TCIAW and continuing to support the organization when it
became the Texas Association for Intercollegiate Athletics (TAIAW) throughout the decade of the seventies. Mary Tindle served on the board of the Texas
Foundation for Intercollegiate Athletics for Women, an organization formed
in 1970 to provide financial support to the Commission. The Foundation
collaborated with the Commission to offer a series of Annual Sport Institutes

---

9   See Chapter 1 for more detail.

throughout the seventies, providing opportunities to enhance the expertise of both women coaches and athletes at the collegiate level. There are extensive records about the work of the TCIAW/TAIAW and the Texas Foundation in the archives of the Women's Collection at Texas Woman's University in Denton, Texas.

The women's intercollegiate competition throughout the 1960s was governed by the Women's Recreation Association (WRA) and the Texas Recreation Federation of College Women (TRFCW) and played under the rules of the Division of Girls and Women's Sports (DGWS) of the American Association for Health, Physical Education, Recreation and Dance (AAHPERD). Within this structure and on an annual basis, universities had the opportunity to enter teams from every sport in a district tournament. First and second place winners at the district level advanced to play in the state tournament. There was no play beyond the state level at this time.

During the 1960s, the Baylor women's extramural program was under the auspices of the Health, Physical Education, and Recreation Department. Initially Dr. Lloyd O. Russell, Chair of the Department, supported having the program and provided financial support for the women. When Dr. Russell died suddenly in the late sixties, Dr. Ted Powers assumed the chairmanship of the Department. He continued the support for the women's athletic program and particularly provided support and advocacy for the women through the 1970s when the women's programs transitioned to the athletic department and during the years when Title IX was implemented at Baylor. He was one of the main people that Olga Fallen leaned on for support and advice during these turbulent years. Ted Powers remained as chair of the Department until 1988.

BASKETBALL

Basketball continued to be the main intercollegiate sport for the women. While won-loss records were sketchy for this team, anecdotal evidence from players during that time suggests the team played individual home and away games. Records indicated Baylor participated in tournaments at Stephen F. Austin University and North Texas State College as well.

Temple Junior College (TJC) provided some of the stiffest competition for the women during this period. Coached by Fran Garmon, TJC offered athletic scholarships to women. As reported in the March 2, 1966 *Baylor Lariat*, Baylor lost to TJC, 59-28. The Bearettes also lost to TJC in the second round of the 1970 TCIAW District IV tournament.[23] Records identified fifteen women who played for Baylor during this period— LaDawn Kemp, Frankie Blaylock, Linda Lene', Ann Weaver, Susan Courtney, Ginny Reed, Margaret Kocek, Joy Massey, Nancy Goodloe, Pixie Mansfield, Sandy Schier, Christine Camp, Barbara Cook, Sue Hickey, and Susie Riechley.[24] Upon graduation many of these women had distinguished careers as physical education teachers and coaches in Texas schools and beyond. I say beyond because Ann Weaver was from Missouri. LaDawn Kemp went on to spend thirty-five years directing Special Olympics in California while Susie Reichley enjoyed a successful professional bowling career.

This group of women were, by and large, physical education majors so there was a wonderful camaraderie within the group because we spent so much time together in our academic classes. The reader will see these names mentioned on most of the teams of the sixties. All of us came from different backgrounds as far as our sport's expertise was concerned. As physical education majors, we learned how to participate and teach/coach every sport. While that didn't make us successful athletes in all sports, it did prepare us well for our chosen profession. We always managed to have fun, encouraging each other in every event to do our best. Even though the group changed from year to year with graduation, we managed to keep our support for each other in tact. I was honored to be a part of this group of women.

BADMINTON

Anecdotal evidence from team players indicated the women's badminton team had strong showings at both the district and state TRFCW tournaments during this period of time. The Baylor team placed first at the 1966 TRFCW District IV tournament.[25] For Baylor to place first as a team, team members would have had to place first in both the singles and doubles competitions. Nancy Goodloe and Sandy Schier were playing for Baylor at that time, both played singles and they teamed in doubles. So, one of those women won the singles, and then Schier and Goodloe won the doubles competition. As a Bearette badminton player, I have vivid memories of my playing years. One was the Friday morning I overslept and didn't show up at Marrs McLean Gym to leave for a badminton tournament. Of course, we were leaving at 4:00 in the morning so to say I overslept might be a stretch. Mary Tindle, coach, was not to be outdone, however, and she came to the dorm and rousted me out of bed in time to leave and make the tournament. I think we were headed to Houston, Texas for that tournament, a four hour drive from Waco, Texas.

My second memory occurred in the mid-sixties when I played both on the basketball team and the badminton team. On this particular weekend, the basketball team was entered in a tournament at North Texas State University, and the badminton team was entered in a tournament at Texas Woman's University (TWU). Both universities were located in Denton, Texas. Sandy Schier, my badminton partner, also played on the basketball team. So the dilemma was how can we (Sandy and I) play on both the basketball and badminton teams this weekend and represent Baylor in both events without either team having to forfeit a match or game? I'm not sure how Mary Tindle and Olga Fallen worked this problem out with tournament officials, but they did. So, Sandy and I would play a badminton match and Mary would taxi us over to the gym at North Texas in time to play a basketball game, then back to the gym at TWU, and so it went the entire day. I don't remember anything about whether we won or lost any match or game, but I do remember changing clothes in the car between trips, and I do remember being pretty tired at the end of the day.

TENNIS

Baylor Lariat reports from March 30 1965 and April 6, 1965 indicated that Baylor women tennis players, Susan Courtney and Barbara Cook, competed in the State TRFCW Tennis tournament along with ten other universities in 1965. They won this berth by winning second place in the District TRFCW Tennis tournament held at Mary Hardin-Baylor. There were six members of the 1965 tennis team, but no identifiable information was available for the other members.

The 1966 tennis team consisted of Susan Courtney, Barbara Cook, Sandy Schier, Sylvia Schier, Sandy Speagle and Martha Smiley. Per a news article in the *Baylor Lariat*, March 25, 1966, Baylor hosted the 1966 TRFCW District tournament with teams from Mary Hardin-Baylor, Temple Junior College, San Antonio College, Trinity University, University of Texas, Texas Lutheran College, Southwest Junior College, and Baylor. The tournament was a one-day event with competition in singles and doubles. Barbara Cook was sick for the tournament. Under TRFCW rules, Libby Johnson, a graduate assistant at Baylor, took her place on the doubles team with Susan Courtney. No record of the outcome was found.

TRACK AND FIELD

Each spring, women physical education majors at Baylor took a class in track and field methods for coaching. The purpose of the class was to help the student develop knowledge and skills in the various track and field events so that she could teach and coach the events in the secondary schools of Texas after graduation from Baylor. As part of the requirements for the class, students had to enter the Southwest Texas Invitational Track meet, competing in two field events and at least one running event. This competitive experience furthered the student's understanding of what is involved in running a track and field meet and how to officiate the various events.

The inaugural season for the women's track and field program was 1965. The team entered and placed first, second, or third in every event at the 4th Annual Track and Field Meet hosted by Southwest Texas State and were paced by LaDawn Kemp, winning the high jump, broad jump and placing second in the 50 yard hurdles. Barbara Cook won the javelin competition. The team finished 2nd to Southwest Texas State College (SWTSC).[26]

As reported in the *Baylor Lariat*, May 3, 1966, the women's track team took second place in the Southwest Texas State Annual Track and Field meet. Connie Sanders paced the Bearettes, placing first in the discus and third in the shot put. Frankie Blaylock placed second in discus while Sue Bennett took second in the javelin and third in the long jump.

LaDawn Kemp shot put

Olga Fallen Collection, Accession 3797, Box 38, Folders 14,
The Texas Collection, Baylor University.

OTHER MEMBERS OF THE 1965 TRACK AND FIELD TEAM WERE:

Jeanne Nowlin – 100, Discus, Javelin, Relay

Barbara Cook – Javelin

Melba Schweinle – 100, 220, Javelin, Relay

Susie Reichley – 100, Discus, Javelin, Relay

Virginia Coffman – 220, Hurdles, High Jump, Relay

Connie Martin – 220, High Jump, Broad Jump, Relay

Susan Courtney – 220, High Jump, Broad Jump, Relay

Elizabeth Cooper – Hurdles, Broad Jump

Janet Holsomback – Hurdles, Discus, Javelin

Connie Sanders – Javelin, Discus, Shot Put

Gwen Landers – Discus, Shot Put

Harriet Rubel – Shot Put, Javelin

Reedelle Muirhead – Javelin, Shot Put, Discus

Janice McSwain – Broad Jump, High Jump, Relay

Susie Isbell – Javelin, Discus, Shot Put[27]

1965 Bearette Track and Field Team

*Olga Fallen Collection, Accession 3797, Box 38, Folder 14,
The Texas Collection, Baylor University.*

Connie Sanders, Shot Put

*Olga Fallen Collection, Accession 3797, Box 38, Folder 14,
The Texas Collection, Baylor University.*

According to the *Baylor Lariat* of May 3, 1966, the women's track team took second place in the Southwest Texas State Annual Track and Field meet. Connie Sanders paced the Bearettes, placing first in the discus and third in the shot put.

Frankie Blaylock placed second in discus while Sue Bennett took second in the javelin and third in the long jump.

At the 1967 SWTSC event, eight teams were entered from Southwest Texas State College, Baylor University, Del Mar College, Trinity University, Tarleton State College, Texas Woman's University (TWU), Mary-Hardin Baylor College, the Austin Track Club and the Austin School for the Deaf. Baylor participants included Ann Sturdivant, Peggy Brooks, Peggy Coppedge, Donna Bussey, Pam Vardeman, Christine Camp, Patsy Tatum, Sandy Schier, Jan Dupree, Connie Sanders, Frankie Blaylock, Nancy Goodloe, Sue Bennett, JoAnne Meffert, Margaret McFadden, Sharon Compton, Jackie Newton, Kathy Debord, Pam Fowler, and Jeannette Lipscomb.[28, 29]

As a participant in that track meet, I don't have a lot of specific memories of the event or how I performed. I do remember being entered in the discus and javelin throws and in the 220-yard dash. Anyone who knows me cannot imagine that I could run anything, especially a speed event. And they would be right about that! The most difficult part of the running was learning how to get down in the blocks and do the whole 'on your mark, get set, gun shot for go` thing. I'd get into the set position, wonder why it took so long for the gun to go off, and then pray that I wouldn't fall flat on my face trying to start the race. I loved the discus and javelin throws, however, and was anxious to perfect the footwork and releases required to get good distances in those events.

I do give credit to Olga Fallen, however, for the learning that occurred by taking that track class and then entering in track meets as an actual participant. That learning stood me in good stead when I coached the Baylor women's track team in the seventies. It also made me appreciate those student-athletes who loved to run, who had the skill and body build to do that well, and the commitment to train hard to be the best in their events.

GOLF

1968 Baylor women's golf team, composed of Lin Blansit, Sharon Wheatley, Sandy Hinton and Nancy Goodloe, was coached by T.D. LIfland. The team practiced at a funky little course on 12th street, not far from the campus. The course had nine holes and featured dead grass greens most of the year and fairways that were mostly dirt and rock. Green fees were cheap, however, and we paid our own way. During dry spells, the cracks in the ground were so big that a few players were known to lose their balls in the middle of the fairway. The men's golf team, however, practiced at Ridgewood Country Club. In spite of efforts by Lifland, the women were not allowed on this course. Naturally, the women supplied all of their own equipment and balls for competitions. In spite of these drawbacks, this team placed second in the 1968 State TRFCW tournament.

TRACK AND FIELD

In 1969 the TRFCW had reorganized itself into the Texas Commission for Intercollegiate Athletics for Women (TCIAW). The TCIAW hosted its first State Track and Field meet this year. Nineteen sixty-nine was also the year for the Commission for Intercollegiate Athletics for Women (CIAW) to sponsor the first ever women's National Track and Field meet.[30]

Over the next few years, Olga Fallen and her staff built a solid program for track athletes at Baylor, utilizing returning students and still requiring class members to participate on the track team. In the decade of the 70s Baylor continued to have a strong Track and Field team demonstrating success in local, state and national track meets.

SWIMMING

Elizabeth Bianchi coached a women swimming team and entered the women swimmers in the TRFCW district meets during these years. The 1969-70 team placed fifth at the TCIAW State meet. No individual event data were found.[31]

Elizabeth Bianchi Coaches a Diver in the Baylor Pool
Olga Fallen Collection, Accession 3797, Box 38, Folder 13,
The Texas Collection, Baylor University.

FINANCIAL SUPPORT FOR
WOMEN'S ATHLETICS

During the decade of the 1960s, the Baylor women's extramural program was under the auspices of the Health, Physical Education, and Recreation Department (HPER). Initially, Dr. Lloyd O. Russell, chair of the Department, supported the program, followed by Dr. Ted Powers, who succeeded Russell as chair in 1966-67. Beginning in 1964 Fallen requested funds for the extramural teams in basketball, volleyball, tennis and badminton. Women's extramurals/athletics was not a line item in the HPER budget, rather it received its funding from a special fund of the Department. According to Dutch Schroeder, the HPER department hosted annually, a boy's high school invitational Christmas basketball tournament in these early years. The proceeds from this tournament went into the fund to support the women's athletic program.[32] When the HPER department quit hosting the basketball tournament, the money for women's athletics continued to flow to the programs. It came from somewhere in the HPER budget. Evidence indicated that in the later sixties and early seventies, Ted Powers would periodically request and receive funds from President Abner V. McCall for the women's athletic program.

During the early years, Fallen's requests primarily were for gas reimbursements to the various tournaments. In 1964 the total cost for all of the teams to do all of their traveling was $210.[33] Athletes paid for their own food, and in sports such as badminton and tennis, their own equipment. The athletes certainly owed a debt of gratitude to all of the parents who provided this level of support and help. Uniforms for basketball and volleyball were supplied by the University and were issued to the students at the beginning of the season and returned at the end. Each student was responsible for keeping her uniform clean and in good repair during the season. Hotel/motel reimbursement was out of the question during this time. When teams needed to stay overnight, team members stayed with friends or family. Some teams stayed in private homes, some were known to sleep in the basements of local Baptist churches. More often than not, the teams traveled late at night and into the early morning hours to return home after a competition. This travel situation prevailed throughout the sixties.

By the mid- to late-sixties, two dollars per day was allocated for meals for the women athletes. Equipment and supplies continued to be shared from the HPER department.

There was no recruiting and certainly no scholarships and anyone who was interested could try out for any of the teams. Many of the teams had 'rookies' playing on a regular basis, women who loved the sport but had never played, but most of the women competitors had played in high school and wanted further opportunity for competition in college. LaDawn Kemp Reichling tells the story of being offered a scholarship to play basketball for the Wayland Flying Queens (1964). Fortunately for Baylor, her heart was at Baylor, so she turned down the scholarship and came to Waco. Her talents did not get past Olga Fallen, however, and Kemp Reichling was placed on the basketball team's starting lineup as a freshman. Fallen then recruited her to compete in track as a hurdler and high jumper. LaDawn had never run track in her life but she was willing to try.[34] Indeed, this attitude was a hallmark of most of the early athletic programs in this country. Women athletes played for the love of the game and for the camaraderie of the team, and, the coaches coached, practiced and traveled because of their dedication to the game and to the athletes.

Through the first seventy years of the twentieth century, Baylor women had a variety of opportunities to participate in sport. Ranging from a vast array of intramural activities to occasional intercollegiate opportunities to compete in badminton, tennis, and fencing, a strong ethic of physical ability and love of the game was laid down for the push to be come a recognized and valued outlet for varsity intercollegiate competition during the 1960's.

As Baylor moved into the decade of the seventies, three events beyond the control of the University and the women's athletic program loomed large and proved to be the important stories in the growth and expansion of intercollegiate athletic programs for women. These events were: The creation of the Association for Intercollegiate Athletics for Women, the first national governing body for women's intercollegiate sport, the passage of Title IX of the Civil Rights Amendments in 1972, and the takeover of women's athletics by the NCAA in 1982.

NOTES ON CHAPTER 3

BEARETTES ARE BORN

1. Baylor University, Round Up 1906 Yearbook, (Waco, TX: [The Senior Class of Baylor University], 1906), The Texas Collection, Baylor University, p. 147.

2. Dutch Schroeder, letter to the author, June 7, 2013.

3. Baylor University, Round Up 1928 Yearbook, (Waco, TX: [The Senior Class of Baylor University], 1928, The Texas Collection, Baylor University), 196, 198.

4. "IM Volleyball, Basketball Letters to Be Awarded In Chapel Next Monday," *Baylor Lariat* Sports, *The Baylor Lariat*, March 16, 1945, 4.

5. "Girls' IM Sports Leaders Announced by Musgrave," The *Baylor Lariat*, September 28, 1945, 4.

6. Ellen Brown, "Milestones in Women's Athletics at Baylor," *The Baylor Line*, Spring 1993, 32.

7. Baylor University, Round Up 1940 Yearbook, (Waco, TX: [The Student body of Baylor University], 1940), The Texas Collection, Baylor University, p. 96.

8. "Badminton Tourney Opens Friday with Big Crowd Expected," *Lariat Daily Sports*, February 15, 1940.

9. Baylor University, Round Up 1941 Yearbook, (Waco, TX: [The Students of Baylor University], 1941, The Texas Collection, Baylor University), 156.

10. Betty Bryant Rogers. Interview by the author, Waco, TX, July 2, 2012.

11. Mary Tindle. Interview by the author, June 25, 3012.

12. "Baylor Olympics," The Olga Fallen Collection, Accession #3797, Box 12, Folder 2, The Texas Collection, Baylor University.

13. "Interschool Activities for Major Students," The Olga Fallen Collection, Accession #3797, Box 12, Folder 10, The Texas Collection, Baylor University.

14. Shirley Poteet. Telephone interview by the author, May 17, 2012.

15. Texas Longhorns, "Jody Conradt Profile," http://www.texassports.com/genrel/conradt_jody00.html. Accessed June 8, 2013.

16. The Olga Fallen Collection, Box 12, Folder 10.

17. Ibid.

18. "Baylor Women to Play in Basketball Tourney," The Baylor Lariat, March 2, 1962.

19. Donna Cleland, email to the author, June 2012.

20. See note 18.

21. "Coed Tourney Draws Baylor Team Saturday," Baylor Lariat, Feb. 9, 1961.

22. See note 19.

23. The Woman's Collection, MSS 77, Box 9, Blagg-Huey Library, Texas Woman's University, Denton, TX.

24. The Olga Fallen Collection, Box 17, Folders 1-2.

25. The Woman's Collection, MSS 77, Box 7.

26. The Olga Fallen Collection, Box 33, Folders 9-14.

27. Ibid.

28. The Olga Fallen Collection, Box 33, Folder 9.

29. The Olga Fallen Collection, Box 38, Folder 14.

30. See note 23 above.

31. Ibid.

32. E.E. Dutch Schroeder, telephone interview by the author, May 21, 2013.

33. The Olga Fallen Collection, Box 36, Folder 13.

34. LaDawn Kemp Reichling, email to the author, May 31, 2012.

CHAPTER 4

◎◎◎

BEARETTES TO LADY BEARS, 1970-1975

Baylor started the decade of the seventies offering opportunities for women athletes to compete in nine sports. Added to basketball, volleyball and tennis were track and field (after a two year hiatus), badminton, fencing, golf, softball and women swimming. All competitions fell under the auspices of the Texas Commission for Intercollegiate Athletics (TCIAW) for Women, the state affiliate of the Commission on Intercollegiate Athletics for Women (CIAW). The organization changed in 1974 to the Texas Association for Intercollegiate Athletics for Women (TAIAW) in concert with the national Association for Intercollegiate Athletics for Women (AIAW).

Throughout the seventies, the women's athletics staff taught in the Physical Education department and coached as part of a full teaching load. This group went through transitions as the number of sports varied and staff turnover occurred. They were:

Olga Fallen—Coordinator for Women's Athletics and Head Coach, Basketball (1970-1979), Softball (1973-1979), Tennis (early seventies), Track and Field, Volleyball (through 1974).

Nancy Goodloe—Asst. Coach Volleyball, 1970–74, Head Coach, Volleyball, 1975, Head Coach, Badminton, 1972–1974, Asst. Track and Field, 1972–1976, Head Fencing Coach, 1970–1971, Head Trainer for Women's Athletics, 1974–76.

Margaret Wooddy—Head Coach Volleyball 1976–1979; Head
Coach Track and Field 1976–79; Sports Information Director
for Women, Head Athletic Trainer for Women, 1976–79

Elizabeth Bianchi—Women Swimming, 1970–1976

Glada Munt—Head Coach Tennis, 1975

John Phelps—Head Coach Tennis, 1977, 1978

Rob Bradshaw—Head Coach Tennis, 1979

Tim Palmer—Head Coach Tennis, 1980, 1981

T.D. Lifland—Golf – middle sixties to early seventies

E.E. "Dutch" Schroeder—Head Coach Badminton, 1975–mid-1990s

It was common practice for the women athletes in the sixties and seventies to participate in more than one sport. For example, Leah Box, playing for Baylor in the mid-seventies was a four-sport letterman. She competed in basketball, volleyball, track and field and softball. In the sixties, the author played basketball, golf and badminton. In the early seventies, Mary Ann Deatley Jewett played basketball and volleyball for the Bearettes, and Carol King played basketball, volleyball and badminton. As late as the early 1980s, Carol Reeves played both basketball and softball.

Beginning with the move of the women under the NCAA umbrella in 1982 and the growth in the ability of colleges and universities to recruit and award athletic scholarships, the opportunities for women to participate in more than one sport dwindled. In today's world of intercollegiate athletics, it is uncommon for women athletes to participate in more than one sport.

BASKETBALL

Basketball was the most prominent of the nine sports across this decade. Forty-five women tried out for the 1970-71 team that participated in three tournaments overall, played several home and away games and hosted the TCIAW District IV tournament. As reported in the *Baylor Lariat*, March 9, 1971, the women finished third in the District tournament, playing four games in a time span of twenty-one hours. Eighteen women comprised the 1970-71 team. They were Carol King, Peggy Hale, Javon Attaway, Mary Ann DeAtley, Becky Futrell, Carol Curtis, Sally Stokes, Norma Pruitt, Henrietta Ridling, Cathy Cundiff, Peggy Bradford, Alita Brown, Judy Power, Jan Story, Kathy Shackleford, Margaret Wooddy, Donna Brooks, and Linda Howard.[1]

1970-71 Bearette Basketball Team

Olga Fallen Collection, Accession #3797, Box 38, Folder 8,
The Texas Collection, Baylor University

The 1971-72 Bearette basketball team participated in six tournaments, winning their first tournament in nine years at the Tarleton Invitational Tournament.[2] They placed third at the North Texas Invitational, fifth in the Houston Invitational, and won the TCIAW District IV tournament. They became the first Bearette basketball team to play in the state TCIAW tournament entering that event with an 11-5 overall record. They lost two of three games in the tournament and finished the season with a 12-7 record. Members of that team were Carol King, Peggy Hale, Mary Ann DeAtley, Sally Stokes, Javon Lechler, Cathy Robinson, Penny Mudgett, Margaret Wooddy, Peggy Bradford, Paula Carroll, Ann Gibson, Jan Camp, Teresa Luttrell, Alice Melendez and Judy Norman. Manager was Paula Love.[3, 4]

1971-72 Bearette Basketball Team

Olga Fallen Collection, Accession #3797, Box 38, Folder 8,
The Texas Collection, Baylor University

The team practiced three hours per day on Monday, Wednesday and Friday. There were no scholarships for women, only the love of the game and a lot of sacrifices. In his *Baylor Lariat* article dated March 11, 1971, David McCollum reported the comments of several of the players, noting their sacrifices and why they played. Mary Ann Deatley: "It's a good feeling working with the team and the coach. Sometimes you come back and are real tired, but I wouldn't give it up for the world." Carol Curtis: "To have time for basketball, I have to double up a lot and study harder, but I really love it (basketball). I played it all through high school and junior high." Carol King: "I like five-man ball because the player has to be skilled in both offense and defense." Becky Futrell: "It's a good way to get to know your team members. I'm going to miss it [going to nursing school] because I have always played."

Reflecting on her years as a Bearette (1970-73), Mary Ann Deatley Jewett shared:

> When it came time for the basketball
> season to begin, I had not even
> considered playing. My level of play for a
> couple of years in high school was less

than basic. I did not have a jump shot,
and did not have basic skills down at all.
I think that Olga [Fallen] saw me both as
an extreme challenge as well as someone
to cultivate into a decent player. It was
tough going. My brain was fried after
being bombarded with all of the different
defenses, learning that you never allow
a player to drive the baseline, to position
and block to grab a rebound....I was
just glad that Olga and the rest of the
team did not give upon me completely.

Back during the early 70s, things were
different. We did not have access to
a nice training room and did not have
a structured program to keep us in
topnotch condition for playing ball....we
went to quite a few away tournaments.
That meant that we had to scrounge up
transportation, food, and a place to stay. I
had a friend on the 5th floor of Collins Hall
from Ft. Worth. When she heard about
it, her parents offered their guesthouse
for our use. That was heaven because it
meant we would have some food provided
by wonderful people, as well as a nice
heated place to stay. Sure, we might have
to use bedrolls, but that was fine..getting
to the tournament was a challenge. I recall
about ten of us crammed into one vehicle
on one particular occasion. I was sitting
in the back seat with someone on my lap.
Sally Stokes was driving. She had to pull
over once because I developed a huge
cramp in my leg—bad timing! We usually

had to pay our own way for meals. On special occasions, Olga might have some money from who knows where to treat all of us for a meal. That was a big deal. One year there was a tournament the same weekend as Baylor Homecoming. We all took a vote and decided to play in the tournament. That was how dedicated we all were….through all the practices, sweat, wrapping injuries, etc. there was nothing but pure joy for me. Carol [King] and I still refer to those days as the 'best times of our lives'. And they were!"[5]

Penny Mudgett, 1971-73, shared that she got hooked into playing when a friend told her they needed someone with experience on the team. She tried out and made it. She remembered that Baylor reimbursed players for gas when they took their own personal cars to tournaments, and verified that players often slept on the floors of any church, home, or apartment they was offered to them. Jewett and Mudgett's words provided a very accurate picture of collegiate athletic experiences during this time. Many women tried out for the teams because they had talent but had never before had the opportunities to compete. They developed their skills while learning to play the game, and they endured all sorts of traveling situations that were less than desirable but produced great memories for many Baylor women.

BADMINTON

Baylor continued its strong tradition of having a men and women's badminton team during the decade of the seventies. The women participated in AIAW events while the men's collegiate tournaments were not sanctioned by a national group.

Baylor badminton was well-represented in tournaments across Texas during this time and continued to host the Baylor Invitational College and Baylor Open Badminton tournaments each year. Players during the 1970-72 stretch were Rachel Cole, Lynn Woodward, Jan Wilson, Carol King and Sally Stokes. Rachel Cole and Jan Wilson placed third at the TCIAW District IV tournament in 1971.[6,7] Rachel

Cole placed third in singles at the 1972 TCIAW District IV TCIAW tournament.[8] Other team members were Jamey Bozeman, Gayle Broome, Kathy Dominguez and Debbie Snyder.[9] Most of these women had never played badminton in their lifetime but got interested in the sport after taking it for physical education credit at Baylor. I had the pleasure of coaching these women and fondly remember the challenge with those who had a tennis background. Our mantra became "use your wrist." Tennis players found that very difficult to do, and more than one of these players accused me of ruining their tennis games forever. They were fun to travel with and a pleasure to know and coach.

Badminton players could use the racquets available through the HPER department but most purchased their own. The HPER racquets were used in the physical education classes and were, for the most part, wooden racquets. Equipment advances in this sport resulted in the lighter aluminum racquets that were strung tighter and contributed to better play. Players furnishing their own racquets would pay upwards of fifty dollars for this piece of equipment, and that was considered a very big investment for the athlete. As a player, I was thrilled when I was able to buy my first aluminum racquet. The team practiced with plastic shuttlecocks. Feathered shuttlecocks were used for competition, and Baylor supplied the team's shuttlecocks for both practice and tournament play.

FENCING/GOLF

As an undergraduate at Baylor, the author took the fencing class as part of her degree requirements and then went on to teach and coach this event as a young faculty member in the early seventies. Fencing was popular at Baylor as one of many choices for a physical education class, and many undergraduates were interested in developing their skills. Records indicated that Baylor hosted the Texas Intercollegiate Fencing Tournament in 1970 and that we had a fencing team in 1970 and 1971. No information could be found to verify any competition, no record of any participation beyond 1971 was found, and I have no memory of spending a lot of time with the fencing team.[10]

The *Baylor Lariat*, March 30, 1971 reported that Baylor's Susan Addy, 1968-1972, took second place in the TCIAW District IV golf tournament, good enough to qualify her for the state tournament. Baylor's Lin Blansit and Pat Freedman placed third and fourth respectively. Addy fondly remembered a special tournament for her.

The girls on the team drove our cars
to practice and to play in tournaments.
We would just show up and play with
no fanfare, no announcement off the
first tee, no nothing! I well remember a
state tournament played in Belton. Mrs.
Lifland's husband was ill so Ms. [Nancy]
Goodloe filled in as her assistant coach.
I was first off the tee with players from
Texas Tech, the University of Texas,
and Sam Houston State. With the last
name Addy and representing Baylor, I
got to go first many times! Nervously,
I drew a driver from my golf bag. Ms.
Goodloe came up to me and asked if
I was really going to use that drover
on the par 3 first hole. When I saw the
yardage, I quickly returned the club
to my bag and chose my 8 iron.

I struck the ball well and turned
to put my club up when the other
participants started yelling. I had made
a hole-in-one and didn't even get to
see it. That, obviously, was the best
start I ever had in a tournament.

Mrs. Lifland arranged the tournaments,
maybe three or four each spring, and
we played on her membership at the
country club with some help from
Baylor perhaps; however, we played
for Baylor and we were proud to do it. I
don't think we even had shirts alike or
anything that set us apart from anyone

**else on the course, but we all knew
we played for Baylor University.**[11]

Lifland continued to coach the women's golf team through the early seventies. There were no records of Baylor women's golf after 1974 until 1988 when Baylor made the decision to drop softball and offer golf as a varsity sport instead. Baylor has had a women's golf team since then. More information about the achievements of this team is available in subsequent chapters.

The women golfers furnished their own equipment—club, bags, shoes, tees—to participate in this sport. Baylor furnished tournament balls through the HPER department, and that was the extent of equipment support.

SOFTBALL

The TCIAW added softball to their list of sports for the 1971-72 year and offered only a state championship tournament. Baylor fielded a softball team for the first time during this year and participated in the TCIAW events. Team members who played in 1970-1971 were: Pat Freedman, Carol King, Diane Henson, Rosemary Patterson, Rachael Cole, Alita Brown, Kathy Wiese, Alice Melendez, Jane Hassan Teresa Luttrell, Peggy Hale, Paula Love, Jeanne Woodfin, Carol Henderson, Jan Storey, Pat Jones, Linda Williams, Annette Henderson, and Cathy Curlee.[12] The team was captained by Kathy Wiese, a sophomore and Waco native. They traveled to Texas Woman's University for one tournament and also participated in the District IV TCIAW tournament. The team had a fifty percent batting average and ended the season with a 3-3 record.[13]

Like other female athletes of the era, softball players furnished their own gloves and shoes and sometimes bats if they did not like what Baylor furnished. Other equipment such as catcher's mask and padding, bats, and balls were furnished by the Health, Physical Education and Recreation Department. And, like all of the other sports, the softball team found themselves often playing two and three games a day with little rest in between.

SWIMMING

There was great interest in the swim team during the early years of the seventies at Baylor. Like the badminton team, both men and women made up the swim team and traveled to several meets around the state each year. Coached by Elizabeth Bianchi, the women's team competed in the TCIAW District and State meets during this time. The March 19, 1971 *Lariat* listed the following team members: Margo Armstrong, Sharon Beasley, Barbara Darling, Diane Donaldson, Gay Langston, Pam Pressley, Kathy Shackelford, Sherry Smith, Judy Seewald, Carol Vaughan, Deborah Huyser, and Sue Root. The 1970 team placed 5th at the TCIAW State meet.[14]

Bianchi coached her 1971-72 women swimmers to a second place finish in the State TCIAW meet that featured two Baylor champions. Paula Love, freshman from Lafayette, Louisiana, took first place in the one-meter diving competition. Linda Frasher, freshman from Houston, Texas, won the 200-yard free style swim. The team had twenty-nine members, men and women, and represented the University in four meets.[15] Other members of the swimming team in these early years were Lynn Woodward, Susan Chalmers, Frances Heard, Carol Vaughan, Judy Crump, and Judy Fitzgerald. Exactly what years they participated on the team could not be determined.[16]

The team practiced in the Marrs McLean gymnasium pool. In the early years taking a swimming class was required of every Baylor student before he/she could graduate. The Baylor Pool was fifty meters long and was used extensively for classes, intramurals and for the swim team. It was called the Swamp.

TENNIS

The women's tennis team played in several tournaments from 1970 through 1972. Candy Hutcheson, Andrews, Texas, won second in the 1971 District TCIAW tournament, as reported in the *Baylor Lariat*, March 30, 1971. This finish qualified her to play in the State TCIAW tournament. Women representing Baylor in tennis 1970 to 1972 were: Candy Hutcheson, Susan Rhoades, Chriss Miller, Patti Sloan, Debbie Routh, Diana Marre, Susan Stoops, Monte Vaughan, Karen Henson, Jennifer Judin, Gail Duncan, Carol Dodson, Susan Smith, and Jan Greer.[17, 18,19]

**Bearette Tennis Players, Diane Marre
and Debra Routh**

*Olga Fallen Collection, Accession 3797, Box 38, Folders 21,
The Texas Collection, Baylor University*

TRACK AND FIELD

The 1969 track and field team placed second at the TCIAW State meet but then the Baylor women experienced a two-year hiatus from competition in these events. Signaling a rebirth of that sport, Baylor fielded a team in 1971-72. Members of the team were Judy Power, Kathy Wiese, Susan Stoops, Paula Love, Marcie Murphy, Kim Alviola, Joan Rogers, and Susan McLendon.[20] No records of their accomplishments were found, but this group formed a core of athletes that went on to great accomplishments before they graduated.

VOLLEYBALL

There is very little information on the 1970 volleyball team, but the starting lineup for that team is pictured below. Members were Janet Bauer, Kathy Shackleford, Sharon Beasley, Alita Brown, Mary Ann DeAtley, and Sandy Edwards. Olga Fallen coached the team and was assisted by Nancy Goodloe.

1970 Bearette Volleyball Team, Starting Lineup

Olga Fallen Collection, Accession #3797, Box 38, Folder 19,
The Texas Collection, Baylor University

According to the *Baylor Lariat,* November 3 and November 9, 1971, the Bearette volleyball team placed third in the TCIAW District IV tournament, losing to the University of Texas in the semifinals. Other teams competing in the District tourney were Southwest Texas, Mary Hardin-Baylor, Trinity, Our Lady of the Lake, St. Mary's, and Incarnate Word. The '71 team also played seven individual matches, traveling to three locations for the out of town games.[21]

Marcie Murphy, a member of that '71 team, recalled that she had not played "real" volleyball in high school and was pretty unfamiliar with the setting and spiking stuff, but she made the team. "I sure had a good time believe it or not, going to practices, but I especially enjoyed the road trips to various colleges. I made some neat friends and learned a lot."[22]

1971 Volleyball Team

Back: Asst. Coach, Nancy Goodloe, Dawn Orr, Teresa Romero,
Javon Lechler, Pat Freedman, Coach Olga Fallen
Middle: Rachel Cole, Marcie Murphy, Kathy Shackelford,
Mary Ann DeAtley, Sally Stokes
Front: Sandy Edwards, Sharon Beasley, Alita Brown, Carol King, Janet Bauer.

Olga Fallen Collection, Accession #3797, Box 38, Folder 19,
The Texas Collection, Baylor University

1972-73—A WATERSHED YEAR FOR BAYLOR BEARETTES

The Baylor women's athletic program exploded in its accomplishments. One reason for this highly successful year was the fact that Mary Ann Deatley Jewett's group of basketball women who started playing basketball together back in 1970 were seasoned performers. They knew what they were capable of, they understood each other's strengths and weaknesses, they had learned to be comfortable with each other on the court. They also had a team chemistry that contributed to their successful year.

As they began their practice and pre-season play in the Fall 1972, there was a confidence that something special could happen this year. And sure enough, in Spring 1973 they won the District IV TCIAW Basketball tournament, the first championship of this type in the history of the basketball team and the Baylor program.[23] This championship advanced them to the state tournament, and while they lost two of three games at the state tournament, they amassed a 19-8 overall record.[24]

1972-73 Bearette Basketball Team

Back: Asst. Coach, Mike Darlan, Cathy Robinson, Ann Gibson, Pattie Peebles,
Margaret Wooddy, Linda Trimble, Sue Hammett, Coach Olga Fallen
Middle: Penny Mudgett, Mary Ann DeAtley, Mary Holliman
Front: Dee Ann Hansen, Nancy Tartaglino, Javon Lechler, Carol King

Olga Fallen Collection, Accession #3797, Box 38, Folder 8,
The Texas Collection, Baylor University

VOLLEYBALL

1972 Bearette Volleyball Team

Back row: Asst. Coach, Nancy Goodloe, Kathy Wiese, Kathy
Shackleford, Jeanine Newland, Mary Ann Deatley, Diane
Herber, Margaret Wooddy, Head Coach, Olga Fallen
Middle row: Chris Miller, Judy Pelzel, Carole King, Judy Power, Paula Love
Front row: Kim Alviola, Veda Smith, Kerry Newhardt
Other participants of record were: Cindy Houck, Teresa Romero, Janet
Bauer, Pat Freedman, Sharon Beasley and Rosemary Patterson.[26]

Olga Fallen Collection, Accession #3797, Box 38, Folder 19,
The Texas Collection, Baylor University

Although no records were available for the 1972 season, the team placed third in TCIAW District play, the best finish ever for a BU volleyball team.[25]

FIRST NATIONAL CHAMPIONSHIP APPEARANCE BY A BAYLOR TEAM

Secondly, the 1972–73 women's track team had an outstanding season, qualifying twelve members to the state track and field meet and four women to the AIAW National Track meet in Hayward, California, another Baylor first. These four women qualified in eight events, most notably the 880-medley relay. The relay consisted of two 110-yard legs back to back, a 220-yard leg, and then a 440 yard leg. Having won all five seasonal meets, setting three meet records along the way, there were high hopes for a strong showing by the relay group.

Members of that team were Susan Stoops, Kim Alviola, Marcie Murphy, and Joan Rogers.

1973 Medley Relay Team, 6ᵗʰ Place Finish

AIAW National Track and Field Meet
Joan Rogers, Susan Stoops, Marcie Murphy, Kim Alviola

Olga Fallen Collection, Accession #3797, Box 38, Folder 15,
The Texas Collection, Baylor University

With the qualification of these students for the national meet, the Baylor administration had a dilemma on their hands. Two questions had to be addressed: (1) do we send these women to the national meet and (2) where do we get the money to pay for this trip? Even though Title IX was in place, there was bare bones financial support for all of the teams at this time, and certainly no one had ever thought that our women athletes might qualify to compete on a national level. The two coaches, Olga Fallen and I, met with President Abner McCall to ask for financial resources to send the six of us to this Meet. Our excitement was soon quelled, however, as very little support was proffered by the President. In fact he indicated that if Baylor could find any money for this trip, only one coach could accompany the team. This meant that I would not be going, since Fallen was technically the head coach of the track team. I had coached the women for three months, training them hard for their season accomplishments. Fallen had been with the team a very short time, having joined them after basketball season ended. I was devastated that I could not make this trip, and Fallen was determined to take me with her. I went home and called my cousin, Al Myers, to ask him to loan me the money so I could make this trip. When I told him the story of our visit with Dr. McCall and that it didn't sound like Baylor was going to provide the funding, Al was flabbergasted. His reponse to me was "Nanny, don't worry about a thing. I'll take care of this." According to Al, he immediately called Dr. Herb Reynolds, McCall's number two man in the administration, to discuss how Baylor could make this happen. Reynolds was supportive of the women making this trip, but there was no funding for anything like this in the athletic budget or in Baylor's budget. Reynolds asked Al to give him a couple of days to talk with his people and figure out how external donations from supporters like Al could be given to Baylor and not present any legal issues for the University. By Al's account, he received a call from Ralph Storm two days later indicating that Reynolds had worked things out and that he and Al were going to fund the trip. Ultimately, their donations were to the Bear Foundation and the funds were designated for the women's track team trip to the National Track and Field meet. By Al's understanding, he and Ralph Storm provided all of the funding for this trip.[27] I remember how excited we all were to be going to San Francisco and to the competition. The four women were proud to represent Baylor and to have reached this pinnacle in their athletic careers.

While none of the women placed in their individual events at the National Meet, their sixth place finish in the 880-medley relay was 1:51.3, a faster time than the previous national record. Finishing in the top six in the nation was a significant feat for Baylor Women's Athletics and started a tradition of strong women's track teams that endures to this day.[28] By today's NCAA standards, these women would have been Baylor's first female All-Americans, but at the time, the women's national governing body, AIAW, was not awarding any All-American honors in any sport.

There is no question that the accomplishments of Baylor women's athletes during the '72-'73 academic year resulted in more awareness on the campus and in the state of Texas of women's intercollegiate athletics at Baylor. There is a marked difference in the number of articles on the Bearettes in the *Baylor Line*, the alumni magazine, and the *Baylor Lariat*, the campus newspaper, beginning in the spring 1973.

SUZIE SNIDER – FIRST FEMALE SCHOLARSHIP ATHLETE, BAYLOR UNIVERSITY, AUGUST 1973

Unquestionably, the arrival of Suzie Snider on the campus was one of the premier events in 1973. At the time she was the most highly recruited high school female athlete in the state of Texas.

Suzie Snider, Women's All-Time Career Scoring and Rebounding Leader

Baylor University, 3861 points
2176 Rebounds

Olga Fallen Collection, Accession #3797, Box 38, Folder 9,
The Texas Collection, Baylor University

Hailing from Robinson, Texas, just outside Waco, she had been on Olga Fallen's radar screen for quite some time in spite of the fact that the governing body for women's intercollegiate athletics, AIAW, did not allow their members to recruit or award athletic scholarships. Snider had an outstanding high school athletic career, helping her basketball team to a 143-9 record, winning the state championship in 1971 and representing the South in the annual North-South All-Star game in Brownwood, Texas in her senior year. At her high school commencement her number 10 was retired.

Snider's first love, however, was Track and Field. At Robinson High School she held state championship honors in the shot put, discus, and high jump. Her record throw of 50' 7" in the shot was a national AAU record, and her throw of

136' 6" in the discus was second in girls AAU competition at the time. Baylor's program was attractive to Snider, and it would enable her to go to school and stay at home, both things she wished to do.

Suzie Snider, Discus

Olga Fallen Collection, Accession 3797, Box 38, Folder 18, The Texas Collection, Baylor University

When approached about helping financially to bring Suzie to Baylor, Dr. Herbert Reynolds, Vice-President, felt the University's hands were tied for two reasons: (1) Baylor did not have athletic scholarships for women and (2) based on the AIAW/TCIAW rules and regulations, Baylor would be deemed ineligible to participate in AIAW events if a scholarship was offered to a woman athlete. What Reynolds did not realize was that the AIAW was under fire from the Kellmeyer lawsuit, filed January 1973. The lawsuit alleged that AIAW discriminated against women athletes with it policy against awarding scholarships on the basis of athletic ability. Little could Reynolds have known that at the November 1973 Delegate Assembly, AIAW members overwhelmingly would vote to reverse this policy.

So, how did Suzie Snider become the first women's scholarship athlete at Baylor University? This answer depends on who's telling the story. Dutch Schroeder, long-time Baylor faculty member, baseball coach, and avid supporter of women's athletics, offered this version. Bill Bradley, Suzie's high school coach, contacted Dutch sometime during the Spring 1973 period with the information that Suzie was interested in staying in the area and playing collegiately for Baylor University. These two men approached Mr. Arch Hunt, Vice-President for Student Financial Aid, with the idea that Suzie could live at home if Baylor could find some grants-in-aid to help support tuition, fees and books. Through a process of filing and review of the application, Mr. Hunt was able to qualify Suzie for the financial aid needed to be able to attend Baylor in the Fall 1973. Then, in a conversation at church shortly after the financial aid was made available to Snider, Mr. Ed. Horner, the chair of the Baylor Athletic Council, discovered that Suzie was coming to Baylor on a financial aid arrangement with the University. Knowing of her talent and skills and how highly recruited Suzie was in the state, Mr. Horner took the discussion to the Athletic Council. Here it was voted to offer Suzie Snider a full athletic scholarship from the athletic department, the first in Baylor history.[29]

So, now Jack Patterson, Athletic Director, had either to create a new scholarship or find one already in place that could be used for Suzie. He went to Clyde Hart, men's track coach and explained the situation. Between the two of them, the decision was made to award a scholarship designated for the men's track team to Suzie. The scholarship agreement was signed on August 31, 1973. At the time of the signing, the athletic award was illegal according to the AIAW rules and regulations for women's sport. Less than three months later, it was legal.

Suzie Snider came to Baylor on a track scholarship and also participated in basketball. She led the Bearette basketball team to appearances in two national championships tournaments and a fifth place finish in 1977. She still holds the career scoring record and rebound record in women's basketball and is the only Bearette to win an AIAW national title in track and field, 1974 Shot Put Champion. Suzie was named to the 1977 Kodak/State Farm/Women's Basketball Coaches Association All-American team and was elected to the Baylor University Athletic Hall of Fame in 1987. During Suzie's career at Baylor, the Bearettes flourished, winning numerous tournaments, accumulating trophies every year, and regularly participating in post-season play in the AIAW Regional tournament. The teams beat powerhouse teams such as the Lady Techsters, coached by Sonja Hogg, the Stephen F. Austin Lady Jacks, and the Wayland Flying Queens during Snider-Eppers career. For home games, the bleachers at Marrs McLean Gym were packed and crowds regularly reached standing room only capacity. It was an exciting time for Bearette basketball.

1973-74

The 1973-74 basketball team had a won-loss record of 23-6, heading into the State Tournament, and posted a scoring average of 68.1 points per game. Snider was surrounded by a talented group of women in Lynnell Pyron, Linda Trimble, Doris Ballew, Sue Hammitt, Pam Mann, Marilyn Williamson, Kim Alviola, Alice Melendez, Linda Trimble, and Margaret Wooddy. The team won the District TCIAW Tournament and went on to place 3rd in the State TAIAW Tournament, losing to Stephen F. Austin (SFA). They placed fourth in the AIAW Regional tournament. In reflecting on the season and the loss to SFA, Fallen commented: "I really did not expect us to do as well simply because they (the Bearettes) were so young." Most were freshman as it turned out, but brought many individual strengths to the game. Fallen cited Ballew's ball handling and Mann's inside shooting as particularly strong in the state tournament but also noted that Snider led the team in every category on the season.[30]

1973-74 BB team with Coach Olga Fallen and Asst. Coach Carol King

First row: Kim Alviola, Audrey Shivers, Sue Hammitt, Alice Melendez, Teresa Epley
Second row: Linda Trimble, Brenda Speer, Kathy Zwald, Doris Ballew
Third row: Carol King, Marilyn Williamson, Margaret Wooddy,
Pam Mann, Suzie Snider, Lynnell Pyron, Coach Olga Fallen

Baylor University, The 1974 Round-Up Yearbook, (Waco, TX: [Baylor University], 1974), The Texas Collection, Baylor University, p. 208.

SOFTBALL

The 1973-74 Softball team played several games and played in the TCIAW Zone tournament. They qualified for the State TCIAW tournament but did not place in that event. Their season record was 8-9-1.[31]

SWIMMING

Baylor swimmers and divers performed very well during the 1973-74 season and sent a large contingent to the State TCIAW meet. The highest finisher for Baylor was Kim Hickey, who finished second in the one-meter diving. Team members are listed below.

1974 Bearette Swimming and Diving Team Members

Terri Calvert, Ricki Cotteral, Patty Hendrick, Kim Hickey, Carla Kuper, Sue Root, Holly Utt, Krissy Utt, Kathy Taylor, Hannie McConnell, Marilyn Williamson and Candace Ferguson[32]

TRACK AND FIELD
BAYLOR WINS E-V-E-R-Y-T-H-I-N-G

This was the headline from Mike Walker in the April 18, 1974 issue of the *Baylor Lariat*. Indeed the 1974 Bearettes did win every event at the District IV TCIAW Track and Field meet held in Waco, Texas. Competing with teams from Southwest Texas State University and Texas Lutheran College, Baylor qualified seventeen women for the State TCIAW Track and Field meet in Canyon, Texas.

The following individual results were reported by Walker in his article:

Bearette	Event	Time/Distance
*Suzie Snider	Shot put	43' 2.5"
	Discus	142' 9.5"
	High Jump	5'6"
	Javelin	109'6"
*Joan Rogers	440 run	1.02.1
	880 run	2.31.8
	880 yd. Medley Relay	1.57.2
	Mile Relay	4.19.4

*Lynnell Pyron	220 yd. dash,	27.5
	440 relay	52.2
	Discus	119"6"
	Mile relay	4.19.4
*Marcie Murphy	220 yd. dash	26.9
	440 yd. relay	52.2
	880 yd. Medley relay	1.57.2
	Mile relay	4.19.4
*Sherry Scheele	100 m. Hurdles	15.4
	440 yd. Relay	52.2
	880 yd. Medley relay	1.57.2
	Long jump	15'11.25"
*Susan Stoops	100 yd. dash	11.9
	220 yd. dash	27.0
	440 yd. relay	52.2
	880 Medley relay	1.57.2
*Susan McLendon	Mile run	5.56.5
	Mile relay	4.19.4
*Diane McNeil	Mile run	5.57.9
	2-mile run	13.06.5
Sue Hembree	Mile Relay	4.42.1
	440 yd. Relay	55.6
Kim Alviola	440 yd. Relay	55.6
	Javelin	93'7"
	High jump	4'6"
	Long jump	15'1"
Sue Hammitt	100 m. Hurdles	19.0
Marilyn Williamson	440 yd. Relay	55.6
	Mile relay	4.42.1
	High jump	4'6"
Paula Love	Discus	n/a
Margaret Wooddy	2-mile run	n/a

Teresa Elliott	Shot put	33'6"
Karen McDaniel	Mile relay	4.42.1
Cathy Lee	440 yd. Relay	55.6
	Mile relay	4:42.1

Table I: 1974 Bearette Track Team/District results

*Qualified for the National AIAW Track and Field Meet

Writing for the *Baylor Lariat*, April 30, 1974, Rick Hale reported that this team placed third at the TCIAW State Track and Field meet held in Canyon, Texas. Records indicated the following state finishes for the Bearettes:

Suzie Snider – first place in shot put, discus, high jump and javelin

Kim Alviola – fifth in javelin

Sherry Scheele – fourth in the 100 meter hurdles

Lynnell Pyron – fourth in the discus

Joan Rogers – third in the 440 yd. dash and second in the 880 yd. run

Diane McNeil – second in the two-mile run; fifth in the mile run

Ricki Cotteral – sixth in the two-mile run

Susan McLendon – second in the mile run[33]

1974 Track Team Members

Left to right: Susan McLendon, Diane McNeil, Sherry Scheele

Olga Fallen Collection, Accession #3797, Box 38, Folder 16,
The Texas Collection, Baylor University

The Bearettes qualified eight members of the team to the National AIAW Track and Field Meet, hosted by Texas Woman's University in Denton, Texas— Snider, McNeil, McLendon, Rogers, Pyron, Murphy, Scheele, and Stoops. At the National Track and Field meet, the team placed 11th out of 150 colleges and universities represented. Other members of the team were Alice Melendez, Teresa Epley, Pam Mann, Ricki Cotteral, Karen Cason, and Joan McDaniel.[34,35]

1974 Track Team Members

Bottom to top: Marcie Murphy, Sherry Scheele, Lynnell Pyron, Susan Stoops

*Olga Fallen Collection, Accession #3797, Box 38, Folder 15,
The Texas Collection, Baylor University*

Baylor women competed in volleyball, badminton and tennis during the 1973-74 academic year but no records of the teams were found.

Sherry Scheele Hands off to Leah Box

Baylor University, The 1975 Round Up Yearbook, (Waco, TX: [Baylor University], 1975), The Texas Collection, Baylor University, p. 136.

MEDICAL CARE FOR THE WOMEN ATHLETES

Another milestone for women's athletics during this time period was the introduction of a women's athletic training program. The Bearette teams were getting more competitive, more talented athletes were coming to Baylor. Up to this point, the head trainer for Baylor, Skip Cox, had welcomed female athletes into his training room for injury evaluations, treatment and rehab. The need to have a medical response on the campus and a preventive approach to athletic injuries was growing and becoming more urgent. I had been serving as liaison between Cox and the women's athletes for a couple of years and had begun to tape basketball players' ankles for practice and for games. I needed some help. In 1974 I decided to approach Cox with the notion of providing me and a couple of students with some in depth training so that we could provide immediate response to female athletes and coordinate a treatment and rehabilitation program on the campus for the women. Cox embraced the idea, and I recruited the first two female student trainers at Baylor University—Cindy Lyles and Diane Johnson. To develop our skills, we attended night sessions that Cox held for all of his male student trainers at the stadium. Diane Johnson tells a great story about how she and Cindy Lyles went out and bought several rolls of masking tape to practice the various ankle-taping techniques they were expected to know. These women were dedicated, spending many extra hours in Cox's classes and at the Baylor training room honing their skills and learning as much as they could. They traveled with the women's basketball team, initially, but eventually expanded services to other women's teams.

I was able to set up a satellite training room in Marrs McLean Gym so that the women athletes were closer for support, evaluation and rehabilitation. That room stocked with taping supplies, a whirlpool, ice packs, and other items needed for use in treating athletic injuries. Cox generously provided the supplies for this satellite facility until 1975 when the women had their own budget for athletic training supplies.

In spite of this support from Cox, no mention was ever made and no offers were ever seen that the athletic department would pay for the extended medical care when women athletes were injured, medical care requiring X-rays and other procedures. That was curious because if there was a female athlete who needed a consult with one of the Baylor team doctors, i.e. the orthopedic surgeon, Cox made those physicians available to me and the women athletes. In that period of time 1974–76, there were several women who required extra treatment from their family physicians or from orthopedic specialist. Fortunately, their families had good health insurance. This situation of families paying for their athlete's medical care continued until it was exposed in 1977 and corrected.

**Nancy Goodloe, Women's Athletic
Trainer, helps Lynnell Pyron**

*Baylor University, Round Up 1975 Yearbook, (Waco, TX: [Baylor
University], 1975), The Texas Collection, Baylor University, p. 128.*

In 1976 Margaret Wooddy took over the program from Goodloe. It continues to this day and stands as one of the first intercollegiate athletic training programs in Texas that prepared women to be athletic trainers.

RECRUITING INTENSIFIES

After the successful 1973–74 basketball season, Olga Fallen found herself deluged with inquiries about athletic scholarships for women at Baylor. The word about Suzie Snider was out. Young women athletes wanted to play on a team with Suzie Snider, or they wanted to attend Baylor and wanted a scholarship for the sport they played in high school. The files in the Fallen Collection are loaded with letters from high school athletes, parents, coaches, and friends of athletes recommending they be awarded a women's athletic scholarship at Baylor. The only problem was no additional athletic scholarships for women at Baylor had been created beyond that of Suzie Snider.

Dealing with all of these letters and inquiries easily overwhelmed Fallen in her capacity as Women's Athletic Coordinator. After all, she was coaching three sports, coordinating the entire program and still maintaining a half-time appointment as a faculty member in the Health, Human Performance and Recreation Department. And, she had no administrative support as the Women's Coordinator.[10]

As a result of the overwhelming interest in Baylor Women's Athletics in the state, and in accordance with AIAW recruiting policy, Fallen and her staff created tryout days for basketball and volleyball, hosting separate events in the spring of each year. Letters of invitation were sent in response to each letter or phone call. It goes without saying that many future women athletic stars were identified during these tryout periods, and the women's program increased both its popularity and its competitive levels over the next five years. Some of the athletes that were recruited during this time were Babette Metcalf, Sarah Davis, Karen Aulenbacher, Leah Box, and Judy Kafer. Karen Aulenbacher and Babette Metcalf actually transferred from other universities to come to Baylor. Aulenbacher came from Texas A&M after her freshman season in which she scored the winning basket at the buzzer to defeat the Bearettes in a tournament. Babette Metcalf was highly recruited by Coach Fran Garmon at Temple Junior College but transferred from there after her first season. All of these athletes provided the support around Suzie Snider-Eppers through 1977 that resulted in two national basketball tournament appearances, many tournament wins, and exciting women's basketball at Baylor University.

---

10 A more thorough discussion of Fallen's work as Women's Athletic Coordinator is found in Chapter 5 as part of Baylor's response to Title IX.

1974-75
BASKETBALL

1974-75 Bearette Basketball Team

Back: Asst. Coach, Glada Munt, Chris Boultinghouse, Linda Gilliam,
Barbara Sulak, Suzie Snider, Lynnell Pyron, Kathy Zwald, Judy Kafer,
Alice Melendez, Student Trainer
Front: Doris Belew, Manager, Linda Trimble, Pam Mann, Marilyn Williamson,
Sue Hammett, Leah Box
Standing: Nancy Goodloe, Trainer, Olga Fallen, Head Coach
Glada Munt, Asst. Coach, Nancy Goodloe, Trainer, Olga Fallen, Head Coach

Olga Fallen Collection, Accession #3797, Box 38, Folder 8,
The Texas Collection, Baylor University

The 1974-75 basketball team posted a 31-11 season record and performed well in several tournaments during the season, bringing home second place finishes in the Tarleton Invitational, the TWU Invitational and their own Baylor Invitational. In TCIAW Zone play, the Bearettes finished as runner-up to Texas A&M, qualifying for the State tournament. Their third place finish at state earned them an invitation to the AIAW Southwest Regional tournament where they missed going to the national tournament by one point, losing to Stephen F. Austin in the semifinals of the tournament. Lynnell Pyron and Suzie Snider received nominations for All-American honors this season.[36]

LYNELLE PYRON

All-American Nominee, 1975

Baylor University, Round Up 1976 Yearbook, (Waco, TX: [The Students of Baylor University], 1976), The Texas Collection, Baylor University, p. 187.

BADMINTON

Members of the 1974-75 badminton team, coached by Goodloe, were Karen McDaniel, Chrisy Kessler, Debbie Schneider, Lydia Goetz, Cynthia Williams and Edie Davis. McDaniel placed second in singles at the TCIAW District IV tournament and partnered with Kessler for third place in women's doubles. Both performances qualified them for the State TAIAW tournament where they won consolation in that event. Schneider and Goetz partnered in district play to take fourth place.[37] These women also played in several other badminton tournaments each year of their careers. Traditionally, the team traveled to the Houston Invitational as well as invitational tournaments at North Texas State University and Texas Woman's University. The Baylor team was always represented in the Baylor Intercollegiate and Baylor Open Invitational.

SOFTBALL

Members of the 1974-75 Bearette Softball team were Alice Melendez, Leah Box, Audrey Shivers, Kim Alviola, Cindi Counts, Cathy Zwald, Debbie Routh,

Kim Rothfus, Kathy Lee, Brenda Speer, someone last name of Caldwell, Marsha Adams, Deana Morrison, and Ty Herrington.[38] No records of their season were found.

TENNIS

Karen Henson

Top ranked Bearette Tennis Player, 1975

Baylor University, The 1975 Round Up Yearbook, (Waco, TX: [Baylor University], 1975), The Texas Collection, Baylor University, p. 146.

The 1975 women's tennis team was coached by Glada Munt, graduate student. Initially Fallen had coached the women's tennis team but by this time she was way too busy with the Bearette basketball team to cover this team as well. Glada Munt was a graduate assistant in the HPER department and was Fallen's assistant coach with the basketball team. There were women who wanted to play, and no other faculty were available to coach the team, so Fallen asked Munt to travel with the group. This assignment became part of Munt's assistantship duties. She was not paid any extra to take on this job.

Participants on the team were Karen Henson, Ann Bowen, and Jennifer Judin. Henson was the top ranked player for the Bearette, followed closely by Bowen. Henson and Jennifer Judin paired to win consolation at the prestigious University of Texas tournament. They placed fourth in the TAIAW District Tournament but did not qualify for state competition. The team had ten members.[39]

TRACK AND FIELD – FIRST NATIONAL CHAMPIONSHIP FOR BAYLOR BEARETTES

1975 Bearette Track Team Display Championship Plaque from the Texas A&M Invitational Track Meet

The 1975 track team, coached by Nancy Goodloe, won the Texas A&M Invitational meet.

At practice the day before the A&M meet, I challenged each team member to consider her events and what she thought her best effort in each event could be for the next day and then set a goal for this meet, a goal she though she could reasonably meet. I asked them to write the goals down on a piece of paper and bring it with them to the meet. I told them not to share their goals with anyone, especially me. I didn't know if they would actually do that or not but my goal was to get them to understand that every effort counted, whether they won an event or came in last place. All I wanted was for them to actualize their athletic potential.

So, we leave the next morning, bright and early, because it was only ninety miles to College Station and the meet didn't start too early. We get there and go through the pre-meet routine of the coaches' meetings, reviewing the rules for the day, making whatever adjustments we need to make to our entries, etc. I distinctly remember that one of the rules was that the coaches could not go onto the field. I had to sit in the bleachers and watch the events. I liked to be on the field with the athletes but not on that day.

As the day goes on, I can see that we are doing really well. Our athletes are performing well and our points are stacking up. I begin to think maybe we can place pretty high at the end of the day. In our track meets back then, the prelims and semifinals were run in the morning and then the finals in the afternoon. The finals for the 100 and 200 hundred meter dashes had finished as I had expected. Two very fast sprinters from Prairie View A&M had the fastest times in both events, and my sprinter, Marsha Talley, had the third fastest time in each event. I don't remember how the 100 meter dash came out but I do remember that the 200 meter dash was a photo finish for third place. I knew that Marsha's foot had crossed the finish line in third place, behind the two Prairie View runners. However, when they announced the results, the officials had given the third place to another sprinter. I immediately went down to the judges' tent and asked for a review of the photo finish. In the meantime, Marsha had come over to me extremely upset because she had finished fourth. She, too, thought she had gotten third place. Well, for what seemed like an eternity the officials reviewed the tape and reviewed the tape. Rules or not, I finally went down onto the field and into the officials' tent. I wanted to see the tape of the photo finish and point out Marsha's foot as it crossed the finish line ahead of the athlete who had been given third place. It was obvious that she had third place but if you weren't looking at the tape just right, you could have missed it. Then the announcement came that the third place would go to Marsha Talley from Baylor University. From way across the infield came this really loud scream of excitement. I look up and Marsha is running toward me with her arms outstretched and gives me the biggest hug. I looked up and saw Marsha running toward me. She looked me in the eye and said something like that was my goal, to win third place in the 200 meter dash. I knew I could beat everyone except the two runners from Prairie View, and I did it! By the end of the day, many of the athletes has shared how they, also, had met their goals for the meet. Many of these were stories of third and fourth place finishes, not victories, but positions that gave us points for the meet. When the results were tallied, Baylor had accumulated the most points and had won the meet. I'll never forget that meet. It was one of the most satisfying days of my coaching career.

This Baylor team went on to finish first in the TAIAW Zone competition, second in the TAIAW State meet and second in the AIAW Regional meet. Marsha Talley, sprinter, anchored a strong Baylor team winning the 100 and 200 meter dash at the TAIAW Zone meet. Suzie Snider won both the shot put and javelin events at this meet[40]

**1975 Track Team Members with the
TAIAW Zone Championship Plaque**

*Standing: Leah Box, Coach Olga Fallen, Lynnell Pyron, Cindy Lyles,
Judy Blalock, Kathleen Matusik, Connie Freeman, Suzie Snider, Joan
Rogers, Carla Lechler, Becky McClenny, Coach Nancy Goodloe
Kneeling: Natalie Gale, Karen Moon, Diane McNeil, Sarah Davis
Sitting: Marsha Talley, Christa Womack, Loretta Buxkemper*

*Olga Fallen Collection, Accession #3797, Box 38, Folder 17,
The Texas Collection, Baylor University*

SUZIE SIDER - AIAW NATIONAL SHOT PUT CHAMPION

Six members qualified for the national meet in Corvallis, Oregon. They were: Suzie Snider, Marsha Talley, Joan Rogers, Chris Boultinghouse, Sherry Scheele, and Leah Box.[41] According to Marsha Talley, a member of that team, several of the team members made a special appeal to Jack Patterson, Athletic Director, to ask that Baylor pay for the athletes to participate in the National Meet. The money must have come from somewhere, though no record of it could be found. The team went to Corvallis, as did both coaches.[42]

Marsha Talley 1975, Bearette Sprinter

Baylor University, The 1975 Round Up Yearbook, (Waco, TX: [Baylor University], 1975), The Texas Collection, Baylor University, p. 134.

Suzie Snider became the 1975 AIAW National Shot Put champion at the Corvallis meet. She also finished 4th in the discus and 8th in the javelin. The 880 medley relay team of Talley, Boultinghouse, Box and Rogers finished 7th in the nation.[43] Again, by today's NCAA standards Baylor would have had five All-Americans, but not under the AIAW structure.

Suzie Snider

AIAW National Shot Put Champion 1975

Olga Fallen Collection, Accession #3797, Box 38, Folder 11,
The Texas Collection, Baylor University

VOLLEYBALL

The 1974 Volleyball team posted a season record of eight wins and nine losses. No other information was available for this team.[44]

By 1975, with a more stable and consistent governing structure for women's intercollegiate athletics,[11] the Baylor Women's Athletic program had established itself as a program of quality. Five women faculty members in the Department of Health, Physical Education and Recreation provided the coaching and support structure for the women's teams. Olga Fallen was the Women's Athletic Coordinator as well as one of the coaches. On the Baylor campus, the word spread about the women's intercollegiate opportunities and each team had larger rosters because former high school athletes wanted to continue their competitive experiences.

The women's track team developed a reputation and was very competitive with their Texas opponents. Members of this team had participated in three AIAW National Track Meets by this time and gained a reputation for quality of performance. The 1973 880 medley relay team brought home a fifth place finish and was the first team to represent Baylor at a national AIAW event. Suzie Snider was the National AIAW Shot Put champion. Indeed, the Baylor program was going places.

Structurally, the program was under the administrative umbrella of the Baylor Athletic Department and more funding was available for the women's programs than ever before. The athletic scholarship support for women had grown steadily since 1973 after Suzie Snider was awarded the first women's athletic scholarship at Baylor. Additionally, there was more funding for travel, uniforms, and equipment. An undergraduate athletic training program for women had been implemented. Baylor University was the first university in the state of Texas to provide this opportunity for their undergraduate women.

---

11   National structure provided by the Association for Intercollegiate Athletics for Women, AIAW. State structure provided by the Texas Association for Intercollegiate Athletics for Women, TAIAW.

Title IX was signed into law in 1972. By July 1975 the regulations for implementation of the law were in place. There is no question that this legislation provided a boost for Baylor's women's athletic program, but it was not well-received on the campus by those in positions of authority and decision-making. That story is told in the next chapter.

NOTES ON CHAPTER 4

BEARETTES TO LADY BEARS, 1970–1975

1. The Olga Fallen Collection, Accession 3797, Box 17, Folder 2, The Texas Collection, Baylor University.

2. David McCollum, "…while Bearettes triumph," *The Baylor Lariat*, February 1, 1972, 4.

3. The Olga Fallen Collection, Box 17, Folder 1.

4. The Woman's Collection, MSS 77, Box 9, Blagg-Huey Library, Texas Woman's University, Denton, TX.

5. Mary Ann Deatley Jewett, personal story shared with the author, June 2012.

6. The Woman's Collection, MSS 77, Box 7.

7. The Olga Fallen Collection, Box 11, Folder 9.

8. The Olga Fallen Collection, Box 7, Folder 11.

9. The Olga Fallen Collection, Box 16, Folder 3.

10. See note 8 above.

11. Susan Addy, email message to the author, November 13, 2012.

12. The Woman's Collection, MSS 77, Box 2 and Box 9.

13. See note 8 above.

14. See note 6 above.

15. See note 8 above.

16. The Woman's Collection, MSS 77, Box 9.

17. See note 8 above.

18. See note 9 above.

19. See note 4 above.

20. See note 9 above.

21. The Olga Fallen Collection, Box 10, Folder 14.

22. Marcie Murphy Paschall, email message to the author, May 21, 2012.

23. Sherry Castello, ed., "Taking a Walk," *The Baylor Line,* August 1973, 16.

24. Ibid.

25. Ibid.

26. The Olga Fallen Collection, Box 7 Folder 11.

27. Al Myers, personal interview, November 9, 2013, Ft. Worth, Texas.

28. See note 23 above.

29. Oral Memoirs of E.E. "Dutch" Schroeder, Baylor University Institute for Oral History, July 1984, p. 122–124.

30. Leah Box, "Women's Basketball: Faster, stronger, better balanced," *The Baylor Line*, December 1975, 23-24.

31. See note 4 above.

32. Ibid.

33. Ibid.

34. Rick Hale, "Weekend Track…a women's record-setter," *The Baylor Lariat*, April 30, 1974.

35. The Olga Fallen Collection, Box 8, Folder 7.

36. Baylor University, The 1975 Round Up Yearbook, (Waco, TX: [Baylor University], 1975), The Texas Collection, Baylor University, p. 181.

37. See note 16 above.

38. The Olga Fallen Collection, Box 32, Folder 5.

39. Baylor University, The 1975 Round Up Yearbook, (Waco, TX: [Baylor University], 1975), The Texas Collection, Baylor University, p. 146.

40. The Women's Collection, MSS 77, Box 9.

41. See note 35 above.

42. Marsha Talley, personal story shared with the author, August 1, 2012.

43. Sherry Castello, ed., "Sports Line." *The Baylor Line*, February 1976, 25.

44. See note 4 above.

CHAPTER 5

BAYLOR UNIVERSITY RESPONDS TO TITLE IX

Dr. Abner McCall, President of Baylor University, 1961-1981, was a fervent supporter of Baylor University and its Baptist heritage. On the Baylor campus there was no card playing, no dancing and no alcohol. Women were not allowed to wear slacks or shorts across campus unless they were covered with a raincoat. This rule was in effect throughout the sixties and well into the seventies. McCall was his own man and despite the women's movement of the sixties, he held fast to what he believed the practices a private Baptist school should be. His decisions were not questioned very often and were supported by the Board of Regents. The number two person in his administration was Dr. Herbert H. Reynolds. Between the two of them, Baylor was managed like a very tight ship. When McCall retired in 1981, Reynolds succeeded him as President.

McCall also believed fervently in the separation of church and state. When Congress passed Title IX of the Education Amendments Act of 1972, McCall was convinced the law violated this premise. Indeed throughout the decade of the seventies and well into the eighties, McCall and Reynolds opposed the legislation as well as the implementation regulations. How this opposition played out and its impact on women's athletics at Baylor is the theme for this chapter.

In 1972 Abner McCall was not a great supporter of any intercollegiate athletic programs. He viewed athletics more as a side business of the university for the benefit of the Waco community and Baylor alums. He was a staunch supporter of Baylor's intramural program and felt that it provided all the opportunities for athletic participation that college students (men and women) needed. For Abner McCall, students came to Baylor for an education. In his mind athletics were not part of the educational mission of the university, so he had little use for them. In fact campus athletic scandals and NCAA investigations were very prevalent on college campuses during this period. Indeed once the NCAA scandals began to emerge in the public domain, it was difficult to see how the NCAA supported any kind of academic focus in intercollegiate athletics. McCall wanted none of this on his campus.

McCall and Reynolds drew a line in the sand with the athletic budget, requiring that the athletic department's revenue streams provide enough funding to operate in the black financially, or at least at a break-even status. They provided little additional financial support from the University. The funding model for athletics at Baylor was similar to other universities, relying heavily on ticket sales, fundraising efforts, and earnings as a result of being in the Southwest Conference. Men's football and basketball were the major revenue generating sources for the athletic department budget since these sports generated ticket sales. Some funding came from the Bear Foundation, a 501c3 structure tasked with fundraising for the athletic department. Fundraising for athletics was not a top priority for the University, so this effort produced minimal revenue. The other men's varsity sports provided little revenue, certainly not enough to support their teams.

Football and men's basketball in turn received the largest allocations from the approximately two million–dollar athletic department budget. The sports of baseball, indoor, outdoor and cross country track and field, tennis and golf were considered minor sports. These teams received minimal support in the athletic department funding model. In effect the funding model for the athletic department discriminated against these minor sports.

Aside from the early seventies when Grant Teaff's football teams were so successful, none of the men's teams posed a threat to win a Southwest Conference championship. As such their ticket revenues and income from the SWC were less than what was really needed for a strong athletic budget most of this decade. This lack of success impacted the amount of funds received from the Conference coffers, as well as the amount of money flowing into the fundraising efforts of the Bear Foundation. Baylor's mantra was 'wait 'til next year'. Students and fans alike adapted to the low expectations for team success. Such was the financial situation when Title IX became law.

Rumor had it that in 1972 when Title IX was passed, Abner McCall did not even realize Baylor University had a women's athletic program. Two items of empirical evidence suggested this was not the case. For one, Dr. Herbert H. Reynolds in a letter to Dr. Ted Powers, Chair, Department of Health, Physical Education and Recreation, April 26, 1972, indicated that the women's athletic program had been extensively discussed by him and McCall. Resultantly, the two men had come to a decision about the program.

> President McCall and I have discussed the "Women's Intercollegiate Athletic Program at some length, with particular emphasis on the implications of establishing and maintaining such a program. After much consideration of this topic, we have concluded that we should continue to offer the sound intramural program that you have always offered in the HPER Department.
>
> Any intercollegiate activity should be a part of the Department of Athletics and it is our belief that the goals of Women's Liberation necessitate being treated equal to men – not having separate programs. Consequently, interested women are invited to go out for any of our athletic teams. Who knows, we might find a tremendous fullback somewhere![1]

Secondly, the women's intercollegiate athletic program was housed in the Department of Health, Physical Education and Recreation prior to Title IX. While it is not clear if this program had its own line item in the HPER department budget, it is clear that, periodically, requests were made to the administration for additional funds for the women's teams.[2] These funds were granted. McCall or Reynolds would have approved these allocations.

Reynolds's letter to Powers reflected one of the controversies surrounding the proposed Title IX legislation that was floating across the national discussion at the time—whether or not allowing women to play on men's team would create equal opportunity required by the legislation. This notion received a lot of discussion nationally, although it was never a serious conversation within the circles of women athletic leaders. As this discussion went forward beyond the passage of the law, however, it became obvious to everyone involved that the intent of Title IX was never to allow women to try out for men's teams. That strategy was not considered effective if equal opportunity for women was to be a reality.

The NCAA was solidly opposed to Title IX implementation, and they rallied athletic directors and college administrators to their cause in large numbers. As the rumors about Title IX moved from speculation and rampant misunderstanding to reality, most colleges and university officials across this country were not prepared for the financial implications for their campuses. Baylor University was no different.

Between the signing of the law, June 23, 1972, and the implementation of the regulations in 1975, Baylor leaders were as confused as everyone about what the regulations for Title IX would be and how they might be interpreted. McCall made no secret of his disdain for the legislation and joined NCAA leaders in challenging the application of the law on college campuses. This opposition took two forms. For one, the leadership argued that the regulations should only apply to <u>programs</u> that received federal financial aid, not to entire universities. Their logic was that since athletic department programs received no federal funding, these departments should be exempt from Title IX mandates.[12] The language of the regulations used the word 'program' so this argument seemed appropriate. However, what this interpretation of the language would have created an inconsistent application of the law on university campuses. The

---

12 Author's note: This was like saying it was alright to discriminate against women in athletic programs but not alright to discriminate against women in the financial aid offices on college campuses.

intent of the law was to apply the requirements to all programs on a university campus, but this argument held up for quite some time.

From 1974 to 1975, Abner McCall mounted a furious letter campaign sending numerous pieces of correspondence to Congressmen and Baylor supporters in an effort to stave off and redirect the regulations. He teamed with Jack Patterson, Athletic Director, and Ed Horner, Chairperson of the Faculty-Athletic Council, to send a personal letter to Athletic Scholarship Donors, Baylor Bear Club members, Baylor Fast-Break Club, and the Baylor "B" Association, on February 28, 1974. Signed by these three men, the letter stated in part:

> "....the proposed regulations could ultimately result in the elimination of the control of collegiate athletic programs in the thousand or so separate colleges and universities in the United States and in the severe restriction and possible elimination of regional and nationwide intercollegiate competition that now exists....it is urgent...that you contact anyone in Washington, D.C. ...who might help defeat the authority grab and prevent the H.E.W. from taking over collegiate and intercollegiate competitive athletics.... we also ask that you get as many of your friends as possible to write to these gentlemen in authority....asking for their help in preventing the enactment of these proposed regulations."[3]

McCall's second argument against Title IX resulted directly from his views on the separation of church and state and his commitment to the Baptist heritage of the University. That argument was that some of the requirements of the law would conflict directly with the tenets of the Baptist church. He took the issue to the Southern Baptist Convention (SBC). The SBC weighed in on Title IX in September 1974, passing an extensive resolution expressing concerns over certain terms in the legislation such as 'comparable,' 'equal,' 'reasonable', and 'proportionate'. There was concern for how the regulations would be interpreted and about what group would be making the interpretation, i.e. would it be the Department of Health, Education and Welfare, or college and university administrators, or perhaps even university students? The SBC noted that actions based on the regulations could become arbitrary and capricious and threaten the internal standards of private universities. These concerns were strengthened by the lack of specificity for many of these terms when the draft regulations were released. These language issues led to national controversy surrounding the regulations. However, two of the more interesting 'Whereas' phrases of the SBC Resolution stated:

> WHEREAS, it is the basic concept and
> conviction of the Association of Southern
> Baptist Colleges and Schools to honor
> and respect each of God's creations; and
>
> WHEREAS, some provisions of
> the proposed regulations for the
> implementation of the provisions of TITLE
> IX of the Education Amendments of 1972
> violate the spirit of positive Christian
> commitment thus creating moral and
> Christian conflict with the same, as it
> relates to the basic health, safety, honor,
> respect, and position of all persons.....[4]

In citing the Higher Education Act of 1965, the Resolution made it clear that SBC members did not believe the government had any right to interfere or exercise any control over educational institutions and proposed the regulations be amended to include the following provisions:

> That there be no unwarranted
> interference or intrusion into the
> internal operations of private institutions
> by members of government;

That members of the SBC be allowed to
interpret the regulations consistent with
their Christian and moral respect for the
individual as taught in the Holy Bible;

That the right to privacy and the right
of safety from harm or being placed
in fear of bodily injury be recognized
and guaranteed in the regulations.[5]

McCall sent this resolution to Casper Weinberger, Secretary of Health, Education and Welfare, October 15, 1974. In a cover letter he noted several pieces of the law that would violate the constitutional rights of individuals and institutions. McCall, clearly had studied the legislation. He made the following salient points:

The proposed regulations were vague
and too subject to interpretation
by bureaucrats. This bureaucratic
lack of understanding about higher
education concerned McCall.

Baylor University, as most universities,
had numerous scholarship opportunities
for its students. Some of these
scholarships were restricted to men;
some were restricted to women.
As McCall understood the proposed
regulations, these scholarships would be
voided once the regulations were in place.
Since many of these scholarships had
been established through wills and trusts,
the regulations discriminated against
the freedom of individuals to make these
decisions about how their property would
be disposed. McCall further believed
that voiding the scholarships given

specifically to train men for the ministry was a violation of the freedom of religion.

3. McCall was concerned that single sex clubs, sororities and fraternities on Baylor's campus would be prohibited under the law. He viewed this as a violation of an individual's constitutional right to freedom of association. He advocated that this restriction only be enforced on campuses where a pattern of discrimination could be proven.

4. The legislation required that men and women's dormitories have the same regulations. McCall argued that these regulations should be different because there were safety issues for women that were not there for men.[13]

5. The legislation required that pregnancy be treated as a disability, eligible for sick leave or absence from classes. McCall's concern rested in the cases of premarital pregnancy since these instances violated the moral standards of Christians. He believed the requirement posed an unwarranted restriction on Baylor's Christian beliefs.

---

13   Prior to Title IX men who lived in the Baylor dormitories had no curfew regulations. All women's dorms had curfews but not all of the curfews were the same. Curfews for men and women in the dormitories at Baylor were adjusted as a result of Title IX and the men students had the same curfew as women after Title IX.

> McCall believed the legislation concerning pensions discriminated against men since women had a longer life expectancy.
>
> Finally, where intercollegiate athletics were concerned, McCall believed the regulations were impractical, unrealistic, and unwarranted since no federal funding flowed to athletic departments. He further described intercollegiate athletic programs as being unrelated entertainment programs for the benefit of the alumni and the public. Given this definition intercollegiate athletic programs had nothing to do with education. By McCall's logic, regulations applied to education (i.e. Title XI) should not be applied to athletic programs.[6]

In contrast to the lobbying against the legislation where it applied to athletics, in 1974 McCall and Reynolds worked with Baylor officials in housing and other programs to ensure Baylor was in compliance with the law. University hiring policies were addressed as were curfews and rules in the men and women's dormitories. Additionally, McCall appointed a campus-wide committee to study the implementation of Title IX and to serve as a grievance committee for any complaints against the University with Title IX provisions. However, students were not allowed to serve on this committee, and the membership consisted of the administrative people in programs where Title IX violations were most likely to occur. On the one hand, these appointments made sense. On the other hand, there was a gross lack of objectivity within this committee and at least a perception that filing a complaint would not be treated fairly. After all, the committee representatives frequently were the bosses of those who might have a legitimate complaint against the university.

By 1975 the proposed regulations were moving forward. In one last effort to stop these regulations from being enacted, McCall sent a letter to forty-three Representatives and fifteen Senators between May 27 and July 20, 1975, urging these Congresspersons to vote against the Title IX regulations before they were signed on July 21, 1975. He stated:

> I believe the…regulations should be
> restricted just to educational programs
> which receive federal aid and not to
> entire school systems….Particularly
> onerous are the regulations concerning
> intercollegiate athletics, which in many
> cases might be called an unrelated
> business conducted by some universities
> for the amusement of alumni and local
> citizens. This business will likely be
> destroyed by these regulations under
> which bureaucrats will inevitably require
> the same expenditures on women
> (sic) as men's sports. The regulations
> should allow the revenue produced by
> a sport to be spent on that sport.[7]

It is fair to say that similar campaigns to McCall's to protest the regulations occurred on most major college campuses across the country. The NCAA had mounted a furious campaign against the legislation and the regulations and had full support of most of their membership. In spite of the numerous letters and phone calls, testimonies and hearings that were held on the regulations, the regulations were approved on July 21, 1975.

In one last effort to have Baylor University restricted from the application of Title IX, McCall wrote to the Director of the Office of Civil Rights, January 1976, six months after the Title IX regulations took effect. In his letter he cited specific sections of the regulations that were problematic for Baylor University because these regulations were inconsistent with the religious tenets of the University.

> Premarital unchastity whether on the
> part of a man or woman is contrary to the
> tenets of the Southern Baptists. Insofar as

**these regulations require Baylor University
to treat the pregnancy of an unmarried
woman as a mere temporary disability
such regulations conflict with the tenets
of Southern Baptists. Such regulations…
are inconsistent with the policies of
the University and Southern Baptists.**

**It is the tenet and practice of practically
all Southern Baptist churches that
only men should be licensed and
ordained for the ministry.**[8]

He noted that the scholarships from the Southern Baptist Convention are for men only, that Baylor matches these scholarships, and that this practice would continue. He further explained that the clubs and organizations on campus designed primarily for ministerial students would continue to operate (without female members). McCall's final point was that the University gave preference in employment in certain areas to licensed and ordained Baptist ministers, i.e. Department of Religion, and that women were not hired for these positions.[9]

Both the argument that the Title IX legislation should apply only to programs receiving federal financial aid and the argument for the separation of church and state were embraced by the Baylor administration until the Civil Rights Restoration Act of 1988 became law, finally putting both issues to rest. Private universities were covered under the law, and all activities of any university receiving federal financial aid were subject to Title IX regulations.

There was no question that the Baylor administration was in no hurry to provide the necessary funding for women's athletics that would provide the equality of opportunity mandated by the legislation. Money was the real issue. In light of the fact that there wasn't enough funding for the men's athletic programs, where to get it for the women's programs seemed like a daunting task. The leadership drug their heels all through the decade of the seventies and into the eighties, taking a very reactive approach to funding, i.e. when extra funds became available, the women received additional financial support. Given the lack of winning seasons for the major revenue generators during the seventies, suffice it to say there were few extra funds circulating in the athletic department during this time. However, by 1974, steady funding was flowing to the women's programs. This increased through the seventies and continued into the eighties. While that funding was more than the women had ever had, it was less than what was needed to meet Title IX requirements.

TWO IMPORTANT DECISIONS

Abner McCall made two decisions resulting from Title IX that had far-reaching implications for women's athletics at Baylor. First was his decision to consolidate the women's intercollegiate athletic programs under the control of Jack Patterson, Baylor's Athletic Director. Documents seem to indicate this move happened sometime between 1972 and 1973 because the first athletic department budget documents for the women's athletic programs were produced in 1973.

The move was consistent with McCall's and Reynolds's early position that if Baylor had a women's athletic program, it should be located in the athletic department, not the HPER department. The move came without any foreknowledge, according to Ted Powers, Chair of the HHPR Department, for him or Olga Fallen, the Women's Athletic Coordinator. By his recollection, Powers said he and Fallen received a letter from McCall indicating the change had been made and it was effective immediately. While the move was practical (and conformed to practices on other campuses after Title IX), how it was done and how it played out was problematic.

At the core of McCall's decisions were two fundamental principles. For one, McCall only wanted one athletic director. That was Jack Patterson. Both he and Herbert Reynolds reiterated this point many times during the seventies. Part of Baylor's tradition not to have women in leadership roles may have contributed to this thinking, but more than likely it was their commitment to a structure with only one athletic director. And that person was not going to be a woman. In their minds, if Title IX required that the women be treated equally to the men, then moving the women's programs onto the same level of the organizational chart as each men's athletic team created that equality. The male coaches answered to Patterson. Under the new structure, Fallen would answer to Patterson.

Secondly, neither Abner McCall nor Jack Patterson understood the philosophy that the Association for Intercollegiate Athletics (AIAW) espoused about women's intercollegiate athletics—that women should govern women's athletic programs. Neither administrator ever went to an AIAW Delegate Assembly, and they, apparently, had no understanding of the AIAW's other philosophical underpinnings. If they did, they certainly did not agree with the premise that women should govern women's athletics. Like most administrators across the country, they believed that managing a women's athletic program was just like managing a men's athletic program. They understood this structure, and they could not see how it could not work for the women.

In my opinion Abner McCalll made two important errors in judgment when he moved the women's programs. He did not take Fallen's title away, and he had no discussions with her about how her role would change under Patterson. I believe his process resulted in the wrong message being sent to Fallen. Continuing to be the Women's Athletic Coordinator meant to Fallen what it had meant for the past twelve years—that she would have autonomy in running her programs, particularly in the decision-making arenas. On the other hand, Patterson believed the women would be moved into his department and would operate in relationship to him like the other men's teams. With that structure, Fallen would be consulted on budget matters for the women's programs, but Patterson would have the final decision in other matters.[14]

According to Ted Powers, the difficulties between Fallen and Patterson were apparent from the first meeting between the two people. Per his recollection, he and Fallen had been invited to Patterson's office to discuss the new athletics structure. Almost before they were invited to sit down, Fallen confronted Patterson and aggressively said something to the effect, "before we start this meeting, I need to know where you stand on women's athletics."[10] Jack Patterson was, by nature, a mild-mannered and soft spoken man, certainly not an aggressive person, while Olga Fallen had more of an aggressive nature. His communication skills were not strong, certainly not the skills that would enable him to deal with an aggressive personality like Fallen's. It is easy to understand why Patterson was completely caught off guard and had difficulty responding to Fallen that day. Needless to say, Patterson's first impression of what working

---

14   I found many pieces of documentation indicating Abner McCall wanted Jack Patterson in charge of all athletic programs. I found no documentation that any conversation with Olga Fallen about this structure ever occurred.

with Fallen was going to be like was not a positive one. It did, however, portend the struggles of the next seven years working together.

This lack of power of the women's athletic coordinator was typical in the men's administrative model of athletics. Hundreds of women across the country found themselves in the same situation as Olga Fallen. The practicalities of this structure did not meet the needs of the women's programs in several ways. For one, Fallen struggled with the lack of flexibility in the way her athletic budget was structured. If she were to grow the women's athletic program, she felt she needed to have the flexibility to move money around as opportunities arose for the various teams. The budget structure in place made that very difficult, and she received little support to make these changes.

Secondly, Fallen had a huge logistical challenge to facilitate communication with Patterson and other athletic department staff. Her office was located in Marrs McLean Gym on the Baylor campus. This made sense because she taught physical education classes in this building as she was still on a half-time appointment to her academic program. Additionally, the women's teams practiced in Marrs McLean and on the fields on the campus. The offices for all of the athletic department staff and coaches were across town in the Floyd Casey Football Stadium. This location made it difficult for her to get to meetings with Patterson. It also necessitated an effective system of phone communication between the two people. Unfortunately, that never happened.

This situation could have been helped if Patterson had installed a staff assistant for Fallen in Marrs McLean gymnasium. Surely managing five athletic teams justified this position. Fallen needed to be able to educate a staff person about the women's programs, the AIAW, the TCIAW, recruiting correspondence, all the issues that were part of a women's athletic program. She needed to be able to teach someone how to answer the phone and take accurate messages. She needed someone who could create appropriate response letters to inquiries and could take care of the myriad of tasks that surfaced on a daily basis with the women's athletic programs. With this person in place, the communication between Fallen and Patterson might have been improved, and Fallen could have managed her administrative load much more effectively. Instead Patterson required Fallen to use the support staff at Floyd Casey Stadium, a structure that just did not work for her. Fallen requested this staff support on many occasions. She never got it. While more funding was flowing to the athletic teams, no funding was coming into the women's budget for secretarial support staff. In addition to a lack of administrative support for Fallen, there was no marketing or public relations personnel hired or assigned to help with the women's programs. All of these elements were part of what was intended by Title IX. None of them happened at Baylor.

When this move occurred, Fallen had her administrative responsibilities in women's athletics and her teaching duties in addition to being the head coach for four of the women's teams—basketball, volleyball, softball, and tennis. There was no funding for assistant coaches for the women's programs, so it fell on the head coaches to do everything for their teams. By the mid-seventies, Fallen had lightened her load, coaching only two teams, continuing her teaching assignment as well as her administrative role. The women's program had four part-time head coaches through the decade of the seventies. Each woman coached but also taught in the HPER department. Adding coaches for the women's program would have brought Baylor closer to compliance with Title IX. It certainly would have helped lighten the workload for these individuals. This never happened. There were no fulltime coaches in the women's program until 1979. There were no paid assistant coaches in the women's program until the early eighties. As the decade of the seventies continued, the problems between Fallen and Patterson intensified. With the growing success of her programs, Fallen needed more support in the form of administrative support staff, marketing personnel, public relations staff and budget development. This support never happened.

What McCall and Patterson and most other male administrators in this country did not get, or ignored, was the notion of gender equity. If they had understood this concept, they would have seen the value in having a woman in charge of women's athletics, of having a voice at the decision-making table that understood what women needed to be successful. This was the seventies and on the Baylor campus, at least, there was only one woman in a significant leadership position—the Financial Vice-President. The cultural revolution of the sixties had not made it to the campus. There was little value for the diversity that women could provide in the campus structure. Title IX mandated gender equity as well as equal opportunity. The seventies were a turbulent time, and administrators were so focused on the equality piece of the legislation that the whole concept of equity was overlooked.

In my mind there is no question that the religious heritage of Baylor was the main reason for such a slow assimilation of these ideas onto the campus. The Southern Baptist Convention was very much a patriarchal structure. Baylor was the largest Southern Baptist University in the world. Women could not wear pants on the Baylor campus. And, female students walking back to the dorms from a physical education class had to wear a raincoat over their shorts. It would be well into the eighties before women began to assume leadership roles on the Baylor campus. It was the early nineties before the conversation about equity in athletics occurred. It was 1996 before a woman assumed autonomous the leadership of women's athletics at Baylor University.

The Fallen-Patterson relationship was neither positive nor productive during the seventies. It was there because it had to be. Resultantly, throughout the seventies, women's athletic programs were an afterthought to the Baylor administration in general and the athletic department administration in particular. In spite of the success of the women's basketball team in 1976 and 1977 and the campus support it generated, there was a sense that the women were being tolerated, that we were there because Title IX said we had to be. Many Bearette fans shared this sentiment and this frustration. Mary Hinton, Baylor alumna and avid Bearette supporter expressed these sentiments in 1978 in a letter to the editor of the *Waco Tribune Herald*. Below is a portion of her letter:

> So, why is it that the women's [athletic] program can not receive recognition from whence it needs it the most — the Baylor Athletic Department? The Director of <u>all</u> Baylor Athletics, Mr. Jack Patterson, had a golden opportunity to help out Saturday afternoon on regional television. When asked about Baylor's athletic program he either intentionally or unintentionally failed to mention the women's program at all…One has to believe that women's athletics in the great Christian institution is merely "a cross to bear" because of HEW guidelines; the Athletic Department seemingly has no intention of providing

**young women with equal recognition. How
sad for the women! How sad for Baylor![11]**

How much the Fallen-Patterson relationship played a role in this feeling of being tolerated and this lack of visible support will never be known. In spite of the obstacles that were put in front of her and the difficulties with Patterson, Fallen continued to lead the women's programs until Spring 1979. Under her leadership, all of the sports teams became more successful each year, more fans were generated from the campus and the community, and a women's sports banquet was held annually beginning in spring 1976.

The number of women's varsity sport teams supported by the athletic department budget declined from nine to five—basketball, softball, track and field, volleyball, and swimming—after the move to the Athletic Department in 1973. The women's tennis and badminton teams continued to play under the AIAW structure. No budget records for those teams were found. What is known is that the HPER Department continued to be the source of funding for the badminton team. How the tennis team was funded could not be determined. In addition fencing had long gone away as a women's sport, and Baylor was no longer fielding a women's golf team.

The first booster club supporting the women's athletic programs was organized during the seventies and was called the Bear Claws. Charter memberships were $50 and were open to anyone interested in supporting the Baylor women's athletic programs. Former players, dating back to 1959 when women first began intercollegiate competition, were given first chance at these memberships.[12] Members followed the team on road trips, provided food and goodies for the women athletes, and conducted fundraisers to support the programs.

In 1975-76, Fallen created the Baylor Bearette Emblem club for the express purpose of having a women's varsity letter club for women. This program effectively matched the men's program where outstanding male athletes were awarded letters each year in their respective sports. There were approximately thirty inaugural members announced at the 1976 Women's Sports Banquet.[13] These women received the first varsity letters awarded to women since 1914. Annual award banquets, sponsored by the Chi's Women's Service organization, were held for the women athletes for three consecutive years 1976–1978. At some point these award banquets began organizing around each women's team.

As of 2012 the Baylor Athletic Department hosts an annual awards banquet for all athletes. Individual teams may be honored by their booster clubs as well.

Those who knew Olga Fallen understood that she had a vision for women's athletics at Baylor, that that vision was broad-based, and that she understood how a women's athletic program should be organized and operated. Unfortunately, Fallen's ability to perform the administrative tasks was hampered, partially because she did not receive the staff support she needed and partially because she may not have had the organizational skills to do the job. Fallen also struggled with health issues that further challenged her ability to manage the demands of her position. She was not the easiest person to work with. Like Patterson, her communication skills were not terribly effective. She was demanding of her players and her staff. She found it difficult to accept responsibility for her shortcomings. Her interpersonal relationship skills were challenging. Even though the women's programs grew in stature and success during the seventies, Fallen's autonomy as the spokesperson for the women's programs eroded steadily. Part of this erosion resulted from her difficulties in managing the job tasks. Some of the erosion came because she was purposefully overlooked in important decisions affecting the women's athletic program.

MCCALL'S SECOND TITLE IX DECISION

A second decision made by Abner McCall illustrates how subtlety forces within the university worked to erode her influence. In 1975 Abner McCall appointed a woman to the Baylor University Athletic Council. Betty Ruth Baker was an assistant professor in the School of Education at the time of her appointment. Not only was she the first woman ever to be appointed to this group, Baylor was the first university in the Southwest Conference to appoint a woman to its Athletic Council.[14] With this move, Baker became Baylor's representative to the women's athletic directors organization within the Southwest Conference. Subsequently, Jack Patterson appointed Baker as Baylor's official representative to the AIAW Delegate Assembly. Olga Fallen had been serving in this capacity since 1973. She had participated in every vote of the assembly since that time. As evidenced by the amount of information available in the Olga Fallen Collection, she stayed heavily involved in the discussions facing AIAW

over Title IX positions, women's scholarship issues, and other governing decisions.[15] While Baker's appointment was a positive move for the University in
terms of Title IX, it further reduced Fallen's credibility as the Women's Athletic
Coordinator and spokesperson for women's athletics at Baylor University.

Certainly Betty Baker was put in an awkward position with her appointment.
To her credit, she worked hard to understand issues and strengthen her ability
to represent those to the Athletic Council and to the AIAW Delegate Assembly.
She consulted with Olga Fallen regularly, became a devoted fan of the Bearettes,
and could be seen at almost every women's event following her appointment.
She even traveled with the 1977 basketball team to Minneapolis to the national
AIAW tournament and volunteered to help Coach Margaret Wooddy wash the
team uniforms between games.[15]

At this time, the Athletic Council was a powerful decision-making body
on the campus. For example, the athletic department budget was heavily scru-
tinized each year before approval of this Council. Additionally, the Council
awarded all athletic scholarships, not the athletic department. Having this
control over the scholarships is what enabled the Council to approve an athletic scholarship for Suzie Snider in 1973. The Council also had the ear of the
President on athletic department issues and advised him regularly. Olga Fallen
was not a member of this body and was seldom included in these discussions.

Betty Baker served admirably in her capacity on the Athletic Council 1975-
84. In reflecting on the significant issues she felt impacted the success and
growth of the women's programs during her tenure, Baker noted the concern
over money. Her comment was there was never enough money for the women.
She indicated the turnover in coaches particularly during the eighties was
problematic. Teams such as volleyball and tennis were challenged to gain any
consistency in their performance because they had so many different coaches.
Finally she noted that the lack of a coordinator for women's athletics who could
be consulted when decisions were going to be made was problematic, someone

---

15 Documentation confirms Fallen knew nothing of Baker's
    appointment as the AIAW Delegate when it was made. If
    Patterson was really interested in knowing what was happen-
    ing in the AIAW, Fallen was certainly the better choice in this
    representative role. Perhaps he was trying to be consistent with
    Baker's representative responsibilities, SWC and AIAW. The
    question remains why he didn't at least tell Fallen what he was
    going to do.

who really understood the programs and the implications of the decisions. She also noted that the lack of adequate facilities for women was a lingering issue and regularly advocated for these on the Council.

THE END OF A LEGACY

On April 24, 1979, Jack Patterson announced that he would not renew Olga Fallen's contract as women's athletic coordinator, head basketball coach or head softball coach for the next year. In a prepared statement for the *Waco Tribune Herald*, he offered this explanation:

> We appreciate the efforts of Miss
> Fallen in the pioneering of women's
> athletics at Baylor University. She did
> a good job during the formative years,
> but the times and methods of handling
> women's athletics have changed and
> we need to move in a new direction.[16]

Evidence showed that Patterson had been dissatisfied with Fallen's performance for quite some time. As early as 1977 Patterson had expressed his lack of satisfaction with Fallen's job performance in a formal letter to her. In February 1977 he stated:

> At first, I believed that our continual
> problems and communication breakdowns
> were the result of your lack of experience
> in running a collegiate athletic program
> and that time would solve these
> problems. However, I have seen very little
> improvement over the last two years.
> Last summer, I felt that I probably had
> not been specific enough with you in
> outlining your responsibilities, and I gave
> you a written list of some of the things
> that I expected from you as Coordinator.
> To date, all that I have received in

response to this list is excuses, deadline delays, and partial compliance.[17]

In this same letter, Patterson went on to indicate that he had set up an office for Fallen at Floyd Casey Stadium where the main athletic administration office were located, and that he expected her to put in regular office hours in this location, 8:30–11:30 am, Monday through Friday, unless her teams were playing out of town.[16] He offered himself and his staff to help her with the administrative details of her position. He further said that he would evaluate her performance again on June 1 [1977] and make a determination at that time of whether or not to maintain her as the Women's Athletic Coordinator. Apparently Patterson decided to leave Fallen in her role as Coordinator after his evaluation in June. She continued as Coordinator beyond this date.

Over one year later, in July 1978, Patterson made the decision to remove Fallen from the Coordinator role. In his mind the structure of the women's program had evolved to a new pattern, and there was no longer a need for a Women's Coordinator. In this new structure, the women coaches would have their own budgets and would report to Patterson in the same manner that the men coaches did. Fallen fashioned a response to Patterson's decision and included Dr. Herbert Reynolds in the loop with this communication. Subsequently, in a letter to Fallen on September 6, 1978, Patterson rescinded his initial decision.[18] This reversal came after a meeting between Patterson, David Taylor, Herbert Reynolds and Abner McCall where Fallen was conspicuously absent. This meeting was more than likely prompted by a long letter from Fallen to Patterson that had been copied to Reynolds. Fallen continued in her role for the 1978-79 academic year.

In 1979 and for the first time in seven years, Fallen had had a losing season with her basketball and softball teams. Evidence suggested there were significant internal conflicts between Fallen and her basketball and softball athletes. Three softball players quit the team in the middle of the season, and one of the highly recruited basketball players also quit the team in January 1979.

---

16 Author's note: Setting specific office hours for Fallen ignored the fact that she had teaching responsibilities and mandated office hours as part of that job. While I can understand Patterson's need to have Fallen at the stadium, this requirement shows how out of touch he was with Fallen's workload demands.

The seriousness of the situation came to a head in early April with the release of a *Lariat* article that led with the headline: 'Growing rift' splits Baylor women's athletics'. The April 4 article was written by *Baylor Lariat* reporters Nancy Dorn and Jeff Barton after a five-month investigation involving current and former athletes, Fallen herself, the athletic community and coaches, and various staff in the athletic administration at Baylor, including Jack Patterson. The information in this article exposed issues that confirmed Fallen was having increasing difficulties keeping up with her obligations as women's athletic coordinator, head coach, and part-time faculty member. Current and former players were interviewed as were opposing coaches, the athletic community, and the Baylor athletic administration. Interviewees were polarized in their support of and dislike for Fallen's performance. Her supporters blamed the administration for failure to support her in her duties and give her the staffing she needed to be successful. Opponents indicated all the support in the world would not have solved the problem. Fallen could be difficult to work with and to work under. There was significant criticism of her coaching style and the way she treated her players.

Administratively, various persons in the athletic community across Texas indicated it was difficult to communicate with Fallen and that she often did not respond to letters from officials. As well it became obvious from this article that recruiting for Baylor was becoming increasingly more difficult as many high school coaches across the state were encouraging their best players not to go to Baylor. From Patterson's perspective it was the last in a long list of problems and issues with Fallen that he had dealt with for several years. His decision was final.

After Fallen's dismissal, the Bear Claws members disbanded themselves. It is unknown if this was a voluntary thing or if the Baylor administration asked them to disband. When Sonja Hogg came to Baylor in 1994, the women's basketball Tipoff Club organized, and Jeanne Nowlin was instrumental in getting several other clubs organized for the women's teams, i. e., softball, soccer, tennis and golf.[19] All of these clubs provided the opportunity for the community and university to come together and support women's athletics at Baylor. Through the years, these groups helped raise significant amounts of money for the various women's teams.

Regardless of motive or purpose, Olga Fallen was no longer the Women's Athletic Coordinator at Baylor University. With her firing, an era of advocacy and leadership for all women athletes and programs by any woman at Baylor University came to an end.

Patterson hired Pam Davis to replace Fallen as women's basketball coach and Bob Brock as women's softball coach. Clyde Hart started working with the women's track and field team and subsequently took over that sport in 1980. Patterson did not appoint anyone to the Women's Athletic Coordinator role but announced that he would assume that position himself. In 1980 Jack Patterson retired from Baylor University. He was replaced by Bill Menefee to lead Baylor athletics into the eighties. Patterson's operational model for all of the Baylor athletic teams remained in place under Menefee's leadership through the eighties. Very little changed for Baylor's women's teams in terms of Title IX support, and no one was in a position to advocate for anything more or better during the eighties. Baylor went into maintenance mode as far as women's athletics was concerned.

Overall, in five years of coaching from 1974 to 1979, Fallen posted a 143-50 won-loss record in basketball, a seventy-four percent winning record, and a 104-87 won-loss record in softball, an eighty-four percent winning record. Her basketball teams appeared in the AIAW National Intercollegiate Basketball Tournament in 1976 and 1977. The 1977 team finished fifth in the nation. She coached one basketball All-American in Suzie Snider-Eppers. Her leadership of the women's athletic program, while rocky and controversial, should be considered effective. Programs grew, teams won, athletes received scholarships, and trophies accumulated. The legacy of women athletic champions at Baylor University grew.

The structure for governing the women's programs that began in 1979 remained in effect until 1996 when Tom Stanton created a new organizational structure and appointed Jeanne Nowlin as the Assistant Athletic Director for Women. In that role Nowlin, was given considerable control over the women's athletic programs, coaches and teams.[20] Nowlin stayed in that role until 2006 when health issues forced her retirement. Her position was renamed Senior Women's Administrator and the responsibilities were altered from those of Nowlin. This position remains within the Athletic Department in 2012.

To this day, no woman in a leadership role in athletics at Baylor University experienced the autonomy and control that Olga Fallen had to run the women's programs from 1960–1972. There are very few athletic departments in the country at the present time that have stand alone women's programs still in their structures.

In spite of the dynamics with Olga Fallen, funding for travel and equipment for the women did increase after the women were moved to the Athletic Department. Additionally, Baylor began providing athletic scholarships to women in 1976, the bulk going to basketball and softball players with some for track and field and volleyball. The results of this financial support and the recruiting surrounding it became obvious as increases in winning seasons and post-season competitions in several sports were noted from 1976 to 1980.

FUNDING FOR WOMEN'S ATHLETICS AFTER TITLE IX

It is easy to understand the threat that the Baylor administration felt with the implementation of Title IX. Here was a private university whose leadership's top priority was to operate in the black and to do nothing that would negatively impact the university financially. The funding model for athletics was weak, relying on revenues from football and men's basketball for most of the department's resources. Assuming debt for anything was not really an option during this period of time. This approach to funding anything at the University began with Dr. Abner McCall (1961–1981) and continued through his second in command, Dr. Herbert Reynolds, President, 1981–1995. At a time when Baylor did not provide a lot of financial support for men's sports, adding dollars for women's programs was a difficult assignment.

In spite of the funding challenges, it was apparent that the women's programs were here for better or worse. To their credit, McCall and later Reynolds did the best they could to funnel money to the women. The women's athletic program budget came under the athletic department, beginning around 1973. The budget chart in Table 1 illustrated that Baylor had a financial commitment to the women's programs during the seventies and that this commitment continued to increase through the decade. Initially, the budget expansion contributed to travel cost like meals and hotel stays. There was also more support for athletic training and team supplies and more funds for equipment and uniforms. Evidence suggested that the women continued to rely on their private vehicles for transportation to and from events. Gas reimbursements for private cars continued until the 1976–77 year. At that time, the women's teams began to travel in university vans or rental vans.

SCHOLARSHIPS, GRANTS-IN-AID, LOANS

Based on guidelines from the AIAW's organizing policy in 1972, scholarship dollars could come in the form of financial aid grants and loans and/or university scholarships (i.e., academic). Additionally, allocation of this money was flexible, meaning that if a full scholarship was worth $1600, that amount could be divided so that several athletes might receive some financial help to attend college. Beginning in 1970 Olga Fallen had begun to develop relationships with her colleagues in the financial aid and housing departments on the campus. Arch W. Hunt, the VP for Student Financial Aid, worked closely with Fallen to see if potential athletes could qualify for some kind of financial assistance, grants or loans or housing. Initially, these were the only funding mechanisms for helping female athletes on the campus. With Hunt's help and advice, Fallen built a very effective structure for supporting women athletes throughout the seventies. Scholarship dollars were inadequate so these additional funding opportunities made it possible to help a lot of female athletes get their degree from Baylor.

The first athletic scholarship awarded to a female student at Baylor occurred in 1973 when the Athletic Council voted to award Suzie Snider a full athletic scholarship to Baylor for four years. Those funds came out of the men's track program scholarship funds and were eventually moved to the women's budget. There is evidence to suggest that the first athletic scholarship allocation ($5000) for women was designated in the 1975-76 academic year, although scholarships were not a line item in this budget year. Additional records indicated as many as eleven women athletes received varying amounts of financial assistance from the Financial Aid office, i.e. grants in aid or loans, totaling $2065 during this year. These awards supported athletes on the basketball, volleyball, and track and field teams. The $5000 allocated for athletic scholarships went to three basketball players. This made the total amount of financial aid available to women athletes at Baylor for the 1975-76 year approximately $7065.

In 1976-77 the scholarship budget received a large increase to $16,000. At the time tuition and fees at Baylor were estimated at $1685/year, indicating that Fallen had ten scholarships to award for that year. Documentation indicated she spread these dollars across fourteen athletes for basketball, softball, track and field and volleyball.[21]

Table 1 illustrates the increasing trend in funding for women's athletics during the decade of the seventies. No documents with exact numbers for each budget year were found, however, so those that are shown are estimates at best. Additionally, some of the numbers reflect the proposed budget for that year, and some reflect amounts that were allocated in a budget year. The important thing to note is that there was a consistent increase in funding support for the women during the years after Title IX. The reader will particularly note the increases in scholarship dollars beginning in 1975-76.

Budget numbers through 1975-76 are based on the total of the line items common to all of those budget years (game expense, awards, banquet, repairs and laundry, supplies, and team travel). By 1978, several line items were added to the women's athletic budget that made the amount of support from the University even greater than what is shown in the Table because personnel costs are not reflected in the Table. Examples of these added items were line items for graduate assistants, team managers, and athletic trainers. One of the women's coaches was receiving a small amount of funding to support her work as a Sports Information director. The large increase in scholarships in 1979 came after Fallen was fired and Pam Bowers was hired. Most of this money supported a full complement of scholarships (12, per AIAW limits) for basketball. Bowers was also hired as the first fulltime women's athletic coach. Part of the budget increase reflected her salary.[17]

---

17   This budget information was gleaned from the Fallen Collection and the McCall and Reynolds collections in the Texas Collection Library on the Baylor campus. Efforts to secure verification of this financial information from Baylor University were denied.

Budget years	1971-72	1972-73	1973-74	1974-75	
Budget amount	$667	$2135	$11,000	$16,152	
Scholarships and Financial Aid*	n/a	n/a	$3000 (Snider)	$3000 (Snider)	
Budget Totals	$667	$2135	#14,000	$19,152	
No. of Students	0	0	1	1	
No. of Sports	9	9	9	9	

Budget years	1975-76	1976-77	1977-78	1978-79	1979-80
Budget amount	$26,648	$37,580	$39.900	$83,610	$92,675
Scholarships and Financial Aid*	$7060	$16,000	#$29,800	$69,680	$119,904**
Budget Totals	$33,708	$53,580	$65,175	$153,290	$212,579
No. of Students	14	12	n/a	n/a	tn/a
No. of Sports	5	5	4	4	4

Table I: Financial Support for Women's Intercollegiate Athletics, Baylor University, 1971–1980.[22]

*Scholarship amounts may include athletic scholarships as well as amounts designated from the Financial Aid Office.
**Reflects increases to athletic scholarships for women's basketball when Pam Bowers was hired in 1979.

Fallen utilized the resources in the Financial Aid office to support her program throughout the seventies, relying heavily on these dollars for students who qualified for financial assistance from the University. In the 1977–78 budget, twenty-four students received some form of financial aid from Baylor, totaling $29,800. A significant portion of that amount, $20,700, was for athletic scholarships.[23]

Early in 1978, the Athletic Council on the recommendation from Jack Patterson made the decision to move volleyball, track and field, cross country, and softball into AIAW Division II status, effective with the 1979-80 budget. More than likely this decision was driven by budget concerns, since costs to support teams in Division II were less than Division I, mostly because fewer scholarships were awarded in Division II. Betty Baker was instructed to support the vote on the divisional structure vote at the upcoming 1979 AIAW Delegate Assembly.

This was yet another decision made without consulting Fallen, another effort to erode her influence and opinions. She strongly objected to Patterson, believing this decision would weaken Baylor's programs. In her estimation, all of Baylor's women's sports teams were positioned to be competitive in Division I. Why move three out of four programs to Division II? It was a move in the wrong direction in her mind. Furthermore, she was adamant because neither she nor any of the women's coaches were consulted about this decision and that she had not been told about the meeting where this decision was made. In a letter to David Taylor, Assistant Athletic Director, February 26, 1978, Fallen expressed her frustration:

> …I had several items of concern
> that I felt should be brought to their
> [Athletic Council] attention. I, therefore,
> was totally surprised to learn that
> they had met and passed a resolution
> regarding divisional structuring with
> very little discussion and input by the
> coaches of the women's sports.[24]

The division change impacted the scholarship dollars in the women's athletic budget for 1979-80. Basketball, the Division I program, saw increased scholarship dollars in this budget because of AIAW requirements. One important problem came out of Patterson's decision. The designated scholarship dollars for volleyball, track and field and softball athletes were based on AIAW policy prior to the divisional structure change. When Patterson made his decision, many of these athletes effectively were put in a position to lose their scholarships because of the move of their sport to Division II. Fallen further explained:

> The scholarships allocated are not
> sufficient to allow any of the sports
> to remain competitive, and divisional
> assignment depends entirely upon the
> University's commitment in this area.
> Basketball, while competing in Division I,
> with slightly less than 3½ scholarships….

cannot even fulfill its responsibilities to
four returning full-scholarship athletes
and will not be able to even recruit for
the next three years…I respectfully
urge a re-evaluation of the budget,
both in the areas of scholarships and
team travel, and a reconsideration
of the divisional structuring.[25]

Nevertheless, the decision stuck. No information regarding the resolution of this dilemma was found. In his response to Fallen's letter, David Taylor, Assistant to Jack Patterson, explained the rationale for the 1979-80 budget decisions stating that the increase granted to the women's athletic budget for 1979-80 was at a rate twice that of other University budgets. He further explained that the divisional assignments were made based on the budget increases for the 1979-80 year. He stated: "These increases are achieved through considerable sacrifice in other areas as there is no corresponding projected increase in revenues from women's athletics."[26] He further indicated that he believed the divisional assignments were in the best interest of women's athletics at Baylor and that there would be no re-evaluation of the decision. Money. It all came down to the money.

Fallen's response, noted above, was to the preliminary budget released by the athletic department. In the final budget, there was a large increase in women's scholarships in the 1979-80 budget, that resulted from the hiring of a new basketball coach and a decision to provide the AIAW maximum number of scholarships—12—moving into the eighties (See Table 1, pg. 18). Fallen had been fired by the time this budget was released. Betty Baker carried the divisional change decision to the AIAW, and the volleyball, track and field and softball teams competed as AIAW Division II teams until 1982 when all of the women's sports were moved under the NCAA structure and into the Southwest Conference.

It is impossible to say how the women's budgets throughout the seventies compared to the men's. Conventional wisdom would suggest the level of funding for each women's team did not compare favorably even with the men's minor sports. There is little doubt that the women's overall funding was in no way comparable to the football program. Is it possible that the men's minor sports suffered because of Title IX? Yes, it is, but not because there wasn't enough funding to go around. Rather, they may have suffered because of the decisions athletic department officials made about how the funds were disbursed. Remember, under the Baylor funding model, football got the most money because that program produced the most revenue. Was football funding extravagant? Possibly. Just one example of this was the number of scholarships allocated to football at this point in time. Under the NCAA policies, the number of football scholarships had no limits like they do in the NCAA policy of today. It would not have been unusual for over one hundred Baylor athletes to be on a football scholarship during the seventies. Funding this many scholarships for football players was not a decision that had to be made by Baylor officials, it was a decision that was made because it was the only decision they knew how to make. Cut back on football scholarships? Not going to happen at this point in time. The same decision was being made at campuses all across America. Another common practice in football programs was to take the team to a motel the night before home games. The thinking was to get them away from campus so they could focus on the game, be with their teammates, etc. Extravagant? Many women leaders in sport thought so, and they sounded the alarm on this kind of spending during numerous Title IX hearings happening during this decade. Were funding priorities in men's sports out of whack? You be the judge. Nevertheless, when funding decisions like these were made in order to protect the football program, women's sports and men's minor sports suffered.

NON-COMPLIANCE AND INEQUITY

Throughout the seventies, Baylor was doing what it could financially for women's sports under Title IX, but the women's programs were not a priority in the eyes of the administration, and as discussed earlier, there was no attention to equity in the women's programs. As a result, numerous Title IX issues as well as compliance details fell through the cracks. This issue surfaced in January 1977 when it became known that several Bearette basketball players had received injuries that required follow-up medical care in the form of X-rays and other medical treatment. These athletes and their families were paying for these expenses. In contrast the athletic department covered these types of medical expenses for the male athletes. David Carter, a student, exposed this situation in a letter to the editor, *Baylor Lariat*, January 27, 2977, when he asked the question "can't Baylor give its female athletes equal insurance protection against physical injury; or are our women athletes of no consequence to Baylor?" In a follow-up phone call with *Lariat* reporters, Assistant Athletic Director, David Taylor, indicated that under Baylor's policy, the University should have incurred these expenses for the women. Apparently there was a communication issue between Taylor and Women's Athletic Trainer, Margaret Wooddy, regarding this issue. Wooddy indicated she had never been told that Baylor would pay these medical expenses. Bad communication or incredible oversight? Who knows? Baylor resolved this issue quickly, and the women athletes were covered for these types of medical expenses.

Clay Morton, in the February 9, 1977 editorial for the *Baylor Lariat* put the incident into context. He stated: "David Carter's question has been answered. But a more important one remains: Why did it take two years and a letter to the editor to end such a blatantly discriminatory practice?"

Another noncompliance area for Baylor was the fact that all of its women's coaches during this period were part-time. They all taught in other areas of the University or held other jobs in addition to their coaching responsibilities. Certainly the spirit of the Title IX guidelines mandated equivalent coaching support for the women as could be found in the men's programs, at least in the major sports of basketball and football. Three of Baylor's minor men's sports— tennis, golf and baseball—had part-time head coaches. Football had upwards of six fulltime assistant coaches, and the men's basketball team had two full time assistant coaches as well as a head coach. None of the women's teams had full-time head coaches, and the only assistant coaches were graduate assistants who were interested in learning more about how to coach the sport. They were not paid for their work until the late 1970s. They volunteered for this experience above and beyond their graduate assistantship responsibilities.

Additionally, the facilities situation for the women, both playing and practice arenas was not satisfactory. During the seventies, Rena Marrs McLean gym was the practice home for both the men and women's basketball teams, and it was where the women's teams played their games. Women's volleyball also practiced and played their matches in this facility, and physical education classes were taught in Rena Marrs McLean gym. Many problems arose with this facility. For one, it was an excellent teaching facility but it was a subpar facility to house an athletic program. There was only one women's dressing room for classes and women's visiting teams. Early in the decade the Bearettes used this dressing room for practice but usually came dressed for the game from their dorms or apartments. By the mid-seventies, men's basketball was practicing and playing at the Heart of Texas Coliseum where they had their own dressing facility. The Bearette basketball team inherited the men's basketball team dressing room at McLean Gym. Visiting teams were a challenge with extremely poor dressing facilities and no quiet place to convene at half time of games. Frequently, a class-room was utilized for this space.

There were scheduling problems for all of these programs. Historically, pri-orities on the schedules for this facility were physical education classes, men's basketball practice, campus intramurals and then women's athletics. The men's basketball practice time was set for the season, and everything else scheduled around it. Women's basketball usually practiced around four o'clock in the after-noon and players frequently had scheduling issues with labs for their classes. At times when the volleyball season overlapped with the starting of men and women's basketball season, scheduling became very challenging. In the early eighties, the women's basketball teams frequently scrambled to find a facility at one of the public schools in town for their early season practices.

Another gender equity issue arose for women's games because there was no event staff to help the women coaches set up for their events. If you were the vol-leyball coach and you had a match in McLean gym, you arrived two hours early to set up the nets, make sure the officials showed up, show them to their dressing room, secure the area from students who were in the gym for recreational basket-ball, and set up for teams. You had also made arrangements to have these officials for the game. If you were the basketball coach, you also arranged for officials and then arrived two hours early to make sure the clock was working properly, make sure the scorers and timers were in place, secure the gym for your game, show the officials to their dressing room. Meet with your team prior to the game and get centered on the game? That was a challenge. The men's basketball and football coaches never had these responsibilities, but anecdotal evidence suggest some of the men's minor sport coaches may have taken on some of these tasks.

The same question posed by Clay Morton to the *Lariat* in February 1977 could be asked in a lot of areas. As a coach, I asked many questions during this time, myself:

- Why did the Baylor women continue to have to provide their own private transportation to events until 1976-77?

- Why did the Baylor women have to compete for athletic facilities for practice and/or competition?

- Why didn't the Baylor women have support from the athletic department for sports information, press releases, etc.?

- Why did Olga Fallen not have the support staff at Rena Marrs McLean Gym to help carry out her duties as Women's Athletic Coordinator?

- Why wasn't Olga Fallen recognized for the position she held, and why wasn't she consulted on issues that impacted the women's programs?

- Why was it always a struggle to arrange sufficient financial support for the women's athletic programs?

- Why was there such an undercurrent of negativity from the Baylor administration about women's athletics?

In spite of all of the questions above and the Title IX issues that might have been raised by the women leadership during this time, in spite of all the problems and communication issues she had with Jack Patterson, in spite of an obvious lack of respect for her accomplishments and for the program she had built, Olga Fallen stated in an interview with the *Baylor Lariat*, November 5, 1976 that she felt Baylor had 'survived' Title IX. She said she was pleased with the situation here [at Baylor]. She recognized that the proportion of scholarships between men and women was not where the law required it to be but she indicated that was too much of a financial burden for the University right away. She stated she believed that the move of the women's program had for the most part been successful but stressed the importance of maintaining a program for women and managed by women.

Within three years of this article, Fallen would be gone. It is fortunate for Baylor University that Fallen had a positive attitude about Title IX and the University's response to the legislation. There is no question that the University could have been sued for failure to comply with Title IX. Administrators had no plan in place to work toward this goal. Indeed, they were still maintaining the position that because they were a private university, they should not have to comply with the law. Anyone, especially Olga Fallen, could have brought a Title IX lawsuit against the institution at any time.

In spite of the struggles brought on by the Title IX legislation, Baylor's women's athletic teams continued to build on their success in the second half of the seventies. The women's basketball team reached the pinnacle of its success in 1976 and 1977 and set the pace in terms of expectations for other teams. The program took on more of the characteristics of a university athletic program. Fallen guided the implementation of an annual Women's Athletic Awards banquet as well as the development of the Bear Claws, a spirit club for the women's basketball team. Women athletes were welcomed back into the ranks of the Baylor Letterman's Association for the first time since 1914. Graduate assistants began to provide coaching support[18] and managers and athletic trainers for the women became eligible for athletic scholarships. While a women's sports information director was designated, this person also taught a halftime load in the HPER department, coached two teams, and managed the athletic training program for the women. Needless to say, the marketing and public relations functions for the women could have used help from those same services that were in place for the men's programs. Very little happened on that front.

18 Whether or not these coaching assignments were part of their graduate assistantship responsibilities could not be documented.

NOTES ON CHAPTER 5
BAYLOR UNIVERSITY RESPONDS TO TITLE IX

1. The Olga Fallen Collection, Box 7, File 11.

2. Dr. J.T. Powers, interview by the author, June 21, 2012.

3. The Olga Fallen Collection, Box 8, Folder 1.

4. *Resolution of the Southern Baptist Convention*, September 26, 1974. BU Records: President's Office: Abner Vernon McCall, 1961-1981, Accession #141, Box 3B372, The Texas Collection, Baylor University.

5. Ibid.

6. Personal letter from Abner V. McCall to Casper Weinberger, Secretary of Health, Education and Welfare, October 14, 1974. BU Records: President's Office: Abner Vernon McCall, 1961-1981, Accession #141, Box 3B391, The Texas Collection, Baylor University.

7. Personal letter from Abner V. McCall to Congressmen between May 27 and July 29, 1975. BU Records: President's Office: Abner Vernon McCall, 1961-1981, Accession #141, Box 3B372, The Texas Collection, Baylor University.

8. Abner V. McCall, personal letter to the Director of the Office of Civil Rights, U.S. Department of Health, Education and Welfare, January 12, 1976. Retrieved with permission from the legal files of Lanelle McNamara, Waco, Texas, October 26, 2012.

9. Ibid.

10. See note 2 above.

11. Mary H. Hinton, personal letter to the editor, *Waco Tribune-Herald*, February 13, 1978.

12. Sherry Castello, ed., "New organization to back Bearettes," *The Baylor Line*, June 1978, 32.

13. The Olga Fallen Collection, Boxes 13 and 14.

14. Betty Ruth Baker, interview by the author, June 21, 2012.

15. Ibid.

16. Michael Lyons, "Baylor Ousts Olga Fallen," *Waco Tribune-Herald*, April 24, 1979.

17. Personal Letter from Jack Patterson to Olga Fallen, February 21, 1977. President's Office: Herbert Hal Reynolds, 1981–1995, Accession #223, Box 3C218–Athletics-Women 1972–1984, The Texas Collection, Baylor University.

18. Personal Letter from Jack Patterson to Olga Fallen, September 6, 1978. President's Office: Herbert Hal Reynolds, 1981–1995, Accession #223, Box 3C218–Athletics-Women 1972–1984, The Texas Collection, Baylor University.

19. Jeanne Nowlin, interview by the author, June 26, 2012.

20. Ibid.

21. The Olga Fallen Collection, Accession #3797, Box 36 and Box 37, The Texas Collection, Baylor University.

22. Ibid.

23. Personal Letter from Herbert Reynolds to Olga Fallen, April 18, 1977. President's Office: Herbert Hal Reynolds, 1981–1995, Accession #223, Box 3C218–Athletics-Women 1972–1984, The Texas Collection, Baylor University.

24. Personal letter from Olga Fallen to David Taylor, February 26, 1978. The Olga Fallen Collection, Box 10, Folder 7.

25. Ibid.

26. Personal letter from David Taylor to Olga Fallen, February 28, 1978. The Olga Fallen Collection, Box 10, Folder 7.

CHAPTER 6

BEARETTES TO LADY BEARS, 1975–1980

Early on Olga Fallen made all of the decisions about how the scholarship dollars would be allocated for the women's teams, rarely discussing this with the other coaches. Consequently, the basketball, softball, and track and field teams received the bulk of the scholarship funding with a small portion going to the volleyball team. All of the women's teams received funding support for travel and equipment and supplies. Overnight stays and meals were now paid for when the teams traveled. However, until 1976–1977 coaches and athletes continued to provide the transportation for the athletes.

There was a direct correlation between the success of the teams and the amount of scholarship dollars flowing to each team. That detail was most evident in the success of the women's basketball program where scholarship dollars allowed Fallen to recruit outstanding players such as Karen Aulenbacher and Babette Metcalf. With these two women complementing the play of Suzie Snider and Lynnell Pyron, the Bearettes were positioned to make a run at the national level.

1975-76
BASKETBALL FIGHTS THEIR WAY TO THE NATIONAL AIAW BASKETBALL CHAMPIONSHIPS!

For the 1975-76 season, Suzie Snider was a junior. She and her teammates had played together for three years. The possibilities were exciting for the team to have an outstanding season. And that they did, winning the Tarleton Invitational Basketball Tournament, the Baylor Invitational and placing second in the prestigious, 24-team Houston Invitational. The Bearettes started the season with an unbeaten record until they played Stephen F. Austin University (SFA) and lost in overtime 74-70. The SFA Lady Jacks had beaten the Bearettes in seven consecutive contests, and the overtime loss was especially painful.

On the season the team posted a season record of 32-6, winning the TAIAW Zone tournament, placing second in the State tournament to Wayland Baptist Flying Queens, the number three ranked team in the nation.[1] They won the Southwest AIAW (SWAIAW) regional tournament to qualify for the national championship tournament at Penn State University.[2]

Babette Metcalf

Baylor University, Round Up 1977 Yearbook, (Waco, TX: [Baylor University], 1977), The Texas Collection, Baylor University, p. 132.

Karen Aulenbacher

Baylor University, Round Up 1977 Yearbook, (Waco, TX: [Baylor University], 1977), The Texas Collection, Baylor University, p. 157.

In the National AIAW Basketball Tournament, March 24-27, 1976, the Bearettes lost to eventual champion Delta State in the second round but finished as one of the top seven teams in the country.

Members of the 1975-76 team are pictured below:

Back: Karen Aulenbacher, Babette Metcalf, Cathy
Hart,Marilyn Williamson, Leah Box, Sarah Davis
Middle: Judy Kafer, Lynnell Pyron, Chris Boultinghouse, Cinda Permenter
Front: Connie Freeman, Manager, Cathy Robinson, Asst.
Coach, Olga Fallen, Head Coach, Suzie Snider
Not pictured: Nancy Goodloe, Head Women's Trainer

Olga Fallen Collection, Accession #3797, Box 38, Folder 8,
The Texas Collection, Baylor University

The trip to Penn State represented a milestone for women's athletics at Baylor. Never before had the University funded anything of this magnitude for women's athletics. In addition to flying the team to Pennsylvania, the Bearettes had a charter bus ride from Waco to the Dallas-Fort Worth airport and from Philadelphia to to the Penn State campus. All expenses were paid for lodging and food and incidentals. Several Bearette backers and parents accompanied the team on this trip at their own expense.

BADMINTON

In the Fall 1975 a young woman enrolled in Dutch Schroeder's beginning badminton class. Her name was Cindy Alty, a sophomore from Corpus Christi, Texas. Schroeder quickly realized this woman had potential and challenged her by entering her in the men's class tournament. She won the tournament.

Schroeder recruited her for the Baylor Badminton team and so began a very distinguished playing career for Cindy Alty. By all accounts Alty was the best female badminton player ever to represent Baylor on the court. Among the women competitors for the 1975-76 season were Cindy Alty and Kathryn Wallace. In her inaugural season Alty placed second in singles in the TCIAW Zone tournament and teamed with Wallace to win the TAIAW Zone doubles championship. Other Baylor players also placed third in singles and third in doubles. Both the singles and doubles teams advanced to the State TAIAW Tournament but no records of their performances were found.[3] Alty, in her debut season, represented Baylor in numerous collegiate and open tournaments, competing in singles, doubles and mixed doubles in both venues. She won singles in the Del Mar Collegiate tournament in October 1975.

Having played badminton as a college student and then as a faculty member at Baylor, I found Alty's accomplishments in her first competitive year amazing. Badminton, when played competitively, is a highly skilled, physically demanding sport. Alty's ability to play all three events in both tournaments and have the skills and stamina needed to win was an incredible feat. The game is also mentally challenging as one has to learn the strategies required to play well in singles, doubles and mixed doubles, all of which are very different games. Many competitors play for years and find it difficult to learn the strategy of all three events, much less develop the ability to execute them in competition. Typically, outstanding singles players find it very difficult to adjust to playing doubles or mixed doubles because these persons are used to playing the entire court, not relying on anyone else. They find it challenging to give up the control of the court that is demanded when playing with a partner in doubles or mixed doubles. Alty made this adjustment with ease.

SOFTBALL

Coached by Olga Fallen, the 1975–76 softball team posted a season record of 17-11, the best all time record for a Baylor softball team. Many of the scholarship players on the women's basketball team also played on the softball team. They were outstanding athletes. The team hosted the Baylor Invitational, winning five games and capturing the championship. They placed second the TCIAW Zone tournament but failed to place in the State tournament.[4] They ended the season having beaten some of the best teams in the state. Fallen contributed much of the success to the pitching of Cathy Hart and Brenda Stahr.[5] Team members were Marsha Adams, Karen Aulenbacher, Judy Blalock, Leah Box, Sarah Davis, Beth Dees, Cathy Hart, Cathy Lee, Karen Moon, Penny Peschel, Judy Pelzel, Lynn ell Pyron, Kim Rothfus, Kara Weldon, Dinah Miller, and Marilyn Williamson. Support personnel included: Debbie Watson, Manager, Nancy Goodloe, Athletic Trainer, Alice Melendez, Assistant Coach, and Margaret Wooddy, Statistics and Sports information.[6]

Leah Box Takes a Swing, circa 1975

*Olga Fallen Collection, Accession #3797, Box 38, Folder 12,
The Texas Collection, Baylor University*

Marilyn Williamson Bearette Softball, circa 1975

Olga Fallen Collection, Accession #3797, Box 38, Folder 12,
The Texas Collection, Baylor University

SWIMMING

Baylor swimmers in the 1975-76 season were Kara Weldon, Alison White, Ana Thatcher, Karen Devitt, and Carol Lamphere. No records of their performances were available.[7]

TRACK AND FIELD

The 1976 Baylor tracksters placed third in the State TCIAW meet. Outstanding finishers for the Bearettes were: Marsha Talley, 3rd in the 100 yard dash, Kathleen Matusik, third in the 880 yard run, Joan Rogers, first in the mile run, Suzie Snider, first in the shot put, second in discus, and third in the javelin. Ten members of the team qualified for the AIAW National Track and Field meet in Manhattan, Kansas. They were Loretta Buxkemper, Sarah Davis, Sarah Martin, Kathleen Matusik, Becky McClenny, Lynnell Pyron, Joan Rogers, Suzie Snider, Marsha Talley and Christa Womack.[8]

The team traveled to Manhattan, Kansas via a Baylor van. That signaled an improvement in terms of financial support, as the women were still traveling in their private cars to these meets. However, as it worked out, flying would have been quicker a lot less stressful.

I was the coach to accompany the team to Manhattan. Olga Fallen was going to fly up in two days. We left Waco in the afternoon and spent the night in Edmond, Oklahoma where we had been invited to dinner at the home of Baylor badminton player Chrisy Kessler's family. The team also had an early breakfast at the Kessler's home and got on the road in what I thought was plenty of time to get to Manhattan, Kansas by 5:00 in the afternoon, the deadline for check-ing in to the national meet. As it happened, the trip took much longer than anticipated. I don't even like to think about how fast we drove that day to get to Manhattan on time, but at 3:00 in the afternoon, I realized we were not going to make the 5:00 deadline. I took the time to stop and call the meet headquarters to report we were running late. My instructions were to get there as quickly as possible. We arrived at 5:30 and I quickly reported to meet officials.

To my dismay, meet officials were having serious discussions about not allow-ing the Baylor team to compete. I was told I would have to make a special appeal to the meet committee for my team to be allowed to compete. I was frantic! On my team were the defending national shot put champion and nine other members who made up relay teams that had the fastest qualifying times in the nation. How could they not let us participate? Nevertheless, I met with the committee and must have said the right things, because we were allowed to compete.

As it turned out, the weather turned nasty the two days of the meet, and the cold running conditions were not conducive to good performances by anyone. The Baylor tracksters did not place in any event at this meet and went home extremely disappointed. Suzie Snider came in second in the shot put. The trip home was long and tiring. At least we were not on a deadline.

VOLLEYBALL

For the 1975 season, Olga Fallen handed the head coaching reins to Nancy Goodloe. She was assisted by graduate student, Margaret Wooddy. According to the *Baylor Lariat*, November 11, 1975 the team earned a season record of 13-16-1 overall. Records indicate the team placed second in the TAIAW Zone tournament. Records of their state tournament play were not available. Team standouts were Marsha Adams, Diane Johnson, and Karen Conrads. Marsha was an excellent setter and anchored the team's offense. Conrads and Johnson were tall and could jump like crazy. They gave the team an offensive capacity with their spiking and shored up the defense with their blocking. Other members contributing to the success of the team were Cynthia Williams, Charlotte White, Barbara Bloemer, Judy Ravesloot, Charlene Cole, Cindy Lyles, Cindy Bartlett, Janet Spivey, Veda Smith, and Karen Nelson. At the 1976 Women's Athletics Award Banquet, the following awards were given: Most Valuable Player, Marsha Adams; Leadership, Charlotte White; "Rookie" Award, Diane Johnson, and Seventh Person Award, Charlene Cole.[9,10,11]

I vividly recall a tournament at Sam Houston State University that year. In our first game, we were playing very badly, no energy, no excitement, no desire to win. I was at a loss as to what to do and say. I'd called a couple of timeouts and talked with the team, trying to encourage them. We lost the first game and were losing like 10-0 in the third game. At that time the team who won the best two out of three games won the match, so we were getting ready to be out of the tournament. I called a final timeout and said something like this: OK, if we lose, we lose. But at least make them work for the match! Don't just give it to 'em! Not sure what happened, but my team went out and won that game and the next game to advance to the second round. That was an exciting moment for everyone, and I will always remember that wonderful comeback victory.[19]

1976-77

By the 1976-77 season, there was no question that women's athletics at Baylor had grown. In a statement for the Baylor Line, Olga Fallen emphasized the reasons for the growth.

> Women's athletics and women's basketball in particular have made tremendously rapid strides in the past year. With increased budgets, more advanced coaching techniques (resulting in better prepared high school players) and, of course, athletic scholarships

---

19 Many of the details of that match have been lost over the years. But I clearly remember what I told the team and how they responded.

> all contributing to a changing scene in
> the world of women's intercollegiate
> athletics, consistent winning seasons
> may be a thing of the past.[12]

Fallen recognized that parity was coming to women's intercollegiate basketball. Teams like Temple Junior College and Wayland Baptist College who had dominated women's basketball for so long because they offered scholarships were on the threshold of losing their powerhouse status. With the advent of athletic scholarships within the AIAW in 1973, all of the intercollegiate programs had had three years to start to catch up. Baylor was competitive with both of these teams by this point in time. While some of these teams may continue to win, they would no longer dominate as they had in the past.

BASKETBALL

Approaching the 1976-77 season, the Lady Bear basketball team was ranked 15th in the nation by Street and Smith Publishers and were anticipating match ups with the Wayland Flying Queens, UCLA, and the No. 1 ranked team in the country, Delta State. The team returned five seniors and five juniors from the 1975-76 season and added seven highly talented freshmen to its roster.

1976-77 Bearette Basketball Team
Seventh in the Nation

Front row: Pam Young, Glenda Holleyman, Asst. Coach, Karen Aulenbacher, Head Coach, Olga Fallen, Suzie Snider-Eppers*
Center row: Suzie Oelschlegel, Judy Kafer, Lynnell Pyron, Jamie Mott, Paula Young, Sarah Davis
Back row: Lark Taylor, Babette Metcalf, Cathy Hart, Rene Verdine, Marilyn Williamson, Beverly Herrington, Leah Box
Not pictured: Margaret Wooddy, Head Trainer

*Suzie Snider married Danny Eppers prior to the 1976 season.

1976-77 BB TEAM

Baylor University, Round Up 1977 Yearbook, (Waco, TX: [Baylor University], 1977), The Texas Collection, Baylor University, p. 157.

AIAW NATIONAL TOURNAMENT – 5TH IN THE NATION FINISH

The women's trip to the AIAW National Tournament in Minneapolis, Minnesota capped a storybook season for the team. Baylor upset No. 2 ranked St. Joseph's 85-75 in the first round but lost to Louisiana State University to advance to the losers bracket in the second round. They posted wins over Missouri and Utah to earn the opportunity to play Southern Connecticut for a fifth place finish. The Bearettes came from 16 points down with eight minutes to go, outscoring the Owls 20–2 in that last eight minutes. With 32 seconds left in the game, Baylor was trailing 69–68. Miraculously, Suzie Snider-Eppers was fouled. As she stepped to the free throw line, she whispered to Lynnell Pyron, then stepped up and sank those two clutch free throws to put Baylor in the lead 70–68. Sarah Davis added one more free throw for the Bearettes in those last seconds, and Baylor sealed the victory. That effort won the Bearettes the game but also the hearts of the 1500 fans in attendance. The team received a standing ovation after the buzzer.

After the game, someone asked Snider-Eppers what she whispered to Lynnell Pyron as she (Snider-Eppers) stepped to the free throw line. Snider-Eppers's reply was "I asked her if she wanted to trade places."[13] I'm sure Lynnell would have stepped up and sank those free throws for Suzie, but that was not an option at the time. Nevertheless, Snider-Eppers came through in the clutch and Baylor left Minneapolis as the best team in Texas, they had the winningest season in the nation and the fifth best team in the country.

According to Fallen, the entire tournament required a team effort. Snider-Eppers, Babette Metcalfe, and Karen Aulenbacher led the team in scoring. Snider-Eppers was recognized as the outstanding center for the tournament, and the Bearettes finished the season 32-12. Fallen commented, "What can I say except this year was the greatest."[14]

1977 KODAK ALL-AMERICAN TEAM

In this year, Suzie Snider-Eppers became the first woman in Baylor history to earn All-American honors as she was voted onto the prestigious Kodak All-American team. Other members of that team were:

Carol Blazejowski – Montclair State
Doris Felderhoff, Stephen F. Austin
Nancy Dunkle, Cal State Fullerton
Rita Easterling, Mississippi
Lusia Harris, Delta State
Ann Meyers, UCLA
Patricia Roberts, Tennessee
Mary Scharff, Immaculata
Charlotte Lewis, Illinois State[15]

Snider-Eppers still holds the career scoring record at Baylor University of 3,861 points. She posted a career rebounding record of 2,176 and was voted into the Baylor Athletic Hall of Fame in 1987.[16]

BADMINTON

Baylor Lariat articles, Fall 1976 to Spring 1977 indicated Cindy Alty returned from her successful 1975-76 debut season winning the women's singles title in four collegiate and open tournaments. She also took home numerous first, second and/or third place trophies in women's doubles and mixed doubles this year. She was joined in many of these women's doubles victories by freshman Sue Butler. Alty won the State TAIAW singles title, qualifying her to go to the National AIAW Badminton tournament in Phoenix, Arizona. However, Alty was unable to attend the tournament because of registration difficulties with the AIAW national office.[17] Records indicate Lydia Goetz represented Baylor in several badminton tournaments during this year.

SOFTBALL

The 1976-77 Bearette softball team, coached by Olga Fallen, posted a 17-11 record during the Fall season and hosted the first Baylor Invitational Tournament in the Spring. With five victories in that tournament, the team took the title, defeating the powerful UT-Arlington 1-0 in the final game. Karen Aulenbacher led the team in batting with a .389 season average. Cathy Hart pitched nine victories, and Judy Blalock posted a .940 fielding average.[18]

The team participated in the State TAIAW Softball Tournament in Nacogdoches, Texas but failed to place in that event. This performance garnered them an eighth place finish in the state rankings. They did play in the AIAW Regional tournament and were seeded third.[19] According to Fallen, it was the finest softball team Baylor had ever put on the field.

1976-77 Softball team with coach Olga Fallen and Asst. Coach Glenda Holleyman, Trainer Cindy Lyles

Front: Gail Kohn, Pam Young, Karen Moon, Paula Young
Middle: Kara Weldon, Judy Blalock, Jan Pennal, Sarah Davis,
Sherry Youngblood, Kim Rothfus
Back: Sheryl Manning, Brenda Stahr, Cathy Hart,
Lynnell Pyron, Karen Aulenbacher

Baylor University, Round Up 1977 Yearbook, (Waco, TX: [Baylor University], 1977), The Texas Collection, Baylor University, p. 136.

TENNIS

There was no record in the state TAIAW archives of the 1976-77 tennis team competing in the TAIAW Zone Tournament. Additionally, there was no mention of a women's team in the 1977 Baylor Roundup or in the Olga Fallen Collection. Additionally, there is no record to indicate that tennis was a part of the athletic department budget after the 1975–76 season. The team continued to compete under the AIAW structure as the reader will see later in this chapter. How they were funded is unknown.

TRACK AND FIELD

Coached by Margaret Wooddy, the 1976-77 Bearette track team enjoyed success in the midst of a rebuilding year. The Bearette Cross Country team debuted in the 1976 Fall season and finished third in the State TAIAW meet. Team members were Natalie Gale, Kathleen Matusik, Becky McLenny, Diane McNeil, Jane Phillips, Joan Rogers, and Allison Welch.[20]

Jane Phillips Hurdles for the 1977 Bearette Track Team

Baylor University, Round Up 1977 Yearbook, (Waco, TX: [Baylor University], 1977), The Texas Collection, Baylor University, p. 172.

Consisting of nine freshmen and two juniors, the 1977 Outdoor team placed second in the TAIAW Central Zone, listing the following team members: Susan Freeland, Karen Moon, Becky McLenny, Cary Smith, Allison Welch,

Janet Stavinoha, Ann Price, Babette Metcalf, Karen Aulenbacher, Sarah Davis, Judy Blalock, Kim Lake, Debbie Bradley, Natalie Gale, Jane Phillips, and Lynn Wheeler. At the TAIAW State meet, the following performances were noted:

Becky McLenny – 2nd, 400 meter dash

Natalie Gale – 5th, 1500 meters, 4th 400 meters

Jane Phillips – 5th, 100 meter hurdles

Debbie Bradley – 5th, high jump[21]

Sophomore Becky McClenny had an outstanding season, running the quarter mile consistently well all year. She won both the prestigious open mile at the Texas Southern Relays and the TAIAW Zone meet, as well as placing second at the TAIAW State meet with a time of 55.7.[22] McClenny was the only Bearette to qualify for the AIAW National meet at UCLA in May. There was no record that she attended this meet.

The Bearettes had notable performances during the season, particularly at the Texas Relays. McCoy reported in the April 14, 1977 *Baylor Lariat* that the mile relay team of Becky Bradley, Susan Freeland, Becky McLenny, and Ann Price clocked a season's best 49.6. Bradley and Kim Lake qualified in the high jump with a best height of 5'2". Kathleen Matusik finished 7th in the 1500 meters. Commenting to McCoy about the meet, Wooddy stated: "Within the state contestants, the girls did well. With the track clubs and schools like Grambling, Texas Southern and others, it made it very tough to win".

1977 Track and Field Team

Front: Coach Margaret Wooddy, Asst. Coach, Chris Mayhew, Kathleen Matusik,
Kim Lake, Alison Welch, Jan Stavinoha, Jane Phillips, Karen Moon,
Cary Smith, Sheryl Manning
Back: Ann Price, Susan Freeland, Becky McClenny, Natalie Gale,
Judy Blalock, Debbie Bradley

Baylor University, Round Up 1977 Yearbook, (Waco, TX: [Baylor
University], 1977), The Texas Collection, Baylor University, p. 173.

VOLLEYBALL

On the strength of several returning starters and outstanding freshman new-comers the 1976 volleyball team, coached by Margaret Wooddy and Chris Mayhew, posted a winning season (22-10-2)[23] and entered the TAIAW North Zone tournament as a third seed. Leah Box, Marsha Adams, and Karen Conrads returned to the starting line-up and were joined by freshmen Janet Stavinoha, Debbie Beyer, and Karen Saunders. The team qualified for the State TAIAW tournament but did not make it out of pool play.[24]

1976 Volleyball Team

*Front: Katie Price, Jan Stavinoa, Karen Conrads, Barbara Dixon, Diane Johnson
Middle: Coach Wooddy, Martha Muckleroy, Vicky Burke, Debbie
Byer, Marsha Adams, Chris Mayhew, Asst. Coach
Back: Laurel Wood, Manager, Siuli Uiagaleiei, Karen Saunders, Leah Box*

*Baylor University, Round Up 1977 Yearbook, (Waco, TX: [Baylor
University], 1977), The Texas Collection, Baylor University, p. 136*

1977-78
BASKETBALL

With losses of significant players to graduation, the 1977-78 basketball Bearettes were faced with a rebuilding season. Gone were Snider-Eppers, Hart, Pyron, and Davis from the 1976-77 roster. However, seniors Babettte Metcalf and Karen Aulenbacher posted season scoring records in double figures and led the Bearettes to a 33-8 season that included a bid to the SWAIAW Regional tournament.

The outstanding play of two freshmen was key for Fallen's squad in this season. Carol Reeves, replacing Snider-Eppers at center, averaged twenty points and eight rebounds per game and had one blocked shot for the season. Ginger Thornton added thirteen points and six rebounds per game.

**Carol Reeves Played Basketball
and Softball as a Bearette**

Baylor University, Round Up 1980 Yearbook, (Waco, TX: [Baylor University], 1980), The Texas Collection, Baylor University, p. 121.

Other players were transfer Mamie Mauch as well as returners Gwen Miller, Stacy Gee, Galyn Zwerschke, Judy Kocurek, Judy Kafer, Jamie Mott, Gwen Miller, Diane Zvara, and Jenny Adams. Fallen was assisted in her coaching tasks by Sarah Davis. Margaret Wooddy was the team trainer.[25] The team placed fifth in the State TAIAW tournament and qualified for regionals but did not return to the national tournament this year.[26] *The Baylor Lariat*, March 15, 1978, handed out the following honors during this season: Babette Metcalf, Outstanding Senior; Carol Reeves, Bearette of the Year; and Ginger Thornton, Reserve of the Year. Other members of the team were: Karen Aulenbacher, Sharon Barnes, Stacey Gee, Beverly Herrington, Judy Kafer, Judy Kocurek, Mamie Mauch, Gwen Miller, Jamie Mott, Susie Oelschlegel, Sharon Rush, Lark Taylor, and Gaylyn Zwerschke.[27]

BADMINTON—SIXTH PLACE IN THE NATION

Three women made up this edition of the Baylor women's badminton team— Cindy Alty, freshman Sue Butler, and Lisa Horlbeck. In an interview for the *Baylor Line* in Spring 1978, Yale Youngblood indicated that Cindy Alty had garnered over seventy trophies or awards during her three year badminton career.[28] In the October 13, 1977 edition of the *Baylor Lariat,* it was reported that Cindy Alty received the Jack Fisher Award for the most outstanding player in collegiate and open tournament hosted by NW Louisiana State University. *Baylor Lariat* articles from 1978 document nine singles championships and three women's doubles titles in collegiate and open tournaments for Alty.

Alty and teammate Sue Butler made it to the AIAW National Badminton Tournament this year and brought home third place honors as a team from that tournament. Alty won the consolation singles event, and the team of Alty/Butler won consolation in women's doubles. The tournament featured sixty competitors from sixteen universities across the country. For their efforts, the Baylor Women's Badminton team finished sixth in the nation at this tournament.[29]

SOFTBALL

"The best softball season Baylor has ever had" summed up Coach Olga Fallen's sentiments about the 1977-78 softball team. Finishing the Fall season with a 20-12 record, the Bearettes took third place at the State TAIAW Tournament, advancing out of the state to the regionals for the first time in history. Karen Aulenbacher, senior, and freshman Carol Reeves proved they were more than one-sport athletes, leading the team in hitting. Aulenbacher posted a season .375 hitting average with Reeves close behind at .333. Other hitters of note were Pam Young, .286 and Cindy Maddox, .286.[30] The squad became the first Baylor softball team to appear in the SWAIAW Regional tournament in Denton, Texas, ending the year with a 28-21 record. Carol Reeves, Pam Young, Paula Young and Cindy Maddox were nominated for the 1979 Summer Pan American games.[31]

SWIMMING—1977-1980

Very few records of the swim team's accomplishments between 1977 and 1980 were found. The only sources for this information were from the *Baylor Round Up* (yearbooks) and the *Baylor Lariats* during these years. A few facts can be documented, however.

Swimmers during the 1977–78 years were: Leslie Mellinger, Kara Weldon, Patricia Managan, Bobby Sue Spencer, Ana Thatcher, Gayle Savage, Karen

Hursh, Barbara Barron, Laura Kramer, Elena Martin, Cheryl Mohr, Jackie Ross, Diane Mellinger, Nan Goulet, Susan Wood. [32, 33, 34] Gayle Savage, the lone diver on the 1977 team, represented Baylor at the State TAIAW meet. At the 1978 Women's Athletic Recognition Banquet, Cheryl Mohr and Leslie Mellinger were recognized for their outstanding performances at the State TAIAW swim meet. No record of those accomplishments was found.[35,36]

TENNIS

The women fielded a team for the 1978 season but no records were available for their accomplishments. Members of the team are pictured below.

Front: Nancy Touchy, Denise Scruggs, Carla Wood

Back: Sandy Hamil, Cindy Ault, Kim Knabe, Susan Walton
Coach was John Phelps

Baylor University, Round Up 1978 Yearbook, (Waco, TX: [Baylor University], 1978), The Texas Collection, Baylor University, p. 101.

TRACK AND FIELD

Coach Clyde Hart took the reins of the Bearette Track team in the Spring 1978, assisted by Coach Margaret Wooddy. At the 1978 TAIAW State Track meet, the Bearettes were led by Jane Phillips, placing second in the pentathlon, Diana

Dunnington, 5th in the long jump, and Kim Lake, 6th in the high jump. Other competitors were Debbie Bradley, Susan Freeland, Carla Lechler, Lucinda Lowry, Maurene Malone, Susan Bicknell, Susan Rouse, Robin Stringer, Becky McClenny, Gina Pruitt, Debbie Alexander, and Charlene Warnock.[37]

The Cross Country team, Fall 1978 was paced by Natalie Gale, Cinda Adams, Becky McClenny, and Joanne Hunter. The Baylor women won a dual meet over North Texas State University in Waco, taking individual placements of second through fifth in the meet. The women competed in several other meets but finished in the bottom half of the TAIAW District standings.[38]

1978 Track Team

Baylor University, Round Up 1978 Yearbook, (Waco, TX: [Baylor University], 1978), The Texas Collection, Baylor University, p. 128.

VOLLEYBALL

Coach Margaret Wooddy's volleyball team won more matches in 1977 than any team in the history of Baylor women's volleyball, finishing with a 26-20 season record. The Bearettes won the Texas Woman's University tournament in October and placed second in the TAIAW Zone tournament. They finished third in the State tournament and qualified for the Southwest Regional AIAW Tournament. Judy Kocurek, Carol Edgar, Debby Beyer, and Katy Price led the team throughout the season.[39] Other team members were Donna Vacek, Karen

Conrads, Karen Saunders, Janice Fields, Sharla Hemmeline, Diane Johnson, Janet Stavinoha, Leah Box, Laurie Kramer, Debbie King, and Marsha Tepe.[40]

1977 Volleyball Team

Front: Debbie Streetman, Eileen Hulme, Debbie King
Middle: Phyllis Spurlock, Mgr., Karen Bond, Angie Phillips,
Janice Field, Charla Dye, Becky Spurlock, Mgr.
Back: Coach Margaret Wooddy, Nancy Moore, Karen Barrow,
Jill Tankersley, Carol Edgar, Katie Price, Mgr.

The Fallen Collection, Accession 3797, Box 38, Folder 19, The
Texas Collection, Baylor University, Waco, Texas.

1978-79
BASKETBALL

Facing an uphill battle because of such a young team, Olga Fallen was joined in her basketball coaching staff by Jackie Junkman. Junkman, having played college basketball and one year of professional ball, knew what it took to build a strong team so Fallen put her in charge of the off-season strength and conditioning program. Fallen knew that having the kind of winning seasons the Bearettes experienced in the past three seasons would be tough. In an interview with staff from the *Baylor Line*, she made this comment:

> "The Baylor Bearettes are not nationally
> ranked this year and justifiably so. We

**may not have a winning season this year
but it will not destroy this team. Their
future is in the next two years. I predict
that great things lie ahead for them.**[41]

Returning starters to the squad this year were Gwen Miller, Carol Reeves, Michelle Cooper and Ginger Thornton. Cindy Gallardo, All-American transfer from Western Texas College, Christi Capps, Mamie Mauch, and Judy Jenkins were also expected to see action. The Bearettes finished the season with a 17-13 record.[42] Signs that something might be wrong in the ranks of the basketball team began to appear in early Spring 1979 when Cindy Gallardo, a junior college All-American, quit the team in January.

The problems with the basketball team were compounded by similar problems with the softball team where three players walked off the team in March. A *Baylor Lariat* article in June exposed a history of problems between players and coaches going back to the early years of the seventies. This article began a series of events that led to Fallen's dismissal as coach of both the basketball and softball teams and her dismissal as Women's Athletic Coordinator (see Chapter 4 for more details).

The 1979 Bearette basketball team received an at-large bid to the Southwest Regional AIAW Basketball Tournament in April but they did not accept the invitation. Research was unable to confirm why this decision was made.

1979 Basketball Team

*Kneeling: Stacey Gee, Michelle Cooper, Debra Garrett, Gwen Miller,
Kim Jamison, Susan Rouse, Jenny Adams, Cile Stokes*

Asst. Coach, Jackie Junkman, Diane Johnson, Trainer, Cindy Gallardo, Christi
Capps, Mamie Mauch, Faith Cederholm, Carol Reeves, Phyllis Gamble,
Judy Jenkins, Ginger Thornton, Mignone Rauch, Sharon Cooper, Mgr.,
Olga Fallen, Head Coach
Baylor University, Round Up 1979 Yearbook, (Waco, TX: [The Senior Class of
Baylor University], 1979), The Texas Collection, Baylor University, p. 107.

BADMINTON—SEVENTH IN THE NATION

By Spring 1979 Cindy Alty was now Cindy Bonilla, having married her mixed doubles partner, John Bonilla. Cindy Bonilla was a graduate student but had one more year of eligibility under AIAW rules. The only records found for the 1978-79 badminton season indicated the team of Cindy Bonilla, Sue Butler and Janet Alty, Bonilla's younger sister qualified for the AIAW National Tournament in Washington, D.C.[43] Alty-Bonilla was also coaching the team this year. Twenty-five teams with over one hundred players were entered in the tournament. All three players entered the singles competition and then Butler/Bonilla entered in women's doubles. Although none of the team members placed in either the singles or doubles events, Bonilla made it to the top sixteen players before losing. The doubles team was eliminated in the quarterfinal round. By virtue of the scoring system used at the national tournament, the Baylor team placed seventh in the nation this year.[44]

SOFTBALL

The softball team posted a 20-14 record during the Fall '78 season, but ran into trouble in the Spring '79 season. Fallen's squad finished with a 26-24 overall record and a trip to the SWAIAW Regional Tournament in Norman, Oklahoma where they lost two games to McNeese State and Central State. The team was plagued with problems during the Spring season. Three of the top athletes on the team—Pam and Paula Young and pitcher Cindy Maddox—walked off in protest of Fallen's coaching tactics and poor handling of team logistics. In the SWAIAW Regional tournament in May 1979, they were coached by a graduate student in light of Fallen's firing on April 23, 1979. The team did not place at regionals.[45]

SWIMMING

Swimming as a sport at Baylor was moved from varsity status to a club sport in 1979. This came as a result of Jack Patterson's decision to create a divisional structure for the women's teams under the AIAW. Swimming was moved to a Division III status, meaning no scholarships would be allocated for this sport. Swimming was moved out of the athletic department budget to the club sport budget at that time.

In spite of this setback for the women's swimming team, they continued to compete in 1979–1981. They coached themselves. Members of the women's team in 1979–80 were Diane Mellinger, Susan Wood, Cherie Mohr, Ana Thatcher, Nan Goulet, Leslie Mellinger, Amy Ogden, Maureen Ferguson, Beth Banter, Christa Corn, Karen Holland, Mary Goldrick, Janet Carpenter, and Robin Hooks.[46]

The 1980 team coached by Nan Goulet and Leslie Mellinger had an outstanding season, perhaps the most successful in the history of women's swimming at Baylor. The team participated in several meets, finishing second in the Southwest Texas meet, the Austin College meet, and the State TAIAW meet. Nan Goulet qualified for the AIAW National Swim Meet in the 400 Individual Medley, the 200 Individual Medley and the 200 Breaststroke. No records were found to suggest she attended these championships.[47]

1981 swimmers were Kennedy Lyon, coach, Cecelia Ciepiela, Lisa Wentnick, Jill Pennal, Michelle McDearmon, Lisa Loftin, Robin Hosks, Beth Ganter, and Patty Neesom. Another successful season ensued for these women as the won the Texas Woman's University and Stephen F. Austin University meets, placed second at the Southwest Texas State University meets, fourth at the Rice Relays and fifth places at the Rice Invitational and the Austin College meet. At the State TAIAW swim meet, Cecelia Ciepiela set an AIAW Division III record in the 100 yard backstroke event. Other team members had two second place finishes and four third place finishes in that meet. This meet was the last TAIAW meet for the women's swim team.[48] As Baylor women's athletics moved under the NCAA structure in 1982, the women's swim team remained as a club sport.

TENNIS

The women's tennis team had a new coach to begin the year, Rob Bradshaw. Led by Nancy Touchy, the team also had outstanding play from freshmen Elizabeth Piland and Rhonda Richards. No information about their season was found.

1979 Tennis Team

Front: Elizabeth Piland, Carla Wood, Vicki Moore, Rhonda Richards
Back: Cindy Ault, Sandy Hamil, Kim Knabe, Denise Scruggs, Nancy Touchy
Coach was Rob Bradshaw

Baylor University, Round-Up 1979 Yearbook, (Waco, TX: [The Senior Class of Baylor University], 1979), The Texas Collection, Baylor University, p. 125.

CROSS COUNTRY/TRACK AND FIELD

No information was available on the Cross Country season. The 1979 spring team placed second in the North Texas Triangular meet, receiving outstanding performances from several women. Phyllis Gamble won the discus with a throw of 97'4". She was joined by Kim Lake, first in the high jump (5'4"). Ann Price posted her fastest time of 11.5 in the 100 yd. dash and Diane Dunnington bested her season with a long jump of 18'9 . The 1978-79 team did qualify for the State TAIAW Track and Field meet. [49] No information on that result was found.

1979 Track and Field Team

First Row: Debbie Sherman, Lisa Cantrell, Susan Moon, Becky McClenny, Diana Dunnington, Cinda Adams, Susan Rouse, Assistant Coach Lisa Bidelspach Second Row: Robin Roach, Abbey Erwin, Kim Lake, Phyllis Gamble, Debbie Alexander, Natalie Gale, Lucinda Lowry, Joanne Hunter, Coach Margaret Wooddy, Coach Clyde Hart

Baylor University, Round-Up 1979 Yearbook, (Waco, TX: [The Senior Class of Baylor University], 1979), The Texas Collection, Baylor University, p. 125.

VOLLEYBALL

Coach Margaret Wooddy's 1978 volleyball squad had a very successful season. They won the Texas Woman's University tournament in September and finished second in the Oklahoma State University tournament in October.[50] The team did not fare well in the TAIAW State tournament, placing sixth, but received a second bid to the AIAW Region IV tournament. At the Tournament, held in Arlington, Texas, the Bearettes dropped matches to Lamar and Tulane. They finished the season with a 22-20 match record.[51] Coach Margaret Wooddy finished her volleyball coaching career with the 1978 season. In her three years at the helm, she posted a won-lost record of 70-60. Her teams participated in the AIAW post-season tournament two of the three years.

1978 Volleyball Team

*Front: Susan Moon, Debbie King, Linda Armstrong, Eileen Hulme
Middle: Katie Price, Anne Byanski, Janice Field, Lynn Wheeler
Back: Ann Blythe, Liz Kalenak, Trainer
Coach Margaret Wooddy, Asst. Coach Jacalyn Junkman*

*Baylor University, Round Up 1979 Yearbook, (Waco, TX: [The Senior Class of
Baylor University], 1979), The Texas Collection, Baylor University, p. 132.*

1979-80
BASKETBALL

Pam Davis took the reins of the Baylor Women's Basketball program in time
to coach the 1979-80 basketball season. When she came to Baylor, Davis had
a very successful coaching record at McLennan Community College (MCC)
in Waco. Her four-year record with the Highlanders was 81-30, and she had
coached two All-Americans. Her squads had won three Northern Texas Junior
College Athletic Conference championships and three runner-up crowns
in regional tournaments. Additionally, MCC had become an arch rival of the
Baylor Bearettes, having defeated Olga Fallen's teams in earlier years.

Pam Davis got off to a rough start in her first year as the Bearette basketball
coach, 1979-80, with a 4-24 overall record. Coaching transitions are difficult
but Davis was dealing with the loss of several key players to graduation with
only two returning starters. In spite of getting late start, she had recruited some

quality players for Baylor, but they were freshmen. Her second season produced a much better won–loss record, reflecting the recruiting that she had done. Team members are pictured below with Coach Davis.

Front Row: Mary Ann Jones, Manager, Cheri Fast, Veronica Hicks,
Gayle Pack, Michelle Cooper,
Cele Stokes, Deb Davis, Gail Kohn, Trainer
Back Row: Coach Pam Davis, Christi Capps, Faith Cederholm, Adele Kennedy, Carol
Reeves, Nancy Davis, Phyllis Gamble, Jackie Valentine, Angie Lambeth, Asst. Coach

Baylor University, Round-Up 1980 Yearbook, (Waco, TX: [Baylor
University], 1980), The Texas Collection, Baylor University, p. 130.

Pam Davis was responsible for changing the name of the Bearettes to Lady Bears, beginning with her tenure in 1979-80. Although there was no formal decision from the athletic department marking this change, Davis began referring to the team as Lady Bears when interviewed by the press.[52] In 1981 Davis supported the decision of University officials to move to the NCAA from the AIAW. This decision was not really controversial within the ranks of the athletic administration. After all, the NCAA was the organization the men knew the most about, the organization they had been supporting all along to take over the women's programs. And, gone was the voice that would have objected— Olga Fallen. In an interview with the *Baylor Lariat* staff, August 31, 1981, Davis indicated she thought the NCAA was a more stable organization than the AIAW and that she was looking forward to the new competition, i.e. Southwest Conference teams.

SOFTBALL—SEVENTH IN THE NATION

Coach Bob Brock

Baylor University, The Round-Up 1980 Yearbook,
(Waco, TX: [Baylor University], 1980),
The Texas Collection, Baylor University, p. 121.

Bob Brock, a member of the McLennan County Sheriff's Department, became the part-time head coach for women's softball for the 1979-80 season. Paula Young, who had walked off the team in the spring was now Brock's graduate assistant coach as well as a player. Her twin sister, Pam, also a walk-off in the Spring, returned for her final season as did pitcher Cindy Maddox. Because of her outstanding play, Pam Young was named the 1980 AIAW Division II Softball Player of the Year. In his debut season, Brock molded a cohesive unit from the turmoil of the previous season. His team won the Division II SWAIAW Regional Tournament and qualified for the national tournament. The women lost their first game at the national tournament but went on to get the wins it took to finish seventh in the nation. This trip to the national tournament marked the first time any Baylor softball team had qualified for this level of play.[53]

Brock, whose tenure extended from 1979 through 1981 was successful in his role, albeit part-time. Over his three years stint, he compiled a 49-46-1 record and took the Lady Bears to three AIAW Division II Regional tournaments and two AIAW Division II National tournaments. He resigned in 1982 and was succeeded by Paula Young.

There were few athletic scholarships for women's softball during the seventies. Fallen had allocated some financial aid for softball players along the way, but those players were few in number. The scholarship situation changed somewhat during the eighties as Brock, and later Paula Young, had 2.3 scholarships for women's softball each year. Brock utilized his scholarships effectively and also relied on the great play of some of the women's basketball players.

While there was no athletic facility for women's softball, the team played their games and practiced at the Little League facilities on the campus where the entire field was grass. Although regulation softball fields required dirt infields, Baylor's team was allowed to use this for their softball facility during this decade. By Young's assessment, the Baylor women had an advantage for home games and a disadvantage for away games because of the configuration of their facilities. [54]

1980 Softball Team

First Row: Kim Jamison, Sharon Cooper, Ann Tucker,
Debbie McDonald, Susan Foster
Second Row: Pam Young, Suzie Oelschlegel, Susan Tipton,
Cindy Maddox, Stacey Gee and Paula Young

Baylor University, Round-Up 1980 Yearbook, (Waco, TX: [Baylor
University], 1980), The Texas Collection, Baylor University, p. 120.

Pam Young, 1980 Division II AIAW Player Of The Year

Baylor University, The Round-Up 1980 Yearbook, (Waco, TX: [Baylor University], 1980), The Texas Collection, Baylor University, p. 121.

TENNIS

1980 Tennis Team

Front: Carla Wood, Pam Foglietta, Rhonda Richards, Lisa Pardo, Alison Hightower
Back: Sheri Endsley, Janda Edwards, Sue Breisch, Tammi Ketler,
Sandy Hamil, Clarice Pick, Head Coach Tim Palmer

Baylor University, The Round-Up 1980 Yearbook, (Waco, TX: [Baylor University], 1980), The Texas Collection, Baylor University, p. 138.

The 1980 Tennis team experienced the highest level of success of any team to date during their season and brought home first place honors from the State TAIAW Division III tournament.[55] This victory qualified them for the Southwest Regional tournament. No results were available for their performance in that tournament.

CROSS COUNTRY RUNS AT THE NATIONAL AIAW DIVISION II MEET

Coach Clyde Hart's 1979 Cross Country team placed second in the State TAIAW Division II Cross Country meet. Cinda Adams placed second in that meet and three other Baylor runners placed in the top ten. The next week the team won the Southwest Regional meet, avenging their state loss to a tough Abilene Christian team, and became the first women's cross country team to qualify for the AIAW National meet in Tallahassee, Florida.

Natalie Gale 1980 Cross Country

Baylor University, The Round-Up 1980 Yearbook, (Waco, TX: [Baylor University], 1980), The Texas Collection, Baylor University, p. 117.

Led by Cinda Adams, who placed 35th in the national meet, the Lady Bears placed fifteenth out of twenty-three schools in the nation. Team members included Kathy Vetter, Kayla Williams, Linda Adams, Cynthia Oliphant, Becky McClenny, Kim Nelson, JoAnne Hunter, and Natalie Gale.[56]

1980 Cross Country Team

AIAW Division II National Qualifiers
Front: Kathy Vetter, Kayle Williams, Linda Adams, Cynthia Oliphant
Second: Becky McClenny, Kim Nelson, JoAnne Hunter, Cinda Adams, Natalie Gale

Baylor University, The Round-Up 1980 Yearbook, (Waco, TX: [Baylor University], 1980), The Texas Collection, Baylor University, p. 117.

TRACK AND FIELD

The Lady Bears competed in a short indoor season, experiencing success in a number of areas. Freshman Kathy Vetter led the effort with victories in the 880 yard run at the Sooner Indoor Relays, the LSU Indoor Invitational and taking second in the event at the Oklahoma Track Classic. Becky McClenny won the 440 at the L.S.U. invitational and Kim Lake won the high jump at that meet. [57]

The outdoor season began with a triangular meet against North Texas State and UT Arlington. Kim Lake won the high jump, Adele Kennedy won the discus, Katie Freeman took first in the 100m hurdles, and Cinda Adams won the 5000m run.[58]

VOLLEYBALL

Judy Jenkins took the reins of the Women's Volleyball team for the 1979 season. Her team finished the season with a 26-29 overall match record and made Baylor's third post-season appearance at the Southwest Regional AIAW Tournament. This was the last post-season appearance for Baylor Volleyball until 2001.[59]

During the decade of the nineteen seventies, the Baylor women's athletic programs grew in strength of schedule as they played tougher competition each year and were able to defeat some of the best teams in the country. The increase in funding for scholarships, travel, and equipment enable the Bearettes to build a quality program.

Numerous athletic champions emerged to lead their teams to championships, both state and national. Many of them have been noted in this chapter, but certainly there were many more who played and represented Baylor during this decade. Of note is that many of these champions played on more than one team during their Baylor years. In the early years, it was necessary to overlap players and teams in order to have the numbers to be able to compete. Many of these athletes were very talented individuals. Some had never played any sport before coming to college and discovered their talents on the courts and fields as Bearettes. Some had only played one sport in high school and then discovered interests and talents for other athletic opportunities.

When asked to reflect on her playing days, one of those champions, Babette Metcalf Eiklenborg, a standout on the Bearette basketball team that went to the National AIAW tournament in 1976 and 1977, shared these thoughts:

> **I have never given much thought about reflecting on my contributions to the Baylor Women's Basketball program until now. It seems very foreign to me that people believe I was special or outstanding as a student athlete. I have never thought much about my talent, in fact I think of myself as a skinny kid with a quick instinct who loved the game and was excited to have an opportunity to continue to play basketball beyond high school. I played basketball for the love of the sport and for the camaraderie of being part of a team. I did not have the**

pressure of playing the sport so that I would hopefully glean honors, tributes, endorsements, or other financial gains—because there were none at that time. I played basketball for the love of the sport.

At the time I was playing basketball and a student athlete at Baylor, I knew nothing about the politics and adjustments that the men and women's programs were having to undergo to peacefully coexist at a time when money for scholarships, uniforms, equipment, travel, coaching salaries, and other expenses related to running athletic programs were tight. I am grateful and very thankful to the university's athletic staff for somehow working it out to give our era an opportunity to make a lasting mark on the history of the women's athletic program at Baylor University. I am proud and honored to be a part of something very special.

Lastly, I am really delighted to see the name changed from the Baylor Bearettes to the Baylor Lady Bears![60]

NOTES ON CHAPTER 6
BEARETTES TO LADY BEARS: 1976—1980

1. Leah Box, "Bearettes post 29-3, take second in state," *The Baylor Line*, February, 1976, 28.

2. Sherry Castello, ed., "Bearettes win berth in national tourney," *The Baylor Line*, February 1976, 28.

3. The Women's Collection, MSS 77, Box 2 and Box 11, Blagg-Huey Library, Texas Woman's University, Denton, Texas.

4. The Women's Collection, MSS 77, Box 11.

5. Sherry Castello, ed., "Softball team posts best season record," *Baylor Line*, November 1976, 28.

6. The Olga Fallen Collection, Accession 3797, Box 32, Folder 6, The Texas Collection, Baylor University, Waco, Texas.

7. The Women's Collection, MSS 77, Box 11.

8. The Olga Fallen Collection, Box 35, Folder 7.

9. The Olga Fallen Collection, Box 36, Folder 7.

10. The Olga Fallen Collection, Box 14, Folder 9.

11. The Women's Collection, MSS 77, Box 11

12. Sherry Castello, ed., "Bearette basketballers get national ranking," *The Baylor Line*, November 1976, 25.

13. Yale Youngblood, "Bearettes end season as top team in Texas, fifth best in the nation," *The Baylor Line*, June 1977, 28.

14. Ibid.

15. WBCA All-Americans: 1975-2013, accessed May 2, 2013, http://sports.espn.go.com/ncw/news/story?id=406268

16. *2011-2012 Baylor Women's Basketball*, Media Guide, Baylor University Athletic Department, Baylor University, Waco, TX., 71.

17. Dutch Schroeder, telephone interview by the author, May 21, 2013.

18. Sherry Castello, ed., "Softball Team Posts Best Season Record," *The Baylor Line*, November 1976, 28.

19. The Olga Fallen Collection, Box 16, Folder 5.

20. The Women's Collection, MSS 77, Box 14.

21. Ibid.

22. Sherry Castello, ed., "McClenny highlights Bearette tracksters 1977," *The Baylor Line*, 28.

23. The Olga Fallen Collection, Box 16, Folder 12.

24. Sherry Castello, ed., "Women's VB earns place in spotlight," *Baylor Line*, November 1976, 28.

25. The Olga Fallen Collection, Box 16, Folder 7.

26. Yale Youngblood, ed., "Bearettes go 33–8, win regional berth" *The Baylor Line*, April 1978, 24

27. See note 25 above.

28. Yale Youngblood, "You never know how far a P.E. Course will take you…, *The Baylor Line*, April 1978, 27.

29. "Baylor women place in badminton tourney," *The Baylor Lariat*, March 8, 1978.

30. Yale Youngblood, "Women's softball takes third in state, *The Baylor Line,* February 1978, 24.

31. Sherry Castello, ed., "Best year ever for BU softball," *The Baylor Line,* June 1978, 32.

32. Baylor University, Round Up 1977 Yearbook, (Waco, TX: [Baylor University], 1977, The Texas Collection, Baylor University, 163.

33. Baylor University, Round Up 1978 Yearbook, (Waco, TX: [Baylor University], 1978, The Texas Collection, Baylor University, 123.

34. "Women swimmers nudged from 1st by TCU in meet," *The Baylor Lariat,* February 9, 1977.

35. "Lone diver to compete at University of Houston," *The Baylor Lariat,* February 24, 1977.

36. "Women athletes honored," *The Baylor Lariat,* April 19, 1978.

37. The Women's Collection, MSS 77, Box 18.

38. David Young, "Cross Country," *The Baylor Line,* November 1978, 23.

39. Yale Youngblood, "So does volleyball," *The Baylor Line,* February 1978, 24.

40. See note 37 above.

41. David Young, "Bearettes building, not nationally ranked, *Baylor Line,* November 1978, 22.

42. Sherry Castello, ed., "Bearettes get to state," *The Baylor Line,* April 1979, 36.

43. Donna C. Smith, "Baylor badminton team travels to Washington for national meet," *The Baylor Lariat,* February 27, 1979.

44. "Baylor badminton places seventh in national final," *The Baylor Lariat,* March 9, 1979.

45. Sherry Castello, ed., "Softball makes regional," *The Baylor Line,* April 1979, 34.

46. Baylor University, Round Up 1979 Yearbook, (Waco, TX: [The Senior Class of Baylor University], 1979, The Texas Collection, Baylor University, 134.

47. Baylor University, Round Up 1980 Yearbook, (Waco, TX: [Baylor University], 1980, The Texas Collection, Baylor University, 143.

48. Baylor University, Round Up 1981 Yearbook, (Waco, TX: [Baylor University], 1981, The Texas Collection, Baylor University, 135.

49. "News Release", *Baylor Sports Service*, Sid Wilson, Sports Information Director, March 21, 1979.

50. Sherry Castello, ed., "Volleyball," *The Baylor Line,* November 1978, 23.

51. The Women's Collection, MSS 77, Box 2.

52. Pam Bowers, telephone interview by the author, July 9, 2012.

53. The Women's Collection, MSS 77, Box 3.

54. Paula Young, interview by the author, June 28, 2012.

55. Baylor University, Round Up 1980 Yearbook, (Waco, TX: [Baylor University], 1980, The Texas Collection, Baylor University, 138.

56. Baylor University, Round Up 1980 Yearbook, (Waco, TX: [Baylor University], 1980, The Texas Collection, Baylor University, 116.

57. Baylor University, Round Up 1980 Yearbook, (Waco, TX: [Baylor University], 1980, The Texas Collection, Baylor University, 151.

58. Ibid.

59. *2011 Baylor Volleyball*, Media Guide, Baylor University Athletics Department 2011, 45.

60. Babette Metcalf, email message to author, August 18, 2012.

CHAPTER 7

ᔕᘐᔓ

BACKLASH FROM TITLE IX

NATIONAL BACKLASH

During the decade of the seventies, opportunities for women to participate in athletics at the high school and collegiate level exploded. The women's athletic program at Baylor were but one example of this growth and development. As the decade drew to an end, there was tremendous momentum for continued growth in all areas addressed by the civil rights legislation of the sixties and seventies.

This progress in civil rights/Title IX implementation and interpretation seemed to come to a halt in 1980 when Ronald Reagan was elected President of the United States. He was swept into office on a wave of a conservative social agenda that featured a backlash from the women's rights and feminism movements of the past twenty years. The religious right was gaining ground in the political arena of this country, and the right to life movement was gaining momentum at a rapid pace. Additionally, Reagan had run on a platform of regulatory reform, promising to cut away the "the thicket of irrational and senseless regulations" in an effort to support large and small businesses. This, he said, would help return America to economic prosperity.

Reagan made two decisions that effectively put a hiatus on the rapid growth of Title IX programs during the decade of the eighties. Opportunities for women in athletics slowed during Reagan's term of office, and many viewed the decade of the eighties as the dark days for women's athletics in this country.

His first decision was to form the Task Force on Regulatory Relief, naming his Vice-President, George W. Bush, to chair this group in January 1981. Members of the Task Force were the Secretary of the Treasury, the Attorney

General, the Secretary of Commerce, the Secretary of Labor, the Director of the Office of Management and Budget, the Assistant to the President for Policy Development, and the Chairman of the Council of Economic Advisors. Title IX, as well as the other pieces of civil rights legislation, was directly in the crosshairs of this Task Force. Reagan charged the Task Force to "review pending regulations, study past regulations with an eye toward revising them and rec- ommend appropriate legislative remedies"[1] All programs receiving any kind of government funding were subject to review.

Secondly, Reagan appointed Terrell H. Bell as his Secretary of Education. Although Bell was a Republican, he was considered a moderate in a very conser- vative environment. Bell had served under Nixon and Ford as deputy commis- sioner of education and ultimately became the U.S. Commissioner of Education. He had served under Casper Weinberger, Secretary of Health, Education and Welfare and was intimately acquainted with the Education Amendments of 1972 and Title IX. He was well-suited for this appointment.

Even though Reagan had made it clear during his campaign that he intended to abolish the Department of Education, Bell accepted the appointment because he believed that Reagan could be influenced not to do this. Weinberger was a Reagan man, and Bell had worked well with him. One thing that Bell was not prepared for was the open hostility of many of Reagan's other cabinet members as well as staff persons toward the civil rights movement and toward Bell's positions.

As Secretary of Education, Bell and the OCR were responsible for the inves- tigation of Title IX complaints, but the Justice Department was responsible for enforcement of the regulations. Education referred cases to Justice when enforcement was necessary. These two departments and the two men who led them were on philosophically and ideologically different ends of the spectrum in the interpretation of Title IX. In his memoirs, Bell reflected on this difference.

> ED's problems with the Department of Justice emerged from differences in reading and interpreting the words in the laws both departments were required to enforce. In ED, we read the law from the perspective of educators who had worked in schools and colleges and

> understood admission, placement, and
> promotion procedures. We read the law
> broadly to assure equal educational
> opportunity. Justice lawyers were reading
> to find ways to "get the government
> off the backs of the people"[2]

It was clear that Bell intended to use the broader interpretation of the Title IX legislation that had been the practice of the Office of Civil Rights during the seventies. If any campus program receives federal funding, then all of the campus was subject to Title IX regulations. This broad interpretation meant that no program on any campus could discriminate against women.

The Department of Justice argued that Title IX regulations should only be applied to programs that received federal funding, a very narrow interpretation of the law. This interpretation essentially meant that one program on campus could not discriminate against women but other programs could. Assistant Attorney General Brad Reynolds made this position clear from the beginning.

The conflict with the Justice Department proved challenging for Bell. Struggling to find balance between his beliefs and how he knew the enforcement process would play out, his decisions often seemed somewhat wishy-washy on Title IX issues in the early years of his tenure. For example, he chose not to appeal U. of Richmond v. Bell, a Title IX lawsuit that had been overturned by the 4th Circuit Appeals Court upholding a programmatic application of Title IX instead of a broader institutional application of the law. Then, he ruled that the University of Akron was in compliance with Title IX (despite numerous violations) because they (Akron) had a plan in place to address Title IX issues. In making this decision, Bell created a precedent allowing athletic departments to take their time in complying with Title IX as long as they had a plan in place with a timeline. Ultimately, Bell was so hot and cold on Title IX and other civil rights issues that The National Organization for Women gave him the "Silver Snail" award for failing to help girls and women.[3]

The Supreme Court's ruling in 1984 in Grove City v. Bell was a landmark decision that tolled a death knell through the halls of civil rights advocates and gutted many hopes of real progress on civil rights issues during this decade. In its ruling, the Court agreed that only programs receiving federal funds should be held accountable for Title IX compliance. Grove City was a small private college. In 1977 Bell ruled they were in violation of Title IX. The college received no federal funding but some of the students received Pell grants indirectly from the government. In reviewing the original case, the Department of Health, Education and Welfare had ruled that because Grove City students received federal aid, the College must comply with Title IX regulations. Four students joined the college in suing over disagreement with the ruling. At the district court level, the college's interpretation of the law was upheld; but in appeal, the Second Circuit Court ruled in favor of the government, making Grove City college subject to Title IX regulation because of these Pell grants. There were inconsistent interpretations of the law between the district courts and courts of appeal across the states. Because of this fact, the Supreme Court decided to hear the Grove City case to sort out some of the inconsistencies prevalent in various court rulings up to that time. In issuing its 1983 decision Justice Byron White quoted:

> We have found no persuasive evidence
> suggesting that Congress intended that
> the Department's regulatory authority
> follow federally aided students from
> classroom to classroom, building to
> building, or activity to activity. Title
> IX should be applied to Grove City's
> financial-aid program, thanks to the Pell
> grants, and nothing else at the school.[4]

This ruling ended all discussion and debates between constituents favoring a broad application of Title IX and others who favored a more narrow interpretation. The "narrows" had won. The law of the land now supported their position. Within the Reagan cabinet, the Justice Department had prevailed. At OCR, the ruling shut down investigations of numerous complaints against educational institutions that were receiving federal aid. It had a profound impact on Title VI and VII of the Civil Rights Act 1972, Section 504 of the Rehabilitation Act of 1973, and the Age Discrimination Act of 1975. The Office of Civil Rights closed their files on several active investigations.

The Civil Rights Commission along with other civil rights advocates in America was concerned, if not alarmed. The sentiment in Congress was that the civil rights of many Americans were in danger. Shortly after the Supreme Court's ruling, Senator Robert Dole and several of his colleagues sponsored a bill titled the Civil Rights Restoration Act, 1984. The legislation laid out a broad application of the law and made it clear that "Title IX, Title VI, Title VII, the Rehabilitation Act and the Age Discrimination Act applied to all programs operated by recipients of federal funds."[5] The legislation was aimed directly at the Supreme Court and was intended to overturn the 1984 Grove City ruling. Reagan's administration was split on the bill and his supporters were concerned about Reagan's re-election hopes if he were to veto the legislation. A similar resolution was passed overwhelmingly in the House. The legislation became stalled in the Senate and was tabled in the final session of 1984. Dole reintroduced the legislation in 1985 and 1987 only to find it rejected by Reagan. In vetoing the 1987 legislation March 16, 1988, Reagan offered a bill that would exempt religious institutions and some private businesses from coverage under all civil rights laws. In his announcement he explained that the civil rights laws unjustly expended the powers of the Federal Government over private organizations such as churches, synagogues, businesses, farms and state and local governments. He felt the law would seriously impinge upon religious liberty.

This proposal garnered the wrath of civil rights and women's rights organizations. As Congress prepared to debate an override of Reagan's veto, members endured an onslaught of protests from Evangelical Christians, particularly Jerry Falwell. Clearly the public was split on this issue. However, it took Congress less that one week to vote and override Reagan's veto. On March 22, 1988, the Civil Rights Restoration Act of 1987 became the law of the land. In response to the bipartisan show of support for the bill, Speaker of the House Jim Wright commented "…the President 'may want to turn the clock back on civil rights, but the American people do not.'"[6] Grove City was struck down. Baylor had to comply with Title IX.

BAYLOR'S BACKLASH

This was the political arena that Baylor University and the women's athletic programs experienced in the eighties. Early on, the Supreme Court's decision in the Grove City case was good news to university administrators. They had opposed Title IX legislation ever since its passage in 1972 and had written many letters to Congressmen, athletic supporters, booster clubs, former students and others in an effort to mount a strong opposition to the legislation. Abner McCall even involved the Southern Baptist Convention and was on record with the Office of Civil Rights in 1976 opposing the legislation because compliance with portions of it was in direct conflict with the religious tenets of the Baptist General Convention of Texas.[7] University officials had long held to the notion supported by the Grove City ruling — that the athletic department received no federal funding, therefore they should not have to comply with Title IX.

As Herbert Reynolds moved into the presidency in 1981, Baylor's financial support for the women's programs could be considered minimal at best. The 1984 Grove City decision represented a reprieve from the law. "When the ruling was made, that took the pressure off", said Dr. James Netherton, Vice-President and Chief Operating Officer at Baylor, 1981–1996.[8] He further indicated in a letter to Taylor August at the Office of Civil Rights, March 1984, that while Baylor intended to move forward with providing scholarship support for their women athletes, the prevailing belief of the university administration was that Baylor was not subject the provisions of Title IX. He stated: "There have been no findings that the Baylor athletic program receives direct federal aid and in our opinion it is not such a recipient. Thus, we are of the opinion that Title IX does not apply to the Baylor University athletic program."[9] However, a funny thing happened later that year that completely changed that point of view for Baylor University. Ironically, it was an NCAA policy that caused this turn-around. The Baylor women's programs had been under the governing structure of the NCAA for two years at this time.

It happened when Basil Thompson, General Counsel and Special Assistant to the President, discovered and subsequently informed Reynolds that NCAA policy <u>required</u> athletic scholarships to be administered through the financial aid office. While athletic scholarships were not federal aid, the policy meant that Baylor was subject to the requirements of Title IX because the financial aid office at Baylor received federal aid. Thompson recommended that the university proceed to ensure that there was no discrimination on the basis of sex in the athletic scholarship program.[10] By 1984 Baylor had a plan to comply with NCAA scholarship regulations for women by 1989 (See Table III).

By 1981 the leadership of the Baylor's Athletic Department had changed. Mr. Bill Menefee was now the Athletic Director. Menefee had been Baylor's basketball coach in earlier days and was teaching in the Department of Health,

Physical Education and Recreation and managing the Baylor Marina at the time of his appointment. In response to questions about Ronald Reagan's Task Force and possible changes to the rules for Title IX enforcement, Menefee felt whatever the new rules were that Baylor would not be affected. In a 1981 interview he stated: "We have followed the guidelines and I think we have a very fine women's athletic program."[11] Assistant Athletic Director David Taylor, in response to the same questions about the possible rules changes, said: "We have always wanted a first-class athletics program in both men and women's athletics and we think we have it now...."[12] Taylor added: "The federal government doesn't have a very big hammer to swing at us because we have complied with them all along"[13]

People connected to women's athletics at the time found these responses laughable. Baylor may have followed the Title IX guidelines, but they were nowhere near being in compliance with Title IX in 1981. In addition Baylor did not have an excellent athletic program at the time. The male sports teams' ability to compete in the Southwest Conference (SWC) showed glimpses of success throughout the seventies but brought home very few SWC championships.

Perhaps it depended on what one's view of excellence or compliance was. The philosophy of the University administration. i.e. Abner McCall, was that athletics were just for entertainment. This position seemed to indicate that whether or not athletic teams actually won anything was immaterial. If this were the case, then Baylor would have had a fine athletics program simply by virtue of the fact that they had an athletics program. However, there is no reasonable way to justify being in compliance with Title IX in 1981. The facts just did not support this assertion. Neither did the budget numbers. There were still funding inequities, even across the men's programs.

Aggregate expenditures for men and women's athletic programs 1980-1984 are reflected in Table I below. These were the allocations being made to every sport at the time Reagan launched his Task Force and at the time the leadership of the Baylor Athletic Department indicated that Baylor had a first class athletic program. Football and men's basketball received the highest allocations because they were the revenue-producing sports at the time. It was the hope of those making budget decisions that if the revenue-generators were given the largest allocations, they would generate more revenue for the next year. This was the thinking pre- and post-Title IX that had resulted in significant funding discrimination in the men's programs. When the women's programs were added, the discriminatory allocations for the men's minor sports came more into focus. Indeed, Table II demonstrates that some of the women's programs received higher allocations than the men's minor sports. Additionally, figures in Table I made it evident that the "we must operate in the black" financial philosophy for athletics had gone by the wayside.

Program Expenditures	1980-81	1981-82	1982-83	1983-84
Football	$1,010,177	1,258,717	1,403,682	1,454,249
Other men's programs	517,043	585,081	1,289,482	2,042,939
All women's programs	180,391	206,795	211,542	237,182
Athletic Department deficit	(202,910)	(123,835)	98,298*	(230,338)

Table I: Aggregate expenditures and deficits for men and women's programs, Baylor University Athletic Department, 1980-1984[14]
*Athletic department went over three million dollars for the first time in 1982-83, producing a budget surplus. Documents showed significant revenue increases for football, men's basketball, fundraising, and SWC support in this year.

Women's athletic programs were being financed at a much higher rate during the period 1980-84, indicating an effort to move in the right direction in terms of Title IX compliance. The numbers in Table II show program expenditures only, items that support travel, scholarships, meals, recruiting, etc. No salary figures are included. When Pam Davis was hired in 1979, her salary was $18,900/yr. At the same time, Jim Haller, the men's basketball coach was making $30,000/yr. Plus, he had a bonus clause in his contract of one month's salary for him and his staff if his teams won a Southwest Conference title or participated in a post-season tournament NCAA or NIT tournament. All of the head coaches for men's sports had this bonus clause attached to their salary. Davis had no such bonus clause. Davis took her team to the Women's National Invitational

Tournament (WNIT) in 1981.[15] There is no documentation of any bonus paid to her for this achievement.

Expenditures per sport (excluding football)	1980-81	1981-82	1982-83	1983-84
Men's Basketball	$272,825	311,020	360,667	360,170
Baseball	108,212	120,434	129,665	146,461
Track	107,254	121,225	172,608	193,403
Golf	12,900	13,700	17,000	16,700
Tennis	15,852	18,702	24,461	36,723
Women's Basketball	95,305	116,216	127,613	140,806
Softball	23,184	26,339	32,177	29,402
Track	42,172	40,487	27,627	28,988
Volleyball	19,730	23,700	26,900	35,221

Table II: Expenditures Per Sport, 1980-1984, Baylor University[16]

In his March 1984 letter to the Office of Civil Rights, Jim Netherton, Vice-President for Financial Affairs, explained Baylor's progress with its athletic scholarship program for women. In Table III, it is noted that all women's sports except tennis and golf were receiving some scholarship support. One point of confusion, however, is that in 1984 women's golf was not a women's sport at Baylor. Why it appears in this table is unknown, unless Baylor had plans to add the sport by 1989. Netherton indicated that if the plan could be actualized Baylor would have eighty percent of the number of allowable NCAA scholarships for women. His plan added thirty-seven scholarships over the next five years to the women's program. These numbers would allow Baylor to be in compliance with Title IX in this area.

Women's Sport	Current Scholarships 1984	NCAA Limit	Baylor Goal by 1989
Basketball	12.0	15	12
Softball	2.3	11	9
Track*	2.3	16	13
Volleyball	2.3	12	10
Tennis	0.0	8	7
Golf	0.0	6	5
Total	19	68	56

Table III: Number of scholarships per sport for women, Baylor University, 1984[17]

Baylor was unable to execute this scholarship plan, but significant progress was made between 1984 and 1990. Per an Athletic Task Force Report, October 12, 1990, the university's total scholarship number for women had grown from nineteen to forty. The NCAA limit, however, had been raised to fifty-seven.[18]

Only one women's program, basketball, had a full-time coach during the decade. Clyde Hart spread his fulltime appointment across the men's and women's track programs. He had one part-time assistant coach and some graduate students to support these coaching needs. This staff provided consistency to the women's track program during this time.

Women's tennis and volleyball experienced significant turnover in its coaching staffs, partly because these individuals had to work other jobs to support their families, and the workload was too demanding. Softball had consistency in its coaching staff from 1981 to 1988 but this position was also a part-time position.

With the exception of track and field that had one paid assistant coach, none of the women's programs had paid assistant coaches during this time. What assistant coaching positions there were resulted from graduate assistantship positions created by the Department of Health, Physical Education and Recreation and shared with the Athletic Department.

Baylor invested more in women's basketball under Pam Davis than they had under Olga Fallen because of the decision earlier in 1979 to put the women's basketball program in Division I of the AIAW structure. Programs in this structure could provide up to 100% of the scholarship aid indicated in the AIAW guidelines, and Baylor made the decision to have 100% scholarship support for this program. Pam Davis started her tenure with twelve scholarships and a graduate assistant coach, Leann Waddell. While this scholarship allotment was the maximum for the AIAW, it fell short of the NCAA limit of fifteen that started in 1982. For most of Davis' tenure, she operated on these twelve scholarships.

For a variety of reasons the excitement and support for women's intercollegiate athletics coming out of the seventies slowed considerably during the eighties. Culturally, the decade of the eighties ushered in a more conservative political arena and a pro-life movement that was a direct reaction to the feminism and women's liberation movements of the sixties and seventies. Politically, Ronald Reagan rode into office in 1980 with the support of profoundly conservative voters, slamming the brakes on moves toward women's equality and women's liberation.[19] With a desire to scale back big government and limit federal initiatives, particularly those pertaining to civil rights, Reagan appointed his Vice-President, George Bush, to lead a study of these initiatives. Title IX was one of the initiatives under review.

Reagan's position, as well as the 1984 Grove City ruling, stifled the growth of women's athletics for most of the eighties. Admittedly, it was difficult to know what to do. In some universities, women's programs and teams were dropped completely. That was not the case at Baylor. It took the Civil Rights Restoration Act of 1988 to restore the broad coverage of Title IX. Congress enacted this legislation over the veto of President Reagan.[20] This legislation set the stage for another growth spurt in women's athletics in the nineties.

NOTES ON CHAPTER 7
BACKLASH FROM TITLE IX

1. Ronald Reagan, *Remarks Announcing the Establishment of the Presidential Task Force on Regulatory Relief*, January 22, 1981. Accessed December 12, 2012. http://www.reagan.utexas.edu/archives/speeches/1981/12281c.htm

2. Terrell H. Bell, *The Thirteenth Man: A Reagan Cabinet Memoir*, (New York: The Free Press, 1988), 107.

3. Welch Suggs, *A Place On the Team: The Triumph and Tragedy of Title IX* (New Jersey: Princeton University Press, 2005), 87.

4. Grove City College v. Bell, 687 F. 2d 691 (3d Cir. 1982), affirmed, 465 U.S. 555 (1984), quoted in Welch Suggs, *A Place on the Team: The Triumph and Tragedy of Title IX*, (New Jersey: Princeton University Press, 2005), 89.

5. Suggs, *A Place on the Team*, 90.

6. Andrew Glass, *Opinion: Ronald Reagan veto overridden, March 22, 1988*. Accessed November 30, 2012. http://www.politico.com/news/stories/0310-34778.htm

7. Personal letter from Abner V. McCall to the Director of the Office of Civil Rights, U.S. Department of Health, Human Services, and Welfare, January 12, 1976. Retrieved with permission from the legal files of Lanelle McNamara, Waco, Texas, October 26, 2012.

8. Paula Price Tanner, "Approaching the Goal," *The Baylor Line*, 55 (2), 78.

9. President's Office: Herbert Hal Reynolds, 1981-1995, Accession #223, Box 3C218, The Texas Collection, Baylor University.

10. Ibid.

11. Keith Randall, "Title IX Burden May Be Eased," *Waco Tribune Herald*, August 13, 1981, 3D.

12. Ibid.

13. Ibid.

14. Files of LaNelle McNamara, *Bowers v. Baylor et. al.,* 862 F. Supp. 142, 1994. Used by permission, October 2012.

15. Ibid.

16. Ibid.

17. See note 9 above.

18. Title IX Focus Group, *Baylor University/Athletic Program Task Force Report,* (Baylor University, October 12, 1990), 3.

19. Pamela Grundy and Susan Shackelford, *Shattering the Glass: The Remarkable History of Women's Basketball* (North Carolina: University of North Carolina Press, 2005), 194.

20. Susan Ware, *Title IX: A Brief History with Documents,* (Boston: MA: Bedford/St. Martin's Press, 2007, 15.

CHAPTER 8

FORWARD THROUGH THE FRAY: LADY BEARS PERSIST

When the NCAA voted to include women's championships beginning in 1982, all of the member universities of the Southwest Conference (SWC) made the decision to move their women's programs to the NCAA. These decisions required the Conference to put a competitive structure in place for the women. The Baylor women competed in five sports – basketball, volleyball, softball, tennis, and track and field, with track and field competing in three seasons, cross country, indoor and outdoor. The teams had some success in the early eighties before competition moved to the NCAA and Southwest conference structure. However, during the decade of the eighties, few teams finished higher than 6th place in any SWC event, and won-loss records were heavily weighted in the loss category.

BASKETBALL

Pam Davis'[20] 1980-1981 Lady Bear team surprised everyone, posting a 29-8 record, placing third in the SWC tournament, and accepting an invitation to post-season play in the National Women's Invitational Tournament in Amarillo,

---

20   During her tenure at Baylor, Pam Davis married Sonny Bowers. Upon her firing in 1992, she was Pam Bowers. She is referred to as Davis-Bowers throughout this chapter.

Texas. Although Davis-Bowers had a full complement of scholarships (twelve by AIAW limits) and stronger budget support for recruiting, things seem to go steadily downhill for Davis after the second season. She ended her Baylor career in 1994 with a 168-257 won-loss record, or .395 percent winning record.

Davis-Bowers coached Jackie Reiter, 1980-84, one of four Lady Bears to post 1000 points and 1000 rebounds in a single season as well as Maggie Davis Stinnett, 1986-91. Davis-Stinnett, the only player in Southwest Conference (SWC) history at that time to score over 2000 points and pull down 1000 rebounds for her career, was a three-time All SWC selection and was named to the SWC All-Decade Team.

Maggie Davis-Stinnett, 1990 Lady Bear Basketball

Three-time All SWC Team
SWC All-Decade Team

Baylor University, The Round-Up 1990 Yearbook, (Waco, TX:
[Students from Baylor's Office of Public Relations], 1990),
The Texas Collection, Baylor University, p. 127.

Davis-Stinnett was inducted into the Baylor Athletics Hall of Fame in 2001.[1] Davis-Bowers also coached Debbie Polk, 1980-82, AIAW Kodak All-Region IV team, averaging 22.5 points and 11.5 rebounds a game in the National Women's Invitational Tournament, 1981.[2,3]

Debbie Polk, 1982 Wade Trophy Nominee

1981 AIAW Kodak All-Region Team

Baylor University, The Round-Up 1980 Yearbook, (Waco, TX: [Baylor University], 1981), The Texas Collection, Baylor University, p. 114.

Early in the eighties the women's basketball team played their games at the Heart of Texas Coliseum (where there were no dressing facilities for the home or visiting teams for the women). Later games were moved to the Ferrell Special Events Center. The women's team had no designated practice facilities, sharing the Ferrell Center with the men when available and utilizing other gyms around the city on occasion, especially during pre-season practices.

1981 Lady Bear Basketball Team

*Front: JoAnn LeFridge, Debbie Polk, Gaye Pack, Jackie
Valentine, Cele Stokes, Veronica Hicks, Sharon Kelley
Back: Marianne Jones, Mgr., Karen Aulenbacher, Asst. Coach, Deb Davis,
Nancy Davis, Jackie Reiter, Marla Tucker, Carol Brandenburg, Adele
Kennedy, Sharon Barnes, Leanne Waddell, Asst. Coach, Pam Davis*

*Baylor University, The Round-Up 1981 Yearbook, (Waco, TX: [Baylor
University], 1981), The Texas Collection, Baylor University, p. 117.*

SOFTBALL

In his second year, Bob Brock's softball team won the 1981 AIAW Regional
tournament and qualified for the AIAW Division III World Series ranked third
in the nation. The team competed well but did not bring home the championship title.

Paula Young assumed the head coaching position for women's softball from
Fall 1981 to 1988 and posted a 41-108 won-loss record. In her first season, the
Bearettes competed for the last time in the AIAW Division II category before
moving to the Southwest Conference in 1982. The team tied for first place in
the regional tournament in Spring 1982 but was not selected to go to the World
Series tournament.

1982 Softball Team

Top row: Coach Paula Young, Debby Waldren, Kay Murphy, LaRisa Tweedy, Robin Wilson, Cheri Ladue, Sue Herzog, Sally Swain, laurel Wilson, Rhonda Davis, Bottom row: Cheri Neumann, Amy Ezell, Debbie Marlow, Cindy Mosteller, Sara Minton, Anne Tucker, Any Burleson, Becky Spurlock, Trainer

Baylor University, The Round-Up 1982 Yearbook, (Waco, TX: [Baylor University], 1982), The Texas Collection, Baylor University, p. 137.

Young's position as head coach was a part-time position. In a 2012 interview, Paula indicated she worked three jobs so she could coach the team. Her salary was $300/month, just enough to make her car payment. In 1984 she assumed full-time status in the athletic department, part-time coaching and part-time academic advising. Paula had 2.3 scholarships for the women players. Under NCAA rules, she was allowed eleven.

All sports competed in the Southwest Conference. The problem with softball was that there were only two other SWC schools who had softball teams— Texas A&M and Texas Tech. Texas Tech dropped their program prior to 1988. Because there were very few softball programs for girls in high school in Texas, the feeder programs for the collegiate teams were minimal. This lack of interest weighed heavily on Baylor's program. Young worked hard to recruit more players on campus and from other sports teams to no avail. Those women that did come out for softball lacked the skills needed to compete at the intercollegiate level. According to Young, she was teaching the basic fundamentals of throwing and hitting, just to field a team. By 1987–1988 softball roster was down to nine players. The team eventually had to forfeit one game that season because they didn't have enough players to compete.

Writing in the Bay*lor Line* in 1987, Sports Editor Ace Collins commented on the forfeiture:

> The plight of the women's softball
> program cannot be ignored. Their forfeit
> due to a lack of participation points
> to problems that center on the lack of
> funding for a number of athletic programs
> at Baylor. Most the programs, which
> lack support, are in the area of women's
> sports. If Baylor is going to continue to
> pursue excellence in both academics
> and athletics, it is time to look at ways to
> ensure that softball coach Paula Young
> and others have something to offer other
> than just a uniform and a schedule."[4]

Officials in the athletic department made the decision to drop softball once the 1988 season finished. At the time, the SWC did not have a championship for women's softball. According to Young, Baylor officials wanted a sport that offered a SWC Championship.

"WE CAN LIVE FOREVER."

Young, knowing the public announcement to drop the team was coming soon, devised a plan to memorialize the team forever. With only one game left in the 1988 schedule, Young called a meeting with the team to tell them the sport would be dropped after the season. As she told the players about the administration's decision, she also shared with them a way the softball team could live forever. The team wanted to know more. How do we do that? She explained: In this final game, we will walk off the field with two outs left. The record would show forever that the game was unfinished. In that way Baylor softball would live forever.[5] With the cooperation of the opposing team, they executed their plan in 1988, walking off in the bottom of the seventh with two outs left in the game. Members of that team are pictured below. Throughout Young's tenure as softball coach, she had 2.3 scholarships.[21]

1988 Softball Team

"We Can Live Forever"

Front: Coach Paula Young, Lorelie McRae, Colette Cole, Brenda Brooks, Shelley Eubanks
Middle: Carrie Walker, Stacie Walker, Babe Helsner, Sheila Symm, Dorothy Payne, Lisa Oliver
Back: Kellie Spivey, Jenny Campbell, Lynn Douglass, Robin Fink, Sharie Summers

Baylor University, The Round-Up 1988 Yearbook, (Waco, TX: [Students from Baylor's Office of Public Relations], 1988), The Texas Collection, Baylor University, p. 131.

The women's softball team was reinstated in 1995 with Young as the head coach. The first order of business for Young and her team in 1995 was to complete the "unfinished" game from 1988. So, she brought back the former players, the same umpires, and the same game ball from the 1988 game, and recreated the ending scenario. Two outs, bottom of the seventh, one Baylor runner left on third base. Young used the 1995 team as substitutes for the 1988 players but all members of the 1988 team were there to watch. "The team had left Cori Hill on base for seven years, so they substituted Lynn Hill, a current player for

---

21   The NCAA limit for softball scholarships was eleven.

Hill. Christine Mayberry Barton was our first batter and she hits a triple."[6] The runner from third base scores, and Baylor wins the game. Young indicated the motto for her teams in the eighties was "never say die." As long as there is one out left, we still live.[7]

GOLF

Golf was added in 1988 when softball was dropped. Baylor moved Paula Young into the head coaching position. She coached the women's golf team until 1993 when Sylvia Ferdon took the reins. Credit must be given to Young for the success she experienced with this team. By her own admission, golf was not a sport that she was proficient in, nor was it a sport that she knew a lot about. Baylor's hiring of Young, however, was indicative of its desire to "take care of its own" so to speak. While this is admirable, one could wonder if Baylor had hired an expert golfer into the head coaching position in 1988, would the women's team have been stronger in the long run?

The 1988 golf team had a full allotment of scholarships for the women—six. Golf was an equivalency sport, meaning that a scholarship could be split and used for more than one athlete. While Young did not use all of her scholarships that first year, Jennifer Neal was one of the first women to receive a golf scholarship at Baylor. There were no assistant coaches, and Young continued to coach halftime. The team finished 6th in SWC play in both 1988 and 1989 very respectable for an up and coming program.[8]

1990 Lady Bear Golf Team

Front: Kathy King, Penni Perkins, Susie Davis, Pam Christianson
Back: Julie Brink, Cristy Sommerfeld, Jenifer Neal, Sherry Dowd
Not Pictured: Kristen Parker, Coach Paula Young

Baylor University, The Round-Up 1990 Yearbook, (Waco, TX:
[Students from Baylor's Office of Public Relations], 1990),
The Texas Collection, Baylor University, p. 282.

TENNIS

The women's tennis team experienced much the same situation as did the volleyball team with a lot of turnover in coaches during the eighties. This made it impossible to have any consistency, and in fact no consistency was really achieved until the hiring of David Luedtke in 1988. Other coaches during this time were Tim Palmer, 1980 and 1981, Paul McLendon, 1982-84, Paul Kidd, 1985-87. All of these coaches had part-time appointments in the athletic department during this decade, and most of them probably worked at least one more job. They coached because they loved the game and they loved Baylor. They wanted to make a difference for their athletes.

The 1981 tennis team started strong in Fall 1980 but faltered in the spring due to injuries to some key players. The team managed an 8-12-1 dual record and took second place in the TAIAW Division III State tournament.

1981 Tennis Team

Front: Rhonda Richards, Pam Foglietta, Lisa Pardo, Emily Judin, Allison Hightower
Back: Coach Tim Palmer, Terri Finley, Laurie Harrell, Janda Edwards,
Julie Barnett, Sue Breisch, Clarice Pick, Asst. Coach, David Peterson.

Baylor University, Round-Up 1981 Yearbook, (Waco, TX: [Baylor
University], 1981), The Texas Collection, Baylor University, p. 133.

From 1983 to 1989 the combined won-lost record for tennis matches for all coaches was 58-149-4 (ties). When the team played in Southwest Conference competition, a total of nine matches (singles and doubles) were played each time Baylor faced an opponent. This meant that in the decade of the eighties, the team played a total of 504 individual matches in SWC play. They won twenty-eight and lost 476. They faced off against SWC opponents on fifty-six occasions during this time and never came away with a team victory in these encounters. None of the teams participated in post-season play during the eighties.

There were no tennis facilities for the women's tennis team, and they practiced and played most of their matches at the Streich Tennis Courts outside of Marrs McLean Gym on the campus. Later in the decade the team moved to the Lee McLeary Tennis center in Waco and ultimately practiced and played at the Lakewood Country club. In 1984 Baylor awarded no scholarships for women's tennis.

**Dave Leudtke Encourages the Women's
Doubles Team Before a Match**

*Baylor University, The Round-Up 1991 Yearbook, (Waco, TX: [Student staff of 16,
both paid and volunteer], 1991), The Texas Collection, Baylor University, p. 131.*

In 1988 Coach Dave Luedtke had one scholarship for women's tennis. He
recruited Waco, Texas ace Mary Lou Castillo with that scholarship and began to
build his program. By 1989 he had two and one-half scholarships[22] and spread
them over four players, Castillo, Kathryn Sale, Stephanie Krenke, and Leigh
Ann Forney. Luedtke's assignment was a part-time position. During this time, a
Waco donor gave $10,000 to support travel expenses for the team. This enabled
Luedtke to enter his team in tournaments with strong competition as well as
to travel to SWC destinations and have hotel, food and gas expenses covered.
Without this donation, these opportunities would not have happened.[9]

---

22   The NCAA limit for scholarships in 1989 was seven.

Kathryn Sale Serves – Ace?

Baylor University, The Round-Up 1999 Yearbook, (Waco, TX: [Student staff of 16, both paid and volunteer], 1999), The Texas Collection, Baylor University, p. 131.

By 1988, Baylor had built a tennis complex on University Parks Drive where the men's varsity team was housed. This facility became the home for women's varsity tennis in 1988.

TRACK

Clyde Hart began to work with Head Coach Margaret Wooddy and the women's track and field team in 1977. According to Hart, he could see no reason not to combine the men and women's programs and coordinate their coaching. Both groups worked out at the same time everyday and used the same facility, but the men had the benefit of much better equipment. Both teams' training regimens were similar enough for the various events, that it just made sense to him to bring the teams together. When he approached Jack Patterson, Athletic Director, with this idea, Patterson could offer no additional salary incentive for Hart and his staff to take on the women. He also pointed out that the women did not compete in the NCAA, but Hart would not be dissuaded. He knew that NCAA affiliation was coming for the women at some point, and he wanted both men and women's teams to be competitive. Patterson agreed to this idea, and Hart began working with Margaret Wooddy on the women's workouts and conditioning regimens. By 1980 the women's program was under the auspices of Hart and his assistant Que McMasters. The women's track team competed in AIAW Division II through the 1981 season.[10]

**Clyde Hart, Women's Track
1977-2005**

*Baylor University, The Round-Up 1996 Yearbook,
(Waco, TX: [Baylor University], 1996),*

The Texas Collection, Baylor University, p. 153.

In 1982, the first year for the women to compete in the Southwest Conference, Hart fielded a women's team in all three track venues—cross country, indoor and outdoor track. Of all of the athletic teams during the 1980's, the track program had the benefit of consistent coaching from Hart, McMasters, and graduate assistant coaches. In spite of this Hart and his staff were unable to show steady progress building all three programs because they only had 2.3 athletic scholarships for the women. NCAA limits were sixteen.

Hart developed his squad on the back of the cross-country season. His teams placed fourth in the SWC Cross Country meets 1982-86. The 1982 Cross Country team went on to become the first women's team to represent Baylor in an NCAA Championship track and field event. In outdoor competition at the SWC meets, the team never finished higher than sixth place overall.

Track letter winners, 1977–1985 were Cinda Adams, Beverly Bechtel, Lisa Baucom, Judy Blalock, Nancy Davis, Veronica Clafferty, Sandy Forsythe, Karen Gentry, LaTressia Holliman, Jacqueline Horn, Christie Householder, Adele

Kennedy, Ann Kishki, Geraldine Lopez, Emmer Lott, Lucinda Lowry, Melanie Muller, Wende McNew, Lola Reescano, Dalaine Roark, Rebecca Stull, Kathy Vetter, Karen Waldman, Manager, Lora Withrow, and Kathy Woika.[11] Sandy Forsythe, 1982–86, was the second female track athlete at Baylor to receive a scholarship.[12]

1979 Cross Country Team

Front: Kathy Vetter, Kayla Williams, Linda Adams, Cynthia Oliphant
Second: Becky McLenny, Kim Nelson, JoAnne Hunter,
Cinda Adams, Natalie Gale

Baylor University, 1980 Round Up Yearbook, (Waco, TX: [Baylor University) 1980), The Texas Collection, Baylor University, p.117.

Within the NCAA structure Division I schools had to maintain a certain number of sports opportunities for their athletes, male and female. On top of that, within each sport there was a minimum number of participants per team, and this minimum number had to participate in a minimum number of events each year in order for the sport to be considered legitimate with the NCAA. If the sport did not meet the requirements, it was dropped from the NCAA roster. If a sport was dropped, it jeopardized the Division I status of the university. On an annual basis coaches had to certify that their team(s) had met this requirement by signing an affidavit from the NCAA. For women's track, the magic number of participants was fourteen. The number of Baylor women's track team members was under that minimum.

In 1987 Clyde Hart had an ethical dilemma. His women's track team could not meet the NCAA standards for participation. Hart and his part-time assistants had recruited hard on the campus in an effort to fine more female athletes. Flyers were posted all over campus, asking interested women to contact their office. This effort had increased their numbers to some extent but they were hanging in the balance. If an athlete got sick and couldn't participate, then the team numbers would fall below the required standard. Hart was struggling to sign the NCAA affidavit because of this dilemma. Not wanting to be the reason Baylor might be penalized, he paid a visit to Dr. Herbert Reynolds, Baylor President, to explain his situation. Hart told Reynolds he couldn't sign the affidavit and then explained the NCAA policy to the President. Reynolds understood the dilemma and asked Hart what he needed. Hart indicated that more scholarship support would enable him to recruit outside the university and build up the numbers on the team. He explained that he didn't necessarily need full scholarships but that tuition scholarships would be very attractive for most families who had women athletes that wanted to come to Baylor.[13] Hart left Reynolds' office in possession of several Presidential scholarships to be used for recruiting female track athletes. Those Presidential scholarships supported the likes of Heather Van Dyke, Natalie Nalepa, Lisa Stone, Kristin Mulliner, Sally Geis, She She Crawford, Kim Nutter, Suzette Scott, Heidi Semmelmann, Mallori Gibbs, Amy Rowell, Patty Sherman and Kristen Barker. These women formed the foundation for a program that won the Southwest Conference cross country team championship in 1990, 1991, 1992, and 1993. They also won many individual honors and earned fourteen All-American designations between 1988 and 1995.[14]

The 1988 outdoor team finished eighth at the Southwest Conference meet but Lisa Stone's performance in the 10,000-meter run was probably the highlight of the meet for everyone in attendance. Running the event for only the second time, Stone finished second in the 10,000 meters. Her time of 36:05.98 was almost three seconds faster than her first try at this distance. Lisa Stone went on to set school records in the 1500, 3000, 5000, and 10,000 meters events during her four years at Baylor. In 1988, Stone finished 8th in the NCAA Championship in the 5000 meters and became Baylor's first woman NCAA All-American in track and field. In this same season, the 400-meter relay team of Barker, Nutter, Scott, and Van Dyke set a school record in the 1600 meter relay, clocking a time of 3:48. Barker had previously set a school record for the 200-meter dash at the Texas Invitation meet, running a time of 24.71 seconds.[15]

In the 1989 indoor season, Lisa Stone became the first Baylor woman to capture a Southwest Conference indoor championship, winning the 5000-meter run and leading her team to a sixth place finish in the meet. Stone repeated the number one finish in this event in 1990.

Lisa Stone
1989 Indoor SWC Champion 5000 meters

Baylor University, The Round-Up 1990 Yearbook, (Waco, TX:
[Students from Baylor's Office of Public Relations], 1990),
The Texas Collection, Baylor University, p. 275.

By 1989, Clyde Hart knew that the women's program had great potential. Stone's successes, along with her teammates, seemed to verify his thoughts. Hart commented: "We have good facilities and a good climate, what we need are scholarships. Then we could win! Right now, Arkansas, Texas, Texas A&M and most of the others have a full sixteen scholarships for women, while we have six. Next year we will get one more."[16]

Kristen Barker, 1988 Long Jump,

NCAA qualifier, 200 meters, Baylor record holder long jump 20' 2.1/4"

Baylor University, 1988 Round Up Yearbook, (Waco, TX: [Taylor Publishing Company) 1988), The Texas Collection, Baylor University, p.134.

The 1990 Cross Country team won the NCAA District IV NCAA Cross Country meet, beating the University of Texas for the first time in a track and field event. The team was led by Lisa Stone, Natalie Nalepa, Kristin Mulliner, and Patty Sherman, all who finished in the top ten to pace the Lady Bears. This finish qualified the women for the NCAA finals, making them the first women's team in Baylor history to qualify for an NCAA final.[17]

1990 Women's Cross Country Champions

Front: Tasha Renfro, Amy Rowell, Mallori Gibbs, Janet Dollins,
Kristi Walkup, Kristin Mulliner
Back: Coach Tom Hill, Sally Geis, Julie Van Vessem, Heidi Semmelmann,
Patricia Sherman, Coach Steve Gulley, SWC Coach of the Year

Baylor University, Round Up 1991 Yearbook, (Waco, TX: [Student staff of 16,
both paid and volunteer] 1991), The Texas Collection, Baylor University, p. 132.

In the face of great odds, there is no question that the women's track team under the tutelage of Clyde Hart and his staff was the most successful women's athletic program at Baylor during the 1980s. As scholarship support grew, the honors for the Baylor women poured in. Hart's program continued to garner honors into the nineties and the turn of the century.

Missy Wolfe

1988 Baylor Women's Record Javelin Throw – 131'10"

Baylor University, 1988 Round Up Yearbook, (Waco, TX: [Taylor Publishing Company) 1988), The Texas Collection, Baylor University, p.134.

VOLLEYBALL

In the decade of the eighties, the women's volleyball team had five different coaches. They were Judy Jenkins, 1979-1980, Marci Matties, 1981, Jackie Swaim, 1982, Mitch Casteel, 1983-88, and Tom Sonnichsen, 1989. The women's volleyball team did not have a single winning season, averaging a fifth place finish in Southwest Conference play during this time. The team finally received some consistency in their coaching when Mitch Castell, 1983-1988, was hired.

There were 2.3 scholarships allotted for volleyball in 1984. The NCAA limit was twelve. No information was available on how this scholarship support was used for the volleyball team or whether or not it increased during this time.

As the decade progressed, Castell's team received more budget support for travel, making appearances in tournaments in Oklahoma, Alabama, Maryland, Arizona and California in addition to Texas tournaments. The team averaged a sixth place finish in Southwest Conference play during this decade. The combined won-lost record of all the coaches during this decade was 96–236. In Southwest Conference play, the team compiled a won-lost record of 5–75. No post-season play was noted.[18] The team played most of their games and practiced in Marrs McLean gym on the campus. Two volleyball standouts 1985–88 were Jana Ranly and Susie O'Malley. Both placed on the All-SWC team, O'Malley in 1985. Ranly was a three-time All SWC performer during her years at Baylor. These honors were particularly meaningful since the team was never a serious contender for the SWC championship during the years these women played.

Jana Ranly All SWC Volleyball, 1986-88

Baylor University, 1988 Round Up Yearbook, (Waco, TX: [Taylor Publishing Company], 1988), The Texas Collection, Baylor University, p. 118.

Early on there were no dressing facilities specifically for the women athletes or visiting teams. Eventually, Marrs McLean gym was remodeled and these facilities experienced some upgrades for the athletic teams. However, Marrs McLean was first and foremost a teaching facility, not a competitive arena for volleyball. As the decade progressed, the team moved some of the home games and practice times to Russell gym on the campus. Interestingly enough, there were no bleachers in Russell gym so portable seats had to be brought in for these contests. By the end of the nineteen eighties, some volleyball games were played in the Ferrell Center.

SUMMARY

Baylor officials made the decision to align their women's athletic programs with the NCAA in 1982. Their funding model from the seventies did not change. The athletic department still operated with the same revenue streams, and funding decision were driven by the needs of the football team. One could make the argument that the stiffer competition in the SWC was one of the reasons for Baylor's women's' teams having such poor winning records during this decade. However, a better argument could be made that Baylor did not support its women's athletic teams at a financial level that allowed them to be successful in their first decade of SWC competition. Only basketball was fully funded in terms of scholarships with twelve. The rest of the teams started the eighties with little scholarship support. It was not until the latter part of the decade that more scholarship money began to flow into the women's programs. At that point, tennis and volleyball appeared to have had 2.3 full scholarships each, track had six. Softball was dropped in 1988 and women's golf began with a full complement of scholarships, six. Except for the basketball and track and field teams, all other coaching positions were part-time and experienced significant turnover.

It was obvious that the steady growth period the women's athletic program witnessed in the decade of the seventies stopped. A better statement is that the women's athletic program was maintained, somewhat in a holding pattern and still a long way from compliance with Title IX. But, what happened at Baylor during the eighties happened at most other universities in the country. The excitement for women's athletic programs generated in the seventies was quelled in the eighties.

Women's basketball received the bulk of funding pouring into the women's programs during this time with a full-time coach and a full complement of scholarships. In spite of this funding, the basketball program of the seventies produced a better won-loss record than that of the eighties…and on much less funding.

The lesser sports of volleyball, tennis, and softball limped along with little financial support, part-time coaches with significant turnover, and inadequate facilities for the women. The coaches took what they could get and trudged on because they loved their work, they loved Baylor, and they wanted to have successful teams. By the end of the 1980s, these sports had more consistency in their coaching staffs. However, all of these coaching positions remained part-time until 1995.

The women's track team had the benefit of being combined with the men's track program in the late seventies. These women had good facilities and consistent coaching throughout the period of the eighties. They experienced steady improvement in terms of performance but it wasn't until the late eighties when the program began to receive more scholarship help from the University that the program began to gain recognition. Entering the 1990s, this team was well-positioned to be very successful.

While there was no one person on the campus, such as a women's athletic coordinator, to advocate for the women and to push the administration for more equity, it is impossible to know if the picture would have looked differently in 1989 than it did. As it was, each coach carried the advocacy responsibility for his/her team.

In addition to the athletes Baylor's women's athletic coaches during the 1980s were real champions for the women's athletic program. They persevered under severe budget restraints that limited funding for athletic scholarships, travel and equipment but most particularly salaries. Additionally, they had no other coaching support for their teams, burdened with all of the tasks required to run a collegiate athletic team. In spite of these limitations, they brought pride to the women's athletic programs and produced women's athletic champions during this time.

When the Civil Rights Restoration Act of 1987 became the law of the land in 1988, the stage was set for another period of growth for women in education and women in athletics during the nineties. At Baylor, the 'perfect storm' was brewing.

NOTES ON CHAPTER 8
FORWARD THROUGH THE FRAY: LADY BEARS PERSIST

1. 2010–2011 Women's Basketball Media Almanac, *Baylor Athletic Communications*, 68.

2. Baylor University, The Round-Up 1980 Yearbook, (Waco, TX: [Baylor University], 1981), The Texas Collection, Baylor University, p. 114.

3. 2011–2012 Baylor Women's Basketball Media Guide, *Baylor Athletic Communications*, 68.

4. "Ace Notes", *The Baylor Line*, June 1987, 56.

5. Paula Young, interview by the author, Waco, Texas, June 28, 2012.

6. Ibid.

7. Ibid.

8. Ibid.

9. David Leudtke, interview by the author, Waco, Texas, July 2, 2012.

10. Clyde Hart, interview by the author, Waco, Texas, October 29, 2012.

11. 2010-11 Track and Field/Cross Country Almanac, Media Guide, Baylor University Athletic Department, Baylor University. 31.

12. See note 10 above.

13. Ibid.

14. See note 10 above, 17, 24.

15. Ace Collins, "Spring sports roundup-It was anything but dull," *The Baylor Line,* July 1988, 27.

16. Ace Collins, "Track coach Clyde Hart, dedicated team members bring honors home to BU," *The Baylor Line,* May 1989, 30.

17. Andy (Ace) Collins, "Women's cross country captures district title," *The Baylor Line,* January 1990, 32.

18. 2010 Baylor Volleyball Media Almanac, *Baylor Athletic Communications,* 44–46.

CHAPTER 9

CHAMPIONS FOR CHANGE: THE PERFECT STORM

As the women's athletic programs moved into the decade of the nineties, it was apparent that while some strides had been made in the nearly twenty years since Title IX was passed into law, Baylor was a very long way from having a program that even remotely approached compliance with the spirit or the letter of the law. Of the seven sports being offered to women, six sports still had part-time coaches. Track (counted as three sports) was being coached by full-time coaches but these coaches split their time between the men and women's programs without any extra compensation. Tennis, golf, and volleyball had part-time coaching positions with no support staff. Badminton and swimming had been moved into the sport club program on the campus.

The scholarship goals laid out by Dr. James Netherton in 1984 had not been met, women's coaching salaries were nowhere near equivalent to the men's in their respective sports, and the total budget for women's athletics paled in comparison to the men's. Even with football taken out of the equation, the total of expenditures for women's sports was far less than the rest of the men's sports.

With the exception of the women's track team, the women's sports teams had posted poor to mediocre won-loss records through the eighties. They were not competitive in the Southwest Conference. Clyde Hart's track team had shown glimmers of success during the decade with outstanding athletes registering strong performances in SWC competition. But even this program had not been able to reach a level of consistency in its performances.

On the surface, the outlook was pretty gloomy for those involved in women's athletics. However, internally at the University, things were happening, and a storm was brewing. During the 1990s new leaders emerged in the Athletic Department and across the University. These individuals would become champions for women's athletics at the University and would stir up quite a storm before the decade was over. That storm would last for ten years, and it would include key events as well as the efforts of key champions at Baylor as it played out. In the end, Baylor would have a significantly stronger athletic department, including a women's program that was in compliance with Title IX. So, what happened?

Several events and individuals between 1991 and 1996 stood out, but the order in which events played out and individuals were hired was what created the "perfect storm" on the campus. Indeed, these events, and the leadership of key individuals, created the power and the momentum for the changes long needed in the athletic department. There was never a decade before or since that impacted Baylor University athletics in such profound ways. This chapter tells that story.

REPORT FROM THE ATHLETIC PROGRAM TASK FORCE TO THE BOARD OF REGENTS AT BAYLOR UNIVERSITY, 1989-1991

In 1989 President Herbert Reynolds appointed an Athletic Program Task Force. Members of the Task Force were from the ranks of the Board of Regents, the Baylor University faculty and staff, and the Baylor administration. A cross section of men and women were singled out for this committee. The Task Force was directed to focus its efforts in three areas: the relationship of academics to athletics, the women's athletic program and compliance with Title IX, and financial operations. They were told to bring back a report to the Board of Regents.

A subcommittee of this Task Force, the Title IX Focus Group, was subsequently appointed and included Emily Tinsley, Chair, Dr. Marianna Busch, Judge Oswald Chrisman, June Johnson, and T.C. (Skip) Cox, Assistant Athletic Director. As part of their work, the Focus Group specifically compared Baylor's programs with numerous Southwest Conference schools and focused on the impact of Title IX legislation. They submitted their report to the Athletic Task Force in November 1990. Subsequently, the Athletic Task Force submitted this report to the Board of Regents on January 18, 1991. Records were not available to document what the Board of Regents did with the report, but evidence suggested that it was formally recognized as a plan for Title IX compliance for the future.

The report consisted of an assessment of the current women's athletic program, a brief history of Title IX and Baylor's response, a compliance assessment and a program-wide assessment. Finally, the Focus Group presented a set of four goals that would bring Baylor into compliance with Title IX. The recommendations carried a heavy price tag, ~$700,000. A four-year phase in process was recommended.

The Focus Group's assessment of the status of the women's program painted the most accurate picture of the status of the women's programs at the time. More than likely, it was the only assessment of this type to have ever been done at the University. In developing its information, the Focus Group talked to each coach for the women's teams, reviewed the history of the women's competition, studied comparisons of other Southwest Conference women's programs, and examined in great depth the Title IX legislation and its compliance measures. The 1989-90 athletic department budget was used for financial comparisons.

Some of the more significant details of the report were the following:

1. The women's athletic budget (1989-90) comprised 10.47 percent of the total athletic budget.

2. Women comprised 55 percent of the total student body but only 27.9 percent of the total number of intercollegiate athletes.[23]

3. Women's athletic participation had increased 28.3 percent in the past eight years; men's participation had declined 8.2 percent because of NCAA adjustments in scholarship limits [for men].

4. Men's non-revenue sports' deficit for 1989-90 was 78.04 percent; the women's deficit was 60.54 percent.

---

23 This ratio was a violation of the Title IX proportionality rule.

5. The women's budget numbers across the categories of personnel, scholarships, operations, and other expenditures were significantly less than the men's. For example, personnel costs for women coaches (salaries) were 2.47 percent of the total budget while men's were 14.92 percent. Scholarship allocations for women's teams were 5.47 percent while the same allocations for men were 22.68 percent. The report also showed that the revenue from women's sports was very low, .003 percent of the total revenue for the department. Football produced one-half of the total revenue while revenue from sources like the Bear Foundation, marketing programs, and summer school camps, etc. produced 43.94 percent. All other men's sports, including basketball, produced 5.16 percent of the total revenue.[1]

Four goals were presented. With each goal, the group provided a rationale for the goal and a price tag for meeting the goal.

Goal 1: To establish the full compliment of women's athletic scholarships and graduate assistants allowed by the NCAA in order for Baylor University to be competitive on the field and in recruiting.

Observing severe shortages in scholarships, the group noted that the scholarship plan, submitted by Dr. James Netherton to the Office of Civil Rights in 1984, had not met with success. While Netherton's plan had indicated Baylor would be awarding fifty-six women's athletic scholarships by 1988-89, the current status of those awards was forty. The NCAA limit for women's sports had increased to fifty-seven. A comparsion of the men and women's athletic scholarships at the time revealed the following:

Baylor awards 100% of the NCAA allowable normal and equivalency men's football, basketball, track, baseball, tennis and golf scholarships, a total of $1,441,578. NO women's sport receives 100% of the NCAA allowable scholarships. Golf receives 83.3%, basketball 76.1%, volleyball 59.9%, track 53.1%, and tennis 41.6% for a total of only 62.2%

(a total of $321,762) of our allowable
women's scholarships being awarded.[2]

Baylor currently awards 13 scholarships
for women's basketball, 8.2 for volleyball,
8.5 for track (indoor, outdoor, and cross
country), 5 for golf and 4.5 for tennis.
NCAA ceilings for these women's sports
are 15 for basketball, 12 for volleyball,
16 for track, 8 for golf, and 6 for tennis.[3]

Severe shortages in scholarship monies
necessitate extensive splitting and
dividing among players. This impacts
morale, player's schedule priorities
and drastically impedes recruiting the
best and brightest women athletes.[4]

The total cost to implement this goal was $221,800 per year. This total would bring all sports up to 100% with their scholarships and would provide the number of graduate assistant positions needed across the women's teams.

Goal 2: To provide adequate, effective coaching, administrative assistance, graduate assistants, and support personnel necessary to a competitive women's athletic program in the Southwest conference and nationally.

The focus group noted that "Baylor University provided fewer administrators, coaches and support staff for its athletic department than any other school in the Southwest Conference."[5] Olga Fallen could have verified this lack of support staffing back in the 1970s. Noting that additional staff had been added by the athletic director and that many of the coaches were enduring significant pressure from lack of support staff, the report indicated that the athletic department needed more Indians, not chiefs and recommended that steps must be taken to ease the pressure on the coaches to a good and reasonable extent.

In order for the women's teams to be competitive, the focus group recommended that all coaches be elevated to fulltime status. At the time, basketball was the only sport with a full-time coach. In order to meet this standard, the following costs were needed to bring each coach to a fulltime salary[6]:

Basketball -- $60,000

Volleyball -- $5000

Track -- $20,000

Golf -- $26,679

Tennis -- $44,348

Additional personnel recommended by the group were (1) a primary women's administrator to serve as a recruiting coordinator, (2) additional secretarial support for the women, and (3) a full-time women's trainer and strength coach. Total costs for these personnel was cited as $97,000. The group noted that it was important to employ enough people for the program, but that it was equally important to employ the very best people available. The total cost to meet this goal was $253,027 per year.[7]

Goal 3: To give the strength and depth to operations necessary in order for Baylor University's women's athletic program to be competitive in the Southwest Conference and nationally.

Items like travel expenses and transportation arrangements, recruiting budgets, adequate and accessible equipment, and facility upgrades to dressing rooms, lockers and showers were discussed in this section of the report. When discussing the equipment needs, the group noted that the women were "handicapped by inadequate equipment, excessively shared equipment, lack of sufficient storage and difficult limits on availability of equipment and facilities."[8] The group noted that their interpretation of equipment referred not only to sport–related equipment but also to athletic training and weight room equipment. Noting that Title IX required equivalency in facilities, the group cited the need for major upgrades to women's athletic dressing room, lockers, and shower facilities for all sports. And, finally, the report recommended that Baylor University pay the insurance and maintenance and operations costs for vehicles for the women's coaches. At the time, only the women's basketball coach had full time use of a car. The focus group estimated that it would take an annual allocation of $164,374 to strengthen operations for the women's programs.

Goal 4: To devote the necessary time, funds, and personnel in order that the women's athletic program is a prominent, highly visible, integral part of university priorities and student life.

The report recommended that the sports information director for Baylor oversee all sports and that funding for an additional staff be allocated so that the needs of the women's program for marketing and publicity could be considered along with the men's programs. The allocation for this goal was $30,000.[9]

In total, the report recommended necessary expenditures of $669,201 for the women's athletic program at Baylor University, over and above what was already being spent on these programs. These monies would be phased in beginning in 1991/92 and reach full allocation by the end of the 1993-94 academic year. In addition the report requested that an annual update of progress on these recommendations be presented to the Board of Regents each year.

This work and subsequent report came on the heels of the passage of the Civil Rights Restoration Act, 1988, the act that mandated ALL institutions, public or private, that received federal funds must comply with Title IX. It also clarified that the mandate was broadly interpreted and included athletic departments even though these departments did not usually receive federal funds.

The Title IX Focus Group and the Athletic Task Force laid out the reality of what it would take for Baylor to comply with Title IX and have a quality women's athletic program. They recommended that by the end of academic year 1993-94, all of these goals be met. Although this deadline was not met, significant progress increasing the funding for women's programs occurred over this four year time period.

At this point in time, having a plan in place helped the institution in a couple of ways. For the first time, Baylor had a grasp of the work that needed to be done. Now, they just had to get it done. Secondly, the plan provided Baylor some measure of insulation from the threat of losing their federal funding in the event of an Office of Civil Rights (OCR) Title IX investigation. OCR had adopted a policy that essentially said: If you have a plan in place and we like the way it looks, we will judge you to be in compliance with Title IX. Even if you have not implemented all of your program elements, we can see that you are headed in the right direction. Once you implement your plan, you will be in compliance with Title IX. So, Baylor had something to show the federal government if it came knocking. The work of this group proved fortuitous as Baylor did undergo an OCR investigation from 1993-1995 and was able to avoid losing its federal funding because of this plan.

It was very apparent that in researching the issues of equity around Title IX, the focus group had developed an appreciation for all the inequities in the athletic department. Some of the issues around coaching staffs, equipment, facilities, and budget allocations were as out of balance in the men's minor sports (baseball, tennis, golf, track) as in the women's programs. Inherent in some of the recommendations (i.e. more graduate assistants, a sports information director for the entire department, not just football, and marketing programs for all sports, etc.) were changes that would strengthen the entire athletic department, not just the women's programs. In addition the report also cited the fact that while Baylor University had the lowest deficit of any other Southwest Conference school in its athletic program, a different funding model was needed for Baylor. The university had to do things differently in its athletic department if (1) Baylor was going to comply with Title IX and (2) if the university was going to have a first class athletic department and address its deficit. It would seem that the Task Force had grasped the reality that college sports were a business and had to be run like a business. The work of this group can not be underestimated. Essentially, they fired the first volley that started the perfect storm.

GRANT TEAFF, ATHLETIC DIRECTOR, 1992-1993

Bill Menefee retired as Athletic Director at Baylor on June 1, 1992. For months after he had made his intentions known, a search committee had been poring over applications and interviewing interested persons. Herbert Reynolds, Baylor President, wanted only one person for that job—Grant Teaff. At the time, Baylor had a policy that an athletic director could not be a head coach, so it seemed unlikely that Teaff would be a candidate for the AD job since he was the head football coach. While he did not want to give up coaching, Teaff was interested in being the athletic director. After many weeks of discussions and negotiations, however, a compromise was reached. It was agreed Teaff would take the AD job and coach one more year. Reynolds approved the hiring of a Deputy Athletic Director to assist Teaff. Teaff actually began working as the athletic director in May 1992 before Menefee's official retirement date. Grant Teaff coached the Fall 1992 season and resigned his coaching position effective in August 1993.

Shortly after Teaff began work, Dr. Richard (Dick) Ellis was hired as the deputy athletic director. Ellis' job was to provide support and backup for Teaff as the Athletic Director, particularly during the 1992 football season. It was understood that Ellis would be a top candidate for the AD position if/when Teaff decided to leave the position. Ellis and Teaff worked well together. They had similar philosophies and both agreed that it would take a lot of work to bring Baylor into compliance with Title IX.

JEANNE NOWLIN - WOMEN'S ATHLETIC COORDINATOR, 1992-2005

One of Teaff's first appointments to his staff was that of a Women's Athletic Coordinator. He asked Jeanne Nowlin to fill this position. In his July 24, 1992 article, 'Nowlin fills new BU post', *Wace Tribune-Herald* reporter Scott Butterworth indicated that Nowlin's appointment would begin August 1, 1992. Butterworth also reported a statement released by Grant Teaff and quoted him as saying, "We are creating this new position in an effort to put Baylor's women's program on a new level." Butterworth further reported that, in this role, Nowlin would represent Baylor at NCAA and Southwest Conference women's meetings. His appointment did not give her administrative responsibilities for the women's programs. Teaff specifically wanted Nowlin to raise money for women's athletics.

Jeanne Nowlin was a Baylor Bear, and as the saying often goes with Baylor supporters, 'her blood ran green and gold". She had graduated from Baylor in 1968 with a degree in education and had played on the women's basketball team during her undergraduate years. She moved to the Dallas/Ft. Worth area where she taught and coached in high school for a number of years. She had come back to Baylor in 1988 as an Account Executive Vice-President in the Bear Foundation office, helping raise money for Baylor athletics. Nowlin made a name for herself among Baylor supporters as an effective fundraiser and marketer. Although Nowlin's background was in education, she had the personal skills and network of contacts needed to be effective in a fundraising effort. While Teaff's appointment did not put Nowlin in charge of women's athletics, it represented the first time in over ten years that women's athletics at Baylor had a voice, a person in a position of responsibility focused on these issues and this program in an effort to make things better for female athletes.

Before Nowlin's appointment as Women's Athletic Coordinator, the coaches for the women's teams were coming to her with requests for funding for equipment, staff, etc. for their programs. According to Nowlin, the requests

were overwhelming, the needs were great. In an effort to organize a fundraising structure for Baylor women's sports during this time, Nowlin created the
Women's Athletic Cabinet (WAC), a statewide network of Baylor alumni who
wanted to see strong women's athletic programs at the University. This group
formed in the late eighties/early nineties while Nowlin was still working in the
Bear Foundation. The mission of this group was to promote women's athletics
at Baylor by engaging in key primary objectives identified by the group:

> To increase public awareness and
> serve as an advocate for Baylor's
> intercollegiate women's athletic program;

> To assist in the development of
> academic athletic and endowment
> scholarships to provide educational
> opportunities for academically and
> athletically talented young women.

> To engage in fundraising activities,
> such as sponsoring a basketball
> tournament and an annual walk-a-thon.

> To serve as a task force to make
> recommendations to the University
> administration, and to serve as a support
> group for the female student-athletes.[10]

Through her contacts and network of friendships as a Baylor alum, Nowlin
had first hand knowledge of female alumni that (1) were in positions of leadership and authority in their professions and (2) had their own network of Baylor
alumni with money and with an interest in women's athletics. By the time she
was appointed the Women's Athletic Coordinator in 1992, Nowlin's vision for a
support force for women athletes had developed into a strong group.

Over the course of its existence, the Women's Athletic Cabinet proved to
be a powerful force for positive gains for Baylor's women athletes as well as
an effective fund raising organization. Their initial fundraising effort, a walk-
a-thon, that supported all of women's athletics raised $24,000. Eventually, the

WAC organized specialized events that supported specific women's sports. For example, Nowlin was able to get Marilyn Smith, famous on the Ladies Professional Golf Association circuit, to participate in a fundraiser for the women's golf team. This event began and ran for several years in the nineties and became the Marilyn Smith Golf Tournament. Smith and alumni of the 1968 Women's Golf Team are pictured below.

1968 Golf team with Marilyn Smith

Left to right: T.D. Lifland, Coach, Nancy Goodloe, Marilyn Smith, Sherry Wheatley, Sandy Hinton, Lin Blansit.

Used by Permission, Lin Blansit, 2013.

The WAC Outreach Committee eventually organized fundraisers for women's tennis and soccer and partnered with Darryl Lehnus on fundraising activities at half-time for women's basketball games. Among many diverse recommendations that came from this group over the years were the following:

Organize a reunion barbecue for former athletes annually, in conjunction with the golf and tennis tournaments.

Have a band play at the women's basketball games.

> Have an annual 'Meet the Lady
> Bears' dinner to honor and
> recognize women athletes.
>
> Host receptions in Waco and in
> other cities where the Lady Bears
> play for team members.
>
> Target the campus newspaper, campus
> radio station, book store, and general
> campus advertisement to raise
> awareness of women's games.[11]

While these recommendations were pioneered in the nineties and considered challenging at best to get full implementation, they are common practice in the present day. If the Baylor band did not show up to a women's game in 2012, people would want to know why. And, if women's programs were left out of any marketing materials or publicity these days, someone would be asking, what happened? Where are the women? These attitudes are great examples of how support for women's athletics at Baylor has evolved over the years. This is gratifying. But, when the WAC first began to push for these kinds of activities in the early nineties, it was an uphill battle to get the right persons to have the conversations.

When Teaff moved Nowlin from the Bear Foundation into the athletic department in 1992, Nowlin's network of professional contacts in women's athletics was vast. She already knew many of the senior women's administrators in the Southwest Conference. She had an excellent working knowledge of the issues for women's sports in the Conference as well as on a national level. This experience and knowledge was invaluable when Nowlin became the Women's Athletic Coordinator.

With her charge from Grant Teaff in hand, one of Nowlin's first acts was to visit the University of Texas (UT) and talk with their women's athletic staff. Why? Because the University of Texas Lady Longhorn basketball team was one of the top ranked teams in America at the time, and the structure for women's athletics at the University was one of the best, if not the best, in the country. The program operated separately from the men's programs and was funded completely independently from the men's. When UT got into the women's athletic business, their officials made the decision to operate the program out of the President's office and fund it with funds not in anyway connected to men's athletics. As a public university, the money was there for such an endeavor, but UT also had an incredible fundraising program.

The Women's Athletic Director at UT was Donna Lopiano, a strong advocate for women and a force for Title IX implementation. The basketball coach was Jody Conradt, a Baylor alum. Also, Sonja Hogg, successful women's basketball coach at Louisiana Tech, was working at UT as a marketer and fundraiser for the women's programs. As Baylor's representative to the SWC women athletic directors forum, Jeanne Nowlin knew all of these women, knew about the successes in the marketing at UT and understood the kind of funding system that was needed for an effective women's athletic program to happen at Baylor. So, it made sense that Nowlin would visit UT to get as much information as she could on how to generate revenue for women's athletics.

One piece of advice Nowlin received at UT was to get the alumni involved in supporting the women's programs. Nowlin already had such a group in place at Baylor, the Women's Athletic Cabinet, so she worked to strengthen its functions and its influence. The success of the fundraising campaigns for the women's athletic teams during this decade are proof of Nowlin's effectiveness with this work.

There is no question that Jeanne Nowlin's work as the Women's Athletic Coordinator was received positively by the Baylor administration, the Waco community and the Baylor extended family. In 1995, Nowlin was elevated to the Assistant Athletic Director for Women/Senior Women's Administrator position and given administrative responsibility for women's athletic programs. She remained in this position until 2006. The Women's Athletic Cabinet continued to work for women's athletics at Baylor until 2004 when it disbanded. By this time, most of the women's athletic teams had their own booster clubs, so the mechanism for supporting the women was in place. Members of the WAC felt there was more work to do, but Athletic Director, Ian McCaw disagreed.

So, why was Grant Teaff's role such an important piece of 'the perfect storm'? First of all, Teaff became the first person in a position of power in the history of Baylor women's athletics to talk about equity for women athletes. And he backed up his words with his actions.

Secondly, he appointed Jeanne Nowlin to her position, giving credibility and visibility to the women's program, the athletes and the coaches. Thirdly, Teaff took the Athletic Task Force report from 1991 and began to systematically implement the recommendations from the report. In reviewing the plan, he stated:

> I found that many goals had been set by the Baylor Athletic Task Force on Title IX; much work had been done, however, it was apparent to me that not only did we need to reach goals in scholarships, coaches funding, recruiting funds, but we needed to go further and find equity in as many areas as possible, and to do that without forcing us into a greater deficit.[12]

In addition to appointing a Women's Athletic Coordinator, Grant Teaff understood what needed to be done to meet Title IX guidelines for Baylor's women's athletic programs. However, his greatest accomplishment may have been to start the conversation with Baylor administrators and athletic department staff about gender equity. He realized that having gender equity in the athletic department and on the campus went way beyond being in compliance with Title IX. The work that he did in a very short period of time demonstrated this understanding.

In his July 19, 1993 report to Dr. Herbert Reynolds, Teaff summarized what had been accomplished since May 1992:

> He had centralized the Sports Medicine Department so that the facilities, care and prevention of injuries for all athletes were a priority.

> He added a full-time, female trainer who also supervised the women athletes' strength and conditioning program in the Ferrell Center.

He hired a female student
strength and conditioning coach
for the women athletes.

He hired a full-time female volleyball
assistant coach and added a graduate
assistant position for volleyball.

He increased funding to the
women's programs, particularly
in the area of recruiting.

He centralized the video department,
hired an Athletic Video Coordinator,
and directed that efforts to support
all of the sports be coordinated.

He directed marketing director, Darryl
Lehnus, to work with all women's sports
to devise a plan to sell sponsorships
for the women's programs.

He implemented a plan to have press
guides for all sports by 1994, and he
began to use his weekly press conference
to promote women's sports at Baylor.

He hired a full-time female Assistant
Sports Information Director for
women to meet specifically the
needs of women's athletics.

He upgraded the women's dressing
rooms at the track and developed
women's dressing rooms for the
volleyball team at Marrs McLean gym.

He added two full-time women's basketball assistants, one in 1992 and one to be added in fall 1993.

He designated funds to hire student managers for the women's basketball team.

He implemented plans to elevate the women's tennis coach to a full-time position.[13]

All of the work that Teaff did in one year for women's athletics came directly out of the recommendations of the Academic Task Force's Focus Group on Title IX. Teaff knew that the only thing holding Baylor back from being in compliance with Title IX was money, and he understood the challenge. He had orders from the President to get rid of the deficit, yet he had an obligation to help Baylor come into compliance with Title IX.

Grant Teaff resigned from his position at Baylor effective August 31, 1993 to become the Executive Director of the American Football Coaches Association. Prior to his leaving, he presented President Herbert H. Reynolds with a comprehensive plan for reducing the athletic department deficit.

Grant Teaff was a visionary. He knew the only way the athletic department deficit could be reduced was by increasing revenues. The old funding model, based primarily on cost-containment strategies would never produce the revenues needed to move forward. Revenues had to increase. In his travels and visits with athletic directors around the country, he saw a lot of different ways for raising money and had picked up new ideas for generating revenues for Baylor athletics. He realized that athletics was a business and had to be run like a business. He was the first athletic director at Baylor University to provide strong leadership and a vision for the future. In the span of one year, he managed to impact the athletic department like no other athletic director before him, and he set the stage for future generations. He got Baylor University moving toward Title IX compliance and a new funding model. He hired Dr. Dick Ellis as his Deputy Athletic Director. Ellis was committed to build on the foundation Teaff had laid. And, finally, Grant Teaff brought female leadership back to women's athletics at Baylor for the first time in thirteen years. Someone was at the helm, pushing for equity and Title IX compliance, pushing for more money, more scholarships, more support. Grant Teaff and Jeanne Nowlin championed women's athletics. Their work enabled the perfect storm to gain momentum.

TITLE IX LAWSUIT, 1993-95

One of Grant Teaff's last decisions before he resigned his position in August 1993 was not to renew Baylor's contract with Pam Bowers, the current women's basketball coach. On the surface, the move made sense. Bowers had been at Baylor for fourteen years and had produced only one winning season. Over that period of time, the bulk of funding going to the women's programs went to the basketball program. Bowers had more scholarships than any other women's team and a larger operations budget. There were still inequities, however, especially between her program and the men's basketball program.

Several problems arose with the firing. For one, the letter to Bowers was dated May 24, 1993 and it was effective May 31, 1993, hardly enough time for Bowers to respond to the action before it became effective. Secondly, there was no mention in the letter of her won-loss record being a factor in the firing. Thirdly, Bowers heard about her firing when a local reporter called to ask her about it. She had no prior knowledge of the pending termination. It had been leaked to the press. According to Bowers she had never had a performance review in all of her years as the head coach, and she had never seen a contract. She was totally shocked when she heard this news.[14]

She immediately hired Waco attorney Lanelle McNamara to intervene for her in the matter. McNamara, after thorough consultation with Bowers, chose as her first action to file an EEOC/Title VII and Title IX complaint with the Department of Education, Office of Civil Rights (OCR). She then intervened with Baylor representatives, who ultimately recanted the termination.

On June 14, 1993 McNamara proposed several items to Baylor as part of a contract negotiation. These conditions shed some light on the inequities that were present in the women's basketball program at this time.

A written contract containing the same terms and conditions of that of Darryl Johnson, men's basketball coach.

The same number of years of employment;

The same salary;

The same benefits, including gasoline card, clothing, and TV show; and

The same support staff and budget provided to the men's basketball program to include:

Two fulltime unrestricted earning assistant coaches with equivalent salaries to the men's assistant basketball coaches;

One restricted earnings coach, same salary as men's restricted earnings coach;

One full scholarship manager;

Two part-scholarship managers;

An athletic trainer to be paid the same compensation as male trainers.

The same marketing services furnished to the men's basketball program, including preparation and dissemination of publicity items, press guides, programs, etc.

The same filming services that are furnished to the men's basketball program with adequate video equipment (TVs and stereo) in the women's dressing room.

Practice time for the women's team in the Ferrell Center will be 2:00 – 4:00 or an alternative schedule that would allow the men and women's teams to share this time slot would be established.

> The method for selecting summer
> camp dates will be changed so that the
> women's one-week date will be selected
> by the women's coach after the men's
> coach has selected his first week camp;
> the remainder of the men's camps will be
> scheduled after the women's selection.
>
> The ticket allotment for the
> women's and men's basketball
> program will be equalized.[15]

Dick Ellis, former Baylor Athletic Director, confirmed the gaps in the women's program as the new Deputy Athletic Director under Grant Teaff in 1992. He observed that Pam Bowers had no assistant coaches, no team managers, and basically no help. The NCAA allowed two assistant coaches and one graduate assistant coach. According to Ellis, she coached and, among other things, also washed and prepared the team uniforms before every game. Ellis thought it odd that Bill Menefee, the former Athletic Director and a former basketball coach, had done nothing to address these issues. Since Menefee had been the head basketball coach at Baylor, he, of all people, knew what it took to manage a college basketball team. He, also, knew that Bowers did not have what she needed to be successful.[16]

Ellis also confirmed that indeed Bowers did have a one year contract with Baylor. This contract was just like every other coach at the University. In her case, Baylor officials decided in 1993 that they wanted to go in a different direction with their women's basketball program. Resultantly, they chose not to renew Bowers' contract. Ellis also confirmed that, when he arrived at Baylor in May 1992, Bower's knew that she was under the gun to win.[17]

Baylor officials denied the legitimacy of Bowers' complaints, but many of them held up when the lawsuit went to court. All of the complaints addressed Title IX compliance issues. Ellis further observed: "The time she [Bowers] was at Baylor, she coached under some hardships. She was somewhat severely handicapped in her ability to coach there."[18]

In her letter of June 14, McNamara further indicated that Bowers would withdraw the EEOC/Title VII and Title IX complaints if certain conditions were met. She outlined conditions of that agreement, two of which were for Baylor to pay Bowers $350,000 salary differential from past years and to pay Bowers' attorney fees.

Baylor's response to this communication occurred on June 18, 1993. In a letter to McNamara, Basil Thompson, Chief Legal Counsel, noted the following demands from McNamara's letter: the $350,000 salary differential, a five-year contract, an increase in salary from $38,000 to $95,000, a doubling of the women's basketball budget, and payment of attorney fees. Thompson included a copy of a proposed two-year written contract as part of his enclosures and noted that the demands laid out in the June 14, 1993 letter, both for Ms. Bowers and for the women's basketball program, were inappropriate and impossible for the University to meet. He further iterated that the University was committed to Title IX compliance as funds allowed and identified several specific budget increases for the 1993-94 academic year that were already in effect. Some of these increases addressed items mentioned in Bowers' complaint (i.e. addition of second coach, addition of a restricted earnings coach, increase in travel funds, etc.).[19]

One would ask why would McNamara include items in her letter that were already a part of the new budget year for women's basketball? Speculation would seem that either Baylor had not finalized it's 1993-94 budget before McNamara's letter arrived and did so afterwards, or Baylor had finalized the budget and Bowers had not been informed about the budget elements. Regardless of the reason, some strides in funding for the women's basketball program were achieved in the 1993-94 athletic budget. Among those were: 15 scholarships for women's basketball, per the NCAA limit set in January 1993, a second full-time assistant coach (the NCAA limit), an increased travel budget from $16,000 to $25,000, one scholarship to be divided among several managers, and the addition of a graduate assistant restricted earnings coach.[20] Thompson asked Bowers to accept either the two-year written contract or a one-year verbal agreement on or before July 5, 1993. Otherwise, the University would consider Ms. Bowers to have rejected both offers.

Having received the written contract, Bowers countered with a request for clarifications on various clauses of the contract. No clarifications came. Ultimately Bowers accepted the one-year contract. There were some clauses of the contract that Baylor refused to negotiate, some that they would not clarify, and Bowers was not willing to sign the written document as presented. The complaint filed with the Department of Education by McNamara precipitated an OCR investigation of Title IX violations. That investigation began in the Fall 1993 and was culminated in August 1995.

Documentation indicated that Bowers received her first performance review (after 14 years at Baylor) on August 30, 1993.[21] Her won-loss record was a part of this review.

Pam Bowers was terminated a second time on March 28, 1994. The termination was effective on May 31, 1994. Bowers' last season was more successful than past years. She finished with a 13-14 won-loss record and actually won the first game in twelve years of SWC tournament competition. According to Dick Ellis, Athletic Director, her termination was based on her overall won-loss record, 168 wins and 257 losses in fifteen years.[22]

Subsequent to these events, McNamara filed a lawsuit against Baylor University on April 6, 1994. As part of the new lawsuit, Bowers also alleged that Baylor was discriminating against her because she had 'blown the whistle' on academic violations in the men's basketball program that resulted in NCAA sanctions in 1994 and the firing of Darryl Johnson and his staff.

Pursuant to filing the lawsuit against Baylor, McNamara filed a preliminary injunction, requesting that Bowers be reinstated as the women's basketball coach until the lawsuit could be settled. The injunction was denied. Baylor filed a preliminary injunction requesting (1) that individual defendants in the lawsuit, Dr. Herbert Reynold, Dr. James Netherton, and Dr. Richard Ellis, be dismissed, and (2) that the Title IX claims be dismissed for lack of subject matter jurisdiction and for failure to state a claim for which relief can be granted. The Court upheld the first request, naming only Baylor University as a defendant in the lawsuit. However, the Court rejected the second motion, citing two Supreme Court case – *Cannon vs. University of Chicago* and *Franklin vs Gwinnett County Public Schools* – where the Court had ruled that (1) Title IX violations as a cause of action were upheld and (2) that monetary damages as a result of Title IX violations could be awarded to plaintiff. Bowers lawsuit sought one million dollars in compensatory damages and in excess of three million dollars in punitive damages.[23] It was settled out of court on August 3, 1995. It took four mediations to reach agreement on the settlement. The settlement amount was undisclosed, and as part of the settlement, Bowers agreed not to discuss the terms of the agreement.[24]

So what was the issue of the whistle blowing accusations? Darryl Johnson, head basketball coach at Baylor, had come to Baylor in 1992 from the University of Tulsa, where he had gained national prominence as the coach of the men's basketball. He was a young, energetic coach, and had become very popular with the Waco and Baylor communities. He had ignited both groups, and there was unparalleled excitement about men's basketball in the Baylor/Waco community. According to Bowers, one day while standing by the fax machine, information from a community college in Florida came in for Coach Johnson. The documents addressed correspondence courses in which certain men's basketball players were enrolled. These men were receiving credit for the classes without actually doing any of the work. Bowers knew at once that these documents appeared to indicate that Baylor might be in violation of NCAA rules and regulations. Some time later, all of the coaches were asked to sign the NCAA pledge that they knew of no violations in the athletic department. Bowers knew she had to report what she knew.[25] When the 'scandal' about the alleged violations hit the media, the response was quick and unpleasant. The Baylor and Waco community had embraced Darryl Johnson, and there was tremendous excitement about men's basketball. Bowers, on the other hand, was heavily criticized in the media and on the Baylor campus. Bowers felt she was unduly blamed for creating the situation and that the focus for the University and the media should have been on the violations instead of the problems caused in exposing a coach and a program that Baylor loved and did not want to terminate. Athletic Director, Dick Ellis confirmed that there were problems. Reflecting on that time, Dick Ellis observed:

> We went through all the mess with the men's basketball program...what they were doing, these correspondence courses for the men's basketball players, students. What Darryl Johnson was doing at Baylor [was] only the tip of the iceberg. It was all over the country, particularly basketball programs. What we did after it was uncovered, we

> self-reported. We implied sanctions
> on ourselves. What the NCAA did, they
> actually accepted our self-imposed
> sanctions on the men's basketball part.[26]

On a side note: As a result of the Johnson affair, his advisors urged Dr. Herbert Reynolds to hire a full-time compliance officer for the athletic department. Sue Glatter assumed this position in January 1995.

As a result of the OCR investigation, Baylor University arrived at a Resolution Agreement with the Department of Education. In that Agreement, Baylor officials agreed to take specific actions to address concerns in the areas of (1) non-financial athletic benefits for men and women, (2) an initial assessment of student interests and abilities resulting in the addition of two women's sports, (3) a periodic assessment of interests and abilities, and (4) submission of reports. Specifically, Baylor agreed to the following assurances:

> that the women's and men's athletic
> teams receive equivalent equipment;

> that the women's tennis storage
> facility will be equivalent in proximity
> to their practice and competitive
> facilities as the men's;

> that the women's and men's practice
> schedules be equivalent;

> that 'doubleheaders' for the
> men and women's basketball
> teams will be equitable;

> that equivalent funding will be
> allocated for travel of all comparable
> men and women's teams;

> that the men and women receive
> equivalent per diem when traveling;

that the men and women's teams have equivalent hotel accommodations;

that the coaches assigned to the women's program, specifically basketball and golf, are as qualified as those in the men's programs;

that the conditions of employment and salaries paid to the men and women's head coaches and assistant coaches provide student-athletes with equivalent coaching quality;

that the women's tennis team practice and competitive facility is equivalent in proximity as the men's tennis team;

that men and women's sports will be provided equivalent sports information coverage, equivalent access to promotional efforts and opportunity, and equivalent media devices;

that sports information will be equitably assigned;

that the support for local externally-sponsored basketball tournaments for men and women's basketball teams will be equivalent;

that recruiting budgets for men and women's basketball programs will be equivalent;

that its intercollegiate athletics program
fully and effectively accommodates
the interests of female athletes;

that it [Baylor] will conduct periodic
(three year) reviews to examine the
options available for and determine the
most effective program for maintaining a
women's intercollegiate athletics program
that accommodates the interests of
current and potential female students;

that each new women's team will
have sufficient funding and support
to provide equivalent athletic
benefits and opportunities; and

that it [Baylor] will submit a written
annual report to OCR through 1998.[27]

Two sports for women were added during this time: softball was brought back from its eight-year hiatus and began competition in 1996 and women's soccer began competition in 1996. Documentation in the 1995 Athletic Department Self-Study indicated that Baylor conducted an interest survey in February 1994 to determine these two teams would be added to women's sports. Compliance with Title IX required meeting one of three criteria: responding to student interests, meeting the proportionality rule (percentage of female in the overall student body equals percentage of female in the overall number of athletes), or the university's demonstration of an historical commitment to equity in women's athletics. Of note is the fact that in 1995 the ratio of women to men on the Baylor University campus was 54:46 among the student body, a similar student ratio as was reported in the Task Force Report in 1991, and at that time only 29.3 percent of the athletic population at Baylor were women. Baylor had to add some women's sports to be in compliance with Title IX.[28]

While Grant Teaff's work had moved Baylor to a more proactive approach where women's athletics were concerned, the OCR investigation also impacted the movement toward Title IX compliance. In reflecting on the significance of the Bowers lawsuit, Dick Ellis provided a context for the events of that period:

> In the 1990s it [Title IX compliance] was evolving and becoming more important. But obviously Pam Bowers finally put everything on the fire, and it went from there. I think Baylor was moving in that direction, but without that little kick in the rear end, we might not have moved as quickly.
>
> In those early stages, there was just not the national emphasis on college sports that there is today. I know Dr. Reynolds cared about women's sports. I think he also knew that Baylor got their biggest bang for their buck from the programs that gave Baylor the most visibility. Those were men's sports, not women's sports. Dr. Reynolds felt a strong obligation as president to properly use the funds that we had. We were not going to overspend on anything, and we were going to live on a very tight budget. It was different having Baylor University with private funds as opposed to the University of Texas with all the public funds. Again, it was a different culture, it was just a different time in the history of our country and in particular in the history of college sports.[29]

By virtue of her EEOC/Title IX lawsuit, Pam Bowers displayed the courage of her convictions and championed the improvement of women's athletics at Baylor. In some circles, she would be called a hero (or heroine). By retaining Lanelle McNamara as her attorney, Bowers effectively insured that her lawsuit was tried in the courts and in the court of public opinion. McNamara had a reputation as a bulldog when it came to suing Baylor University for Title IX and employment inequity issues. Baylor supporters were eager for Bowers to be out as coach and wanted the lawsuit to fail. Bowers' supporters felt she had been treated poorly by the University and were eager for her to get her reward. Bowers got her settlement as a result of her EEOC complaint. The Baylor women's athletic program moved closer to Title IX compliance because of the OCR investigation. While it cost the university millions of dollars to get rid of Bowers, in the end the University was a winner as well. They had met the letter of the law, and they had met their moral obligations to all of their female students, faculty and staff. After almost twenty-eight years, compliance with Title IX was becoming more of a reality at Baylor University.

Baylor officials were eager to satisfy the Department of Education as a result of the investigation and made very clear to OCR a willingness to address any concerns even without a formal OCR determination regarding compliance. According to the 1995 Self-Study Report, OCR's response to this offer was: "It should be noted that the commitment made by BU includes not only areas of potential violation but also areas of concern that might not have resulted in a violation when fully evaluated."[30]

At the time the OCR investigation was completed at Baylor University, the Department of Education had a policy in place that provided a mechanism for universities to be deemed in compliance with Title IX. Essentially, a university where inequities were found, had to develop a plan that addressed OCR concerns, put some timelines on the work, and agree to implement that plan. If OCR was satisfied with the plan, the university was judged to be in compliance with Title IX (even though elements of the plan had not yet been implemented). Because of the work of the Athletic Task Force report in 1990, Baylor had a plan. OCR, resultantly, ruled Baylor to be in compliance with Title IX in 1995. Timelines for Baylor's plan indicated that all of the actions necessary for Title IX compliance would be implemented by 1997.[31] Anecdotal information gained through conversations with women's coaches at that time, the Assistant Director of Athletics for Women, and the new athletic director, Tom Stanton, seemed to indicate that by the year 2000, Baylor University had taken these necessary steps and had been judged in compliance with Title IX.

When the Court denied McNamara's injunction that would have preserved Bowers' job in 1995, Baylor officials were pleased. It meant that they could move forward with their desire to hire a new women's basketball coach and set that program on a new course. Their fondest hopes were that the program could be competitive in the Southwest Conference and that it could be a winning program. Little did they know what was about to happen in women's basketball at Baylor University.

SONJA HOGG COMES TO BAYLOR, 1994 – 2000

Dr. Dick Ellis appointed the search committee to recommend a new women's basketball coach for Baylor University. Chaired by Dr. Mike Rogers from the Baylor Law School, the committee consisted of representatives from the Faculty Athletic Council, the administration, and the university faculty. I was fortunate to be a part of that committee. Jeanne Nowlin, in her capacity as Assistant Women's Athletic Director, helped the committee identify potential candidates for the position and secure applications and information from each candidate. One of those candidates, identified, contacted, and interviewed for the job was Sonja Hogg. Hogg had been retired from coaching and had worked in marketing/fundraising for women's athletics at the University of Texas for several years. When contacted by Jeanne Nowlin, Hogg, having decided to come out of retirement, was visiting a university in Georgia, interviewing for their head women's basketball coaching job. Nevertheless, the Baylor job was intriguing to Hogg for several reasons. For one, Hogg's family was Baptist, and her mother had wanted Hogg to attend Baylor as an undergraduate. But the family could not afford the costs to attend. Secondly, Hogg knew Nowlin very well and knew of the struggles Baylor had been having with their women's basketball program. She understood there was very little commitment to the women at Baylor. Hogg promised Nowlin that she would interview with Baylor before she made any decision. In retrospect, Nowlin's phone call to Hogg was providential. Hogg completed the Georgia interview and was offered that job, but she told them she had promised to talk to Baylor before she made a decision. According to Hogg, she told the president of that university, "I'm 90% sure, but I have promised Baylor that I will come and take a look."[32]

Hogg's reputation as one of the most successful women's basketball coaches in the United States while at Louisiana Tech was well-known in the women's athletic world. Having begun the LaTech program in 1974, her teams rose to national prominence during the seventies and early eighties and won over 300 games. They won the AIAW national championship in 1982 and the NCAA national championship in 1983. During that period of time, Hogg's team consistently played in post-season, appearing in the Final Four six times between 1978 and 1984.

Beyond her ability to build winning teams, Hogg, along with peers such as Jody Conradt at the University of Texas and Pat Summitt at the University of Tennessee, consistently packed the gym at LaTech with fans for every women's home game. She understood putting a winning team on the floor was critical for success. She also understood that the relationships built with a community were equally as important to developing a fan base that packed the gym when the team was at home. And, she had the personality needed to develop these relationships.

The few days Sonja was on the campus interviewing were extraordinary. In a very short period of time the excitement for women's basketball at Baylor, its potential, rose exponentially with every person who talked with her. On the final day of the interview, the search committee met for her final 'grilling', I guess you could say. We had many questions and many concerns from past experiences that we wanted to address with her. We wanted as many assurances as we could get that if she were hired, Baylor would have a winning program. She, on the other hand, wanted assurances that she would be supported, that there was a commitment at Baylor to build a strong women's basketball program. At one point in the very lengthy interview, Dr. Herbert Reynolds, Baylor President, came in to listen and participate. Not able to stay for the entire interview, he expressed his thank you to the committee and to Coach Hogg and explained that he had to leave. As he turned to exit, Hogg stood up to shake his hand and asked: "If I should be your head coach, will you be at our first basketball game?" There was a very pregnant pause. Reynolds responded: "Coach, I shall." And the rest, as they say, is history.

But, I remember so well my response to that short exchange between Hogg and Reynolds. It was like "Wow, Dr. Reynolds likes her! Maybe we can get her here at Baylor." I think that was the first time I, as a member of that search committee, really had any hope that things were going to be different at Baylor, that we really could have a winning basketball team for the women, that we really could attract a nationally known coach to come to our university.

Sonja Hogg's first season at Baylor began in the fall 1994. Dr. Reynolds came to the first game. Ultimately, he came to all of the women's games over the next six years and became one of the strongest supporters for the women's team. He supported Hogg with funds for the things she needed to make her program bigger and stronger. Hogg helped Reynolds realize that investing in a winning program at Baylor could have big paybacks for the University, paybacks that included never before experienced community support for women's basketball. Community support meant large crowds at games. Large crowds at games meant revenue coming in to support the program. No administrator at Baylor prior to this time ever thought the women could 'carry their weight' and produce revenue. That was one of the reasons so little financial support had been given to the women.

In Hogg's first year at Baylor, the Lady Bear Tipoff Club was formed. The Club grew tremendously over the six years of Hogg's tenure at Baylor and continues to be driving force in support of women's basketball to this day. The success of this group eventually prompted all of the women's sports to have such a support club, and those are still in existence today.

Hogg had very specific ideas about the kind of media guide she wanted for women's basketball, working with Darryl Lehnus to contract with the Whitley company to publish the guides. It just so happened that the company was owned by a family that were major Baylor fans and supporters. Resultantly, the groundwork for higher quality in all the women's media guides was laid during Sonja Hogg's tenure at Baylor.

In addition to the Tipoff Club, media guides, etc., Hogg wanted Lady Bear Basketball fans to have the opportunity to be season ticket holders. She convinced Dick Ellis to implement this program. Yours truly bought some of the first season tickets ever sold for Lady Bear basketball and had a guaranteed front row seat at center court until I left Baylor in 2000. Giving up those seats was one of the hardest parts of leaving Baylor!

In Hogg's second year, she debuted the Sonja Hogg television show. Airing weekly, the show was set in the living room of Hogg's home. Darryl Lehnus helped her raise the funds for the show. It aired on one of the local television channels. Hogg was a master at public relations and used the show to highlight the play of the Lady Bears but also to build relationships with the Waco community. While her television show helped her outreach to the community, Hogg worked tirelessly for her program. She once indicated to me that she would go anywhere and do anything if it would allow her tell people about Baylor and about the women's basketball team. Her appearance on the Charley Pack Show, a weekly television show about fishing, evidenced her commitment. These efforts paid off big time for Hogg and Baylor.

While crowds at games during the eighties averaged around one hundred per game, these numbers grew every year after Sonja Hogg came to Baylor. She had the winning combination of personality, a winning team, the smell of popcorn when fans walked into the Ferrell center, and the sounds of the Baylor band playing in the arena. All of these things contributed to an atmosphere that excited fans and drew people to Lady Bear games.

In 1998, one of Hogg's best seasons, the Lady Bears hosted the National Women's Invitational Tournament final game. The Lady Bears played the Lady Lions of Penn State in that game. And, while Baylor lost the game, the most amazing event of the season happened that night when the Ferrell Center sold out their seats for a women's basketball game! Obviously, today, the Lady Bears many sellout crowds at the Ferrell Center, but, in 1998, that event was one of the most riveting things that happened at Baylor University that year. I can still remember the electricity in the air upon entering the arena. People were jazzed by the fact that the Lady Bears were playing for a national championship (albeit the NWIT, instead of the NCAA), but also by the fact that there was standing room only in the arena. It was magical!

Sonja Hogg coached at Baylor for six seasons. Her won-loss record was not stellar (83-91), but her contribution to the program was priceless. She elevated the Lady Bear game, showing that Baylor teams could compete in the Big 12 Conference. She built it and WE CAME! Tom Stanton, athletic director at Baylor, 1995–2002, credited her with developing a strong foundation for Baylor's future. Marsha Sharp, Texas Tech women's basketball coach, may have said it best:

I have so much respect for her and the things she's done for women's basketball. If you look back on some

of the personalities who were so
instrumental in taking women's basketball
to a different level, Sonja has to be
included in that group. The things she
did at Louisiana Tech and the excitement
she brought to Baylor will be a great
legacy for her. It's a loss to our sport.[33]

When she retired for the second time from coaching in 2000, Sonja Hogg stayed at Baylor University, working in the development office, continuing to build Baylor and Baylor athletics. She received the Naismith Women's Outstanding Contribution to Basketball award in 2004. In 2009, she was inducted into the Women's Basketball Hall of Fame and the Louisiana Sports Hall of Fame.[34]

Hogg's replacement was Kim Mulkey, a former player whose history with Hogg went all the way back to Hogg's days at Louisiana Tech. Mulkey was an outstanding point guard on Hogg's national championship teams at Louisiana Tech in the early eighties. Mulkey stayed at Louisiana Tech after graduation and in 2000 was coaching there when Hogg retired as head coach at Baylor. There are a lot of stories about how Kim Mulkey, her replacement, got to Baylor, depending on whom you talk to. At the least, it seems to me it was a team effort involving Hogg, Stanton and Jeanne Nowlin.

Sonja Hogg initially suggested to Tom Stanton that Kim Mulkey would be the perfect replacement for her. While Stanton was very interested in Mulkey, he did not think he would not be able to pry her away from Louisiana Tech. She was, however, on his short list that also included Gary Blair, the University of Arkansas head coach, and Jim Davis at Clemson University. Stanton wanted a top 20 women's basketball program. Of Mulkey, Stanton said:

She was the kind of hire that the
university needed to make in order
to break a string of 25 years in which
Baylor was just a training ground. She
had the leadership skills that I wanted.
She had integrity. She was intelligent
and accomplished. From a leadership

standpoint alone, you could envision her
one day running a Fortune 500 Company.[35]

It goes without saying that Mulkey's hire was great for women's basketball and great for Baylor University. Some of her accomplishments are highlighted in Chapter 12.

1995 ATHLETIC DEPARTMENT SELF-STUDY AND ACCREDITATION

In 1995 Baylor University conducted its regularly scheduled accreditation process with the Southern Association of Colleges and Schools (SACS). As part of that process, the athletic department combined this review with the first required NCAA accreditation process. Forty-two faculty, staff and administration formed the committee to conduct this accreditation review. It was officially launched on February 15, 1995. The NCAA Division I Athletic Certification Self-Study Report that evolved from this was released in time for an NCAA site visitation team in February 1996. The work of this group and the process they utilized played a significant role in moving the Baylor Athletic Department forward. In addressing the certification process, Don Edwards, chair of the Self-Study Committee, indicated included these remarks in an update to the process.

Although the certification Self-Study
will require a monumental effort on
the part of the committee, the process
will benefit Baylor considerably by
increasing awareness and knowledge
of the intercollegiate athletics program
campus-wide, confirming its strengths
and developing plans to improve areas
of concern. As the University stands
on the brink of entering the Big 12
Conference and a new era in the history
of its participation in intercollegiate
sports, the timing could hardly be
better for conducting an in-depth
assessment of its athletics program.[36]

Edwards' words rang true and the Self-Study Committee issued the most comprehensive document on Baylor Athletics ever developed. It not only looked at strengths of the department but also issued numerous recommendations for program improvement and infrastructure. Some of the more significant recommendations from the report were the following: For one, the report specifically gave the responsibility, including timelines, to the President, Vice-President and Chief Operating Officer, the Director of Athletics and the Assistant Athletics Director for Women/SWA, to implement the OCR recommendations and come into compliance with Title IX. Secondly, the report recommended the establishment of a Commitment to Equity committee to develop a gender-equity plan for the athletic department and included the process to establish the committee as well as the responsibilities of the committee. This committee would be established by the Athletic Council to monitor the activities of the Athletic Department. Thirdly, the report made significant recommendations regarding how minority issues should be addressed on the campus going forward. Among these recommendations were upgrading the position of Advisor to the Office of the President for Minority Affairs and establishing an Advisory Committee on Minority Recruitment. Several additional recommendations to improve student athlete welfare on the campus came out of this report.[37] The recommendations also implemented a system of checks and balances for this work. The Self-Study Report stoked the fire that was building for women's athletics and Title IX compliance.

BAYLOR JOINS THE BIG 12 CONFERENCE

February 23, 1996 was an historic day for Baylor University. It was on this day that the Board of Regents accepted an invitation to join the Big 8 Athletic Conference. The invitation culminated months, if not years, of negotiation with Big 8 officials between Baylor University and Big 8 officials. The conversations began in the early nineties when it became obvious that the Southwest Conference structure was falling apart. That Conference, representing four public universities and four private universities, had been in existence since 1914. The invitation to join the Big 8 was sent to Texas Tech University, the University of Texas and Texas A and M University as well. These four schools would join the University of Missouri, University of Nebraska, University of Kansas, Kansas State University, University of Colorado, Iowa State University,

Oklahoma State University and the University of Oklahoma. The Conference would be known as the Big 12 Conference. The move was huge for Baylor University, and conventional wisdom was that Dr. Herbert Reynolds had really pulled off a coup by getting Baylor in the mix of invitees. After all, it was the only private university in the newly formed conference, and Baylor's record of athletic excellence was less than stellar at the time. Left behind in the old SWC were Texas Christian University, Rice University, the University of Houston and Southern Methodist University. Baylor insiders were jubilant to have 'made the cut' but sorry for those excellent schools and traditions that would be left behind with the move. Each of these schools subsequently found new conferences and the SWC was dissolved.

Why was this move so crucial to Baylor? In a word: money. The expanded Big 8 entered into television agreements with ABC sports for an estimated revenue of one-hundred million dollars beginning in 1996 and spread over five years. This was football revenue only. Baylor leaders knew there was more to come once the other sports were included in a television deal. Steve Hatchell, Executive Director of the defunct SWC, said of the television package, "It is the best in college sports, the best of any conference anywhere."[38] To put this event into context, consider this: At the time unofficial sources at Baylor indicated that Baylor's 1993 television income for all sports was a little less than $400,000 in the Southwest Conference. As a member of the Big 12, Baylor could anticipate an annual average of close to 1.6 million, and this was only revenue for the football program.[39]

The dye was cast, so to speak. Baylor University had committed itself not only to produce excellence in women's athletics, but also for that excellence to spread across the entire athletic department. Somewhere Baylor officials and the Board of Regents would have to find the money to do the things necessary for compliance with Title IX and to strengthen the athletic department across the board.

TOM STANTON, ATHLETIC MARKETING CZAR 1995

While the individuals and events discussed above provided the momentum for Baylor's move toward Title IX compliance as well as its elevation of the entire athletic department for Big 12 play, two players instrumental in making the dream happen were Dr. Robert Sloan and Mr. Tom Stanton.

Robert Sloan became President of Baylor University in June 1995 when Herbert Reynolds retired and became Chancellor of the University. While Sloan's tenure at Baylor was fraught with controversy, his legacy was in the expansion of academic and athletic facilities while at Baylor. Sloan can be credited with loosening the philosophy on funding or spending, depending on one's view, for facility development. Under former presidents McCall and Reynolds, the philosophy advocated a 'cash and carry' type of mentality. Nothing was built, and no programs were developed unless Baylor had the money up front to pay for the endeavor. To the credit of McCall and Reynolds, the University was on good financial footing during this twenty-year period, but the argument could be made that much needed projects, both academic and athletic, were put on hold, waiting for the money to emerge. The frustration that came out of this type of funding philosophy was evident in the athletic department staff. Upon his arrival and subsequent conversations with athletic department personnel, Stanton found many leaders of vision within the department that were frustrated because there were no resources to support their dreams. Dick Ellis was one of these persons.

Robert Sloan supported men and women's athletics and understood the potential for revenue and donor support these programs had. He also realized the role a strong athletic marketing program could play in building the athletic department and "selling" the university to prospective students and parents. Baylor did not currently have anyone with the skills and talents needed for this job. Toward that end, Sloan brought in a former Baylor athlete, Tom Stanton, in the Fall 1995. While Stanton didn't really have a title, he became known on the campus as the athletic marketing czar. His job was to raise money. Stanton had a direct line to Robert Sloan, bypassing Athletic Director, Dick Ellis.

According to Dick Ellis, President Sloan let him know shortly after Stanton was hired that he (Sloan) intended to have his own people in the leadership role in the Athletic Department, specifically Stanton. Ellis acknowledged that this was a common practice in universities, but also noted that the timing of this conversation put him in a bind to find another job in collegiate athletics. Since it was already Fall and programs were already staffed up, it was unlikely that he could find a position at that time. After retaining legal counsel, Ellis and Sloan finally agreed that Ellis would stay in his role until Spring 1996. Ellis agreed to look for a new position at that time.[40] Stanton subsequently replaced Dick Ellis as the athletic director at Baylor University in the summer 1996. His tenure lasted six years.

TOM STANTON, ATHLETIC DIRECTOR, 1996–2002

Stanton came back to Baylor, where he had played basketball and baseball for the university in the seventies, from a twenty-two year marketing and management career at Word Incorporated and the Texas Sports Hall of fame. He had extensive experience in organizational development, strategic planning, marketing and management. However, he had never been an athletic director at a university. While some were critical of this perceived weakness, Stanton saw this as a strength. His lack of experience as an athletic director freed him to bring a new and different perspective to the job, to see the weaknesses inherent in the structure and to capitalize on the strengths. He knew he could learn the information that a Big 12 AD needed to have. He also knew that some of the skills he brought to the position were lacking in many of the Big 12 athletic directors and that he could make a contribution to that group.

Stanton saw two major challenges for his work to be successful. First, he had to change the culture in the athletic department and within the Baylor community from one that expected to lose to one that expected to win. Baylor University desperately needed that shift. The culture of losing was a habit at Baylor. From the athletic department staff to the coaches to the student body to the fans, the slogan for Baylor was `wait 'til next year'.

CULTURE SHIFT

Tom Stanton was a winner, and his enthusiasm for Baylor and Baylor athletics was contagious. To turnaround the culture to a winning mentality, he asked the coaches and staff to do five things: recruit, coach, win, graduate your players, and do all of this with integrity and honesty. His pitch was, if you will do these things, I will raise the money and get you the things you need to do your job. He also believed every team was important to developing this winning mentality, and he treated every team with the same respect and urgency. Gone were the days when football and men's basketball had priority on the funding or were considered the only programs of importance in the athletic department. These two programs still had their importance, but Stanton knew that the only way Baylor would have a winning tradition and a strong athletic department was if every team could win. He particularly believed the women's programs could be very competitive in the Big 12. Toward that end, he elevated Jeanne Nowlin as the Assistant Athletic Director for Women's Sports and actually gave her the power to manage those programs. Stanton and Nowlin formed the core of a strong leadership team over the next six years, hiring the coaches needed to win and securing the funding needed to build the athletic facilities. Included in this team, was Jim Trego, Assistant Athletic Director for Men's Sports. According to Stanton, Trego was instrumental in pushing the facility projects through to completion.[41]

STRONG COACHING

An important piece of this culture change was ensuring that the best coaches were in place for Baylor's programs. His first task was to elevate the women's tennis and golf coaches to full-time status with the full complement of assistant coaches allowed by the NCAA. He hired Paula Young as the full-time softball coach during this time and also supplied her with the staff structure she needed to be successful. Systematically, over the next six years, as some of these coaches stepped aside, Stanton hired a strong lineup of coaches, many of whom are still at Baylor. Quality with consistency became the new mantra, and Stanton and Jeanne Nowlin made it happen in the women's programs. Among those who were hired during this time were: Randy Waldrum, soccer, Glenn Moore, softball, Tim Hobby, men's golf, Sylvia Ferdon, women's golf, Matt Knoll, men's tennis, Joey Scrivano, women's tennis, and Kim Mulkey, women's basketball. Randy Waldrum coached three years, winning the first Big 12 championship for Baylor University in women's soccer in 1998. Ferdon retired in 2011, and the rest of this group is still in place. In eighty-two years in the Southwest Conference, Baylor University teams won eighteen championships. In less than twenty years in the Big 12 Conference, the number of athletic championships number twenty-five.[24] The coaches hired by Stanton and Jeanne Nowlin

24 As of December 2012

accounted for twenty-two of those championships. Twelve of those twenty-one championships were in women's sports.[42]

A WINNING STRATEGY

Stanton asked the coaches to develop and prioritize a wish list of what they needed to win and be the best. According to Stanton, the first time he did this, the combined lists had a thirty-two million dollar price tag. So, he asked the coaches to prioritize the list and give him the top two items. Each year he went back and asked for their top two priorities and then worked to make these happen. Stanton was committed to doing everything in his power to give each coach one or two of their priorities every year, and continue to chip away at the list until everything was done. He recalled the story that, on their first lists, the baseball and softball coaches wanted thirteen million dollars for a new ballpark and softball complex. During Stanton's tenure, they got it. Stanton said it took four to four and half years for every coach to check everything off of their list.[43] He found the funding they needed, and he did it by changing the culture of giving that had entrenched Baylor for decades.

FUNDRAISING STRATEGY

According to Stanton, Baylor's move to the Big 12 had put them behind the eight ball with their athletic facility plans because other members of the conference were planning major capital campaigns. Something had to be done to bring Baylor into the game, and Stanton was put on the hot seat to make these facilities happen. He fashioned a vision that addressed gender equity and athletic excellence with every project.

The fundraising strategy that Stanton presented to the Board of Regents required a shift in their thinking on two fronts. Traditionally, the Board of Regents had taken a very conservative approach to funding projects on the campus, and generally had held to the notion that groundbreaking on new facilities would not happen until the money to pay for the facility was already in hand. Because of this strategy, Baylor was in good financial shape, and Stanton felt the University was in a position to take some financial risks. With a vision in hand and renderings of the athletic complexes to be built along the Brazos River, Stanton approached the Board of Regents realizing that his first big task was to convince the Board to allow him to move forward with groundbreaking with financial pledges in hand and not cash in hand. His strategy was to identify donors with financial means that were willing to make a specific pledge over a specific time period toward specific facility projects. With pledges in hand, groundbreaking could begin on various projects. According to Stanton, convincing the Board of Regents to make this shift was a formidable challenge, and he credited David Sibley, member of the Board of Regents at the time, with turning the tide in his favor. By Stanton's recollection, Sibley simply asked the question of the Board: How many Baptist churches have been built with all of the money in hand? Apparently, the lights went on in the Regent's understanding and Stanton's strategy had the approval of the Board.[44]

A second shift in thinking for the Board of Regents occurred when Stanton asked permission to approach major donors to the University for financial gifts to support athletic department projects. Past practices of the University had prevented access to major donors for athletic department projects out of fear that these projects might take funds away from future academic projects that major donors would support. Stanton's intent was to ask major donors for additional funds beyond those already committed to the University. So, if a donor had given $50,000 to build a science building, Stanton would ask him/her to donate $20,000 more for athletic projects. Stanton was so convincing that Sloan and the Board of Regents granted his request to have full access to all donors with his fundraising efforts.

As part of this relaxing of the traditions, Stanton was given full access to development officers across the state. He developed what he called a niche marketing strategy in his approach to each development officer. Essentially he asked each officer to identify potential donors to Baylor University that had an interest in sport. Within each group he then segmented his requests so that when he met with the prospective donor, he could match the donor's interest to the donation he was requesting. For example, when Stanton knew the donor was interested in basketball, he structured his request for funds to support a basketball project. In exchange for their help in identifying donors, Stanton enabled the development officers to strengthen their portfolios by giving credit to each officer when the pledges/donations came in. He covered the state of Texas in this manner, traveling and talking with Baylor alumna and fans. According to

Stanton, he had never raised a penny before he came to Baylor, but he obviously changed that track record in his time at the University.

NEW ATHLETIC FACILITIES

The first phase of Stanton's facility vision was to construct new baseball and softball facilities adjacent to the Ferrell Center parking lot and build nine new courts as part of a new tennis complex. However, there was a slight problem. The Little League World Headquarters sat squarely in the middle of the land where this initial project would go. The challenge was how to get rid of the Little League facility. That challenge was met in fine fashion by Stanton, and over the next two years, he became good friends with the folks in Williamsport, Pennsylvania in an effort to solve this problem. Ultimately, a collaborative effort involving numerous Baylor and Waco constituents as well as representatives from Williamsport resulted in moving the Little League fields to another location in Waco, Texas. Jim Huey, one of Baylor's development officers, played a major role in securing the land for the new facility, getting it donated. Williamsport officials agreed to a contract deal that secured the land for their facility but also ensured that Baylor would get the land back if the Little League ever moved from Waco. Although it took two years, the path was clear for the first phase of Stanton's vision to begin.[45]

BAYLOR BALLPARK AND
GETTERMAN STADIUM

A multimillion dollar gift from Matt Miller was made to the baseball stadium. Ted and Sue Getterman pledged over one million dollars to the softball complex. Stanton sold naming rights to courts and spectator stands to get the tennis complex underway. At a critical juncture in the process when construction was about to be shut down because the funding had run out, Stanton approached Jim and Julie Turner, Baylor alums, for bridge funding that enabled construction to continue and allowed Stanton to continue fundraising. Jim and Julie Turner had attended Baylor in the sixties and Jim was a star on the Baylor basketball team. At the time, Turner was CEO of Dr. Pepper in Dallas. When approached by Stanton, Turner indicated he and Julie discussed it with their family and decided they wanted to make this commitment to Baylor. The Turner family's willingness to step forward with a financial commitment enabled all of the projects to continue and be completed in a timely manner.

Stanton wanted a plaza to connect all of the projects together and wanted to honor E.E. Dutch Schroeder, his former baseball coach, for his fifty-plus years of service to Baylor athletics. Rick Hawkins, a former baseball player for Schroeder, gladly put forth the funding for that plaza, named in honor of Schroeder and still in use. The softball field was dedicated in 2000 as Getterman Stadium. It continues to be one of the premier softball stadiums in the nation.

Getterman Stadium

Used with permission, Baylor University Athletic Department, 2013.

The baseball field was named the Baylor Ballpark. For their willingness to fund the completion of the baseball, softball, and tennis complex, Stanton recommended to the Board of Regents that the complex be named the Jim and Julie Turner Riverfront Complex.

In contrast to traditional fundraising practices where one building at time was financed and built, Stanton's fundraising strategy raised the necessary funds so that the first three projects in his vision for an athletic complex on the campus could be completed at the same time. He worked for this approach to save the University as much on inflationary costs as possible and to create excitement about athletics within the Baylor community. Stanton credited his success to the willingness of the Board to support his new ideas and strategies, to the work of the Administrative committee of the Board that approved building designs and groundbreaking schedules, and to the internal management of the financial systems by Dr. Harold Cunningham, interim financial officer for the University. Between 1996 and 2002, Tom Stanton accomplished what some residents in Waco said was an impossible task. His fundraising and subsequent athletic facility construction changed the face of the Baylor campus, but more importantly changed the losing culture of Baylor athletics to that of excitement and an expectation to win.

Other projects that happened during Stanton's tenure as Athletic Director were not as big as the Riverfront complex but just as important to the coaches and teams involved. A major renovation at Ferrell Center resulted in a new men's locker room and a new dressing room facility for women after Kim Mulkey was hired in 2000. Tom approached Winston Wolfe, who singlehandedly funded major renovations for both men and women at the Baylor track and resulted in the Hart-Patterson Track stadium on Clay avenue. That stadium continues to be used by both men and women's indoor and outdoor track and cross country teams.

BAYLOR TENNIS FACILITY

Originally part of the Turner Riverfront Complex, the Baylor Tennis center consisted of twelve courts and a clubhouse. Opening in 2001, the facility was made possible by a generous gift from Mark Hurd, Baylor alum and former tennis player, and his wife, Paula, an Alumna-by-Choice. Since its opening, an additional large gift by Hurd financed significant renovation to the facility, including VIP seating, shaded spectator seating over the Hulse grandstands, a new scoreboard allowing spectators to watch matches on every court, and a videostreaming system to air the Baylor matches. In 2009 the facility was officially named the Hurd Tennis Center in recognition of Hurd's generosity.[46]

SOCCER STADIUM

In 1999 a new facility was built adjacent to, but as part of, the Riverfront Complex on the banks of the Brazos River with funding provided by Troy and Betty Mays, Amarillo residents and longtime supporters of the University. Mays attended Baylor in 1941 before joining the Navy during World War II. Troy and Betty Mays have made significant contributions to Baylor over the years, supporting student scholarships, the establishment of the Agnes Mays Professorship of Entrepreneurship, and the Winfred and Elizabeth Moore Center for Ministry Effectiveness. A few of the capital projects that have received their support are the McLane Student Life Center, the Grant Teaff Plaza and Walkway, and the Bill and Eva Williams Bear Habitat.

The initial gift of the Mays family to the stadium came in 1998, and the facility was officially dedicated as the Betty Lou Mays Soccer Stadium in 2000. It replaced the original soccer stadium built in 1996. The facility has undergone numerous upgrades through the years, including an upgraded sound system, thanks to the generosity of the Troy Mays Foundation.[47,48]

Betty Lou Mayes Soccer Stadium

Used with permission, Baylor University Athletic Department, 2013.

GOLF

The women's golf team was housed at Lake Waco Country Club during the 1990s. In 2001, both the men and women's golf teams moved to the Twin Rivers Golf Club. The Bill and Roberta Bailey Golf Center houses the clubhouse for both Baylor teams and includes locker rooms, space for team meetings, and coaches offices. It features an indoor practice area with state-of-the-art video equipment for analyzing players' swings. The course was originally dedicated as Bear Ridge Golf Club in 2001. The Golf Center was added in 2002.[49]

By 2000, new facilities for the women in softball, tennis and soccer had been built. The women's basketball team had found a permanent home at the Ferrell Center, and the Ferrell Special Events Center underwent significant upgrades between 2002 and 2004 resulting in state of the art lockers rooms, a new hardwood floor for the facility, six new scoreboards, and two new 8X10 video replay screens, all for the men and women's basketball teams. A state-of the art press box was added to Getterman Stadium as well as a video board.

Stanton's vision also included additional upgrades to the Ferrell Center, namely the Lt. Jack Whetsel Jr. Practice Facility. The massive facility connects to the Ferrell Special Events center and features the Hawkins practice courts, the Getterman office suites for the basketball coaching staffs, and Gray's gym. Named in memory of R. B. Gray, the gym features a state-of-the-art weight room facility utilized by men and women athletes. This facility became part of Ian McCaw's Vision with Integrity plan and was dedicated in 2006 after he left his position.

All of these facility projects addressed compliance issues with Title IX and strengthened Baylor's position with the Department of Education. According to Stanton, he had a mandate to move toward Title IX compliance and gender equity within the athletic department. His approach to all of the facility construction was viewed through this lens.[50]

SUMMARY

Grant Teaff had started the conversation about equity for the women's program. Pam Bowers forced Baylor's hand with Title IX. Herbert Reynolds made the move to the Big 12 happen. Sonja Hogg's basketball team proved that a community could get excited about women's sports. Robert Sloan opened the doors, and Tom Stanton supplied the skill and leadership to make things happen. For women's athletics in particular, Baylor University was finally in compliance with Title IX.

Each of these people played a part that positioned Baylor University Athletics, particularly the women, on the verge of greatness entering the twenty-first century. They were all champions. While not all were viewed with favor at the University, they, nonetheless, contributed to the momentum of the perfect storm. Additionally, alumni champions began to emerge in this timeframe that provided the funding Baylor needed to move toward gender equity, contributing significant amounts of money for women's athletic facilities.

There is no question that entering the new century, Tom Stanton's positive focus, his commitment to equity, his vision for winning and his ability to bring much needed funding for facility development had changed the culture in the athletic department. New facilities, a full complement of scholarships in every sport, fulltime coaching staffs and exponential increases in the women's athletic budgets for travel, recruiting, equipment and support staffing contributed to these winning ways. Baylor University Athletic programs took off like a rocket in the decade of the nineties, and the University has never looked back.

NOTES ON CHAPTER 9
CHAMPIONS FOR CHANGE: THE PERFECT STORM

1. Title IX Focus Group, *Baylor University/Athletic Program Task Force Report,* (Baylor University, October 12, 1990), 115.

2. Title IX Focus Group, 5.

3. Ibid.

4. Title IX Focus Group, 2.

5. Title IX Focus Group, 6.

6. Ibid.

7. Ibid.

8. Title IX Focus Group, 7.

9. Title IX Focus Group, 8

10. Self-Study Committee on Intercollegiate Athletics, "NCAA Division I Certification Self-Study Report," Baylor University, Section 4, Commitment to Equity,1995, 182-183. The Texas Collection.

11. Women's Athletic Cabinet Outreach Committee, "Recommendations—Women's Athletic Program," 1991.

12. Grant Teaff, "Athletic Department Deficit Reduction and Elimination Plan, Women's Programs and Title IX, July 19, 1993."

13. Ibid.

14. Pam Bowers, interview by the author, July 9, 2012.

15. Lanelle McNamara, Personal letter to Mr. Basil Thompson, Jr., General Counsel, Re: Pam Bowers, Baylor University, June 14, 1993. Used by permission, October 2012.

16. Dr. Dick Ellis, interview by the author, October 10. 2012.

17. Ibid.

18. Ibid.

19. Basil H. Thomson, Jr., Personal letter to Ms. Lanelle McNamara, Re: Pam Bowers, June 18, 1993.

20. Ibid.

21. *Bowers vs. Baylor et al., 862 F. Supp. 142; 1994.*

22. See note 16 above.

23. See note 19 above.

24. See note 14 above.

25. Ibid.

26. See note 16 above.

27. Self-Study Committee, 219-220.

28. "Baylor Trends Fall 1989–Fall 1995," Volume 7, Prepared by the Office of Institutional Research and Testing, February 1996.

29. See note 16 above,

30. Self-Study Committee, 180.

31. Ibid.

32. Hogg, Sonja, interview by the author, July 2, 2012.

33. *So Long, Sonja,* Lubbock Online. Lubbock Avalanche-Journal, February 22, 2000. http://lubbockonline.com/stories/022200/spo_022200096.shtml

34. Jerry Byrd, "LA Sports Hall of Fame – Sonja Hogg,"*Bossier Press-Tribune,* June 29, 2009, http://www.latechsports.com/sports/w-baskbl/spec-rel/062909aab.html.

35. Kim Mulkey with Peter May, *Won't Back Down: Teams, Dreams, and Family,* Philadelphia, PA: De Capo Press, 2007, 105.

36. Don Edwards, "Self-Study and the NCAA," *Baylor University Self-Study Updates,* Spring 1995, 7.

37. Self-Study Committee, 219-227.

38. Dave Campbell, "The Next Level," *The Baylor Line,* Summer 1994, 42.

39. Ibid.

40. See note 16 above.

41. Stanton, Tom, interview by the author, Waco, Texas, April 4, 2013.

42. Ibid.

43. Stanton, Tom, interview by the author, Waco, Texas, June 26, 2012.

44. Ibid.

45. Ibid.

46. "Tennis Center to be Renamed in Honor of Hurd Family." *Baylor Media Communications,* http://www.baylorbears.com/sports/m-tennis/spec-rel/072211aab.html. Accessed May 23, 2013.

47. Betty Lou Mayes Field. http://www.baylorbears.com/facilities/loumays.html. Accessed May 23, 2013

48. "Baylor Honors Troy Mays With 2006 Founders Medal." *Baylor Media Communications,* January 31, 2006. http://www.baylor.edu/mediacommunications/news.php?action=story&story=38694.

49. "Par Excellence." *Baylor Magazine.* http://www.baylor.edu/alumni/magazine/0102/news.php?action=story&story=7320. Accessed May 23, 2013.

50. See note 43 above.

CHAPTER 10

~~~~~

WINNING TRADITIONS BEGIN: LADY BEARS, 1990 – 2000

The decade of the eighties were difficult years for the women athletes and coaches at Baylor. Competing for the first time in the Southwest Conference, the teams were challenged to be more competitive. Funding needs to accomplish this demand were not met by the University. However, Baylor had two things going for them in the eighties that enabled the women's programs to hang on—great coaches and great athletes. By 1990 the women's athletic teams at Baylor had reached an important level of consistency with their coaching staffs. Except for basketball, the effects of this consistency could be seen in stronger won-loss records and individual honors for the athletes. [25]

Starting in 1988, more consistency in the coaching staffs and increased budget support, particularly scholarship dollars began. By 1990 the women's teams were positioned to turn from their losing ways of the eighties to a pattern of more success. This chapter tells that story, highlighting the coaches and athletes who began the winning tradition that is still found in the women's programs at Baylor University.

BASKETBALL

The most visible program for women's athletics has always been the basketball program. This was true at Baylor and at many other universities during the nineties. Traditionally, this program was the most well-financed because of its high visibility. From Olga Fallen's firing in 1979 to Pam Bowers' firing in 1994,

---

25 Southwest Conference and NCAA honors.

the women's basketball team had not had a winning season. Fallen finished her career in 1979 with a .741 record for wins. Pam Bowers posted a .395 winning percentage in fifteen years as the second women's head coach.[1]

Sonja Hogg was the third women's basketball head coach for Baylor University and began her tenure with the 1994 season. Hogg posted a .477 percentage record, tying for fifth place in the Big 12 in 1997 and 1998. Her 1998 team qualified for the Women's National Invitational Tournament and placed second in the nation. Hogg started Baylor fans down the road of expecting to win, and she generated a loyal fan base and community excitement around the Lady Bears. During Hogg's tenure, attendance at Baylor women's games rose to an average of over 3100 fans per game. Her 1998 team, playing for the National Women's Invitational Tournament championship, drew a record crowd to the Ferrell Center. Over ten thousand fans saw Baylor lose that game to Penn State. Hogg set the winning stage for Kim Mulkey, who began her tenure at Baylor in 2000.

1998 BB, WNIT Runner-Up

Sonja Hogg Instructs Her Team During a Timeout

Baylor University, The Round-Up 1998 Yearbook, (Waco, TX: [Baylor University], 1998), The Texas Collection, Baylor University, p. 92.

GOLF

The women's golf team was coached by Paula Young in the early years of the nineties. Young was still a part-time coach but she did have a full scholarship allocation with increased travel money and recruiting budgets. The team did not perform well in Southwest Conference play. At the time there were six teams competing in SWC play, and Baylor placed fifth or sixth in each of the seasons Young coached. The golf team called Lake Waco Country Club home but they never hosted a meet. The team practiced most often at Cottonwood Country club in Waco, Texas.

Sylvia Ferdon took the reins of the Baylor team in 1994, coaching the women until 2011. Ferdon was initially a part-time coach but was elevated to fulltime in 1996. During her tenure, Baylor competed in the Big 12, averaging an 8th place finish out of twelve teams during that five-year span.

Collectively in the nineties, Young and Ferdon's teams won four tournaments and had 12 top four tournament finishes, but neither coach had a postseason NCAA appearance during this decade. The only Lady Bear to garner Big 12 or SWC honors during this time was Ali Brewer.

Ali Brewer

1999 All-Big 12; All-Big 12 Tournament Team

Baylor University, The Round-Up 2000 Yearbook, (Waco, TX: [Baylor University], 2000), The Texas Collection, Baylor University, p. 253.

Brewer was named to the 1999 All-Big 12 and All-Big 12 Tournament teams. Mary Hornsby and Erika Iannariello received honorable mention on the 1997 Academic All-Big 12 team as did Christy Miller in 1998. Jennifer Egan was named to the first team Academic All-Big 12 team in 1998.[2] Ferdon's recruiting efforts were starting to pay off. The program was gaining strength and recognition.

SOCCER

Soccer was added to the women's program in 1996 after the OCR investigation showed that Baylor was not complying with the Title IX proportionality rule. Jeanne Nowlin hired Randy Waldrum as the first women's soccer coach at Baylor, serving in that capacity from 1996 through 1998. Waldrum got the women started off in fine fashion, not only posting winning seasons in his three-year stint but also winning the Big 12 Conference championship in 1998. Prior to this season, the team had placed third in the Big 12 conference tournament in the first two years. The Big 12 championship was the first for any women's sports team since entering the Big 12 in 1996. Randy Waldrum was named Big 12 Coach of the Year for the 1998 season.[3] Waldrum left Baylor in 1999 for the University of Notre Dame. He continues as the Fighting Irish head coach in 2012.

1998 Soccer Team, Big 12 Champions

Molly Cameron, Gina Castellano, Meghan Crona, Jennifer Eden,
Dawn Greathouse, Danielle Gurney, Nikki Hales, Lori Johnson,

*Megan Jones, Rachel Kacsmaryk, Sarah Koch, Jerri Konlande,
Julie Larson, Alyson Miles, Christina Nguyen, Courtney Saunders,
Britt Talley, Megan Townes*

The Texas Collection, Accession 999.1070, Box 14.01, Baylor University

The team, coached by Nick Cowell from 1999-2002, posted a winning record in 1999 and finished fourth in the Big 12 Conference.[4] In 2000, the team experienced their first losing season since beginning play. This year began a long line of losing seasons that would last until 2009.

Several outstanding women played soccer for Baylor during the 1996-2000 period. Some of the standout players were Nicki Hales, Meghan Crona, Sarah Koch, and Lori Johnson. Courtney Saunders and Dawn Greathouse achieved national recognition for their play.

Courtney Saunders

*All-Big 12 Conference team, 1996-97, 993
SOCCER BUZZ All-Region First Team, 1998-99
NSCAA All-Central Region First Team*

Baylor University, The Round-Up 1999 Yearbook, (Waco, TX: [Taylor Publishing Company], 1999), The Texas Collection, Baylor University, p. 222.

Dawn Greathouse

All Big-12 Conference Team, 1998-20004
SOCCER BUZZ All-Region, 1998
NSCAA All-Central Region First Team, 1998
All Big-12 Tournament Goalkeeper, 2000

Baylor University, The Round-Up 1999 Yearbook, (Waco, TX: [Baylor University], 1999), The Texas Collection, Baylor University, p. 223.

SOFTBALL

Women's softball was also resurrected in 1996 with a full complement of scholarships and a full coaching staff. Paula Young was hired to restart the program.[26] Young coached for four seasons, taking the Lady Bears to winning seasons in 1996, 1997, and 1999. Although the team did not fare well in Big 12 play, they did make one post-season appearance at the National Softball Invitational Tournament in 1999. Outstanding players for Young are listed below.

Player	Years	Honors
Kristin Barton	1996	1st Team *NFCA All-Region
Shelly Green	1996	2nd Team *NFCA All-Region

---

26 Readers will recall that Young was coaching the team in 1988 when it was abandoned.

Jennie Vargas	1996	2nd Team *NFCA All-Region
	1997	All-Big 12 Conference-1st team
Bri Chambliss	1997	2nd Team *NFCA All-Region
Michelle Sorrels	1999	2nd Team *NFCA All-Region
Stacy Allison	1997	All-Big 12 Conference – 2nd team
Misty Perry	1999	All-Big 12 Conference – 2nd team
Naomi Fitzgerald	1998	Big 12 Conference All-Tournament

Table I: 1996-1999 Baylor Lady Bear Softball Outstanding Players[5, 27]

TENNIS

When Dave Luedtke took over the women's tennis team at Baylor in 1988, he brought a sense of stability to the position for the first time. He stayed with the team through the 2002 season.

1990 Women's Tennis Team

Front: Kathy O'Toole, Karen Bishop, Jessica Chen
Second: Stephanie Krienke, Rachel Forney, Leigh Ann Forney, Dave Leudtke
Back: Gina Gibson, Mary Lou Castillo, Kathryn Sale,
Andrea Guy, Asst. Coach Dave Vinsant

Baylor University, Round Up 1990 Yearbook, (Waco, TX: [Students from Baylor's Office of Public Relations], 1990), The Texas Collection, Baylor University, p. 281.

---

27 *National Fastpitch Coaches Association

In his fourteen years Leudtke made significant strides producing a winning tradition with this program, posting the teams first winning seasons in 1989 and 1990, and then for eight consecutive seasons, 1992-1999. When money began to flow into the program after Tom Stanton became the athletic director, scholarships appeared, travel budgets increased, and recruiting thrived. Luedtke was elevated to full-time status in 1996. His teams appeared in the NCAA post-season tournament from 1998-2001. Although his team never won a SWC or Big 12 championship, they finished in the top five positions in the Big 12 race starting in 1996. The 2001 team made it to the round of sixteen in the NCAA tournament before losing to the University of Georgia. Luedtke was named SWC Coach of the Year in 1997.

Leudtke recruited and worked with outstanding tennis players. In addition to winning numerous academic-athletic awards during his tenure, Luedtke recruited and worked with the following outstanding athletes.

Player	Year	Honor
Barbara Navarro	1997	All Big 12 Singles
	1997	Big 12 Newcomer of the Year
Jahnavi Parekh	1999-01	All Big 12 Singles
Katja Kovac	1999-02	All Big 12 Singles
Vida Mulec	2002-03	All Big 12 Singles
Carolyn McGrath/ Vanessa Abel	1997	All Big 12 Doubles
Katja Kovac/ Jahnavi Parekh	1999, 2001	All Big 12 Doubles
Katja Kovac/ Vida Mulec	2000, 2002	All Big 12 Doubles
Melissa Castro	1993, 1995	Arthur Ashe Sportsmanship & Leadership Award
Sarah Chester	1996	Arthur Ashe Sportsmanship & Leadership Award
Carolyn McGrath	1997	Arthur Ashe Sportsmanship & Leadership Award

Table II: 1990–2002 Lady Bear Outstanding Tennis Players[6]

Jahnavi Parekh

Baylor University, The Round-Up 2001 Yearbook, (Waco, TX: [Baylor University], 2001), The Texas Collection, Baylor University, p. 283.

TRACK

Consistency was the byword for the women's track and field program during the 1990s. Beginning with the scholarship athletes recruited in the latter years of the 1980s, Clyde Hart and his coaching staff built an incredibly strong program in all three track and field programs (cross country, indoor, and outdoor). Along the way they recruited and coached numerous All-Americans.

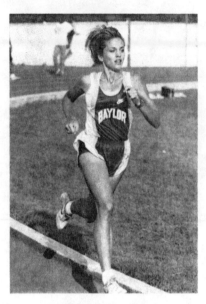

Natalie Nalepa

1991 – First place, SWC Cross Country Championships,
5th Place NCAA Cross Country Championships,
First Baylor Female Cross Country All-American[7]

Baylor University, The Round-Up 1991 Yearbook, (Waco, TX:
[Students from Baylor's Office of Public Relations], 1991),
The Texas Collection, Baylor University, p. 132.

During the nineties, coached by Steve Gulley, the women's cross country team were the SWC champions 1990, '91, '92, and 1993.[7] They placed second as a team in the 1994 and 1995 conference meets. After entering the Big 12, the team averaged a fifth place finish in 1996-1999.

Stacey Bowers (Smith)

*1999 NCAA Champion Triple Jump, Most Decorated Female Trackster
in the History of Baylor University*

1999 Baylor Media Guide, Track & Field, front cover

Clyde Hart's Indoor teams placed in the top five in the Southwest Conference and Big 12 Tournament meets in every year during this decade, and his Outdoor teams placed in the top five finishers in every year 1990-1999. Baylor saw its first women's individual NCAA champions during this decade in 1999 with Stacy Bower's NCAA victory in the Triple jump and in 1998 with the women's 4x400 relay winning the NCAA Indoor championship. Interestingly the men's indoor 4x400 indoor relay team also won the NCAA championship in that year. Both teams are pictured below.

1998 4X400 Indoor Relay

National Champions
Back: Stephan Bragner, Brandon Couts, Mario Watts, Damian Davis
Front: Yulanda Nelson, Angelique Banket, Alayah Cooper, Jennifer Jordan

1999 Baylor Media Guide, Track & Field, front cover

No other Baylor women's team demonstrated the winning tradition like the women's track and field program. Along the way several women gained All-American honors in their specific events. Those individuals are listed below.

Runner	Event	Year	NCAA Place
Quanta Anderson	Indoor	1999	6th -- 4 X 400 Relay
	Outdoor	1999	7th – 4 X 400 Relay
Angelique Banket	Indoor	1999	6th – 4 X 400 Relay
	Outdoor	1997	6th – 4 X 400 Relay
		1998	2nd – 4 X 400 Relay
		1999	7th – 4 X 400 Relay
Jill Chertudi	Indoor	1995	5th – 800m
Alayah Cooper	Outdoor	1997	6th – 4 X 400 Relay
		1998	2nd – 4 X 400 Relay

She She Crawford	Outdoor	1992	5th – 100m
		1994	4th – 4 X 100 Relay
		1994	6th – 4 X 400 Relay
Demonica Davis	Outdoor	1994	4th – 4 X 100 Relay
Janet Dollins	Indoor	1991	4th – 4X800 Medley Relay
Karen Ernstrom	Indoor	1999	3rd – 5,000m
	Outdoor	1998	8th – 5,000m
		1999	3rd – 5,000m
Sally Geis	Outdoor	1995	7th – 10,000m
Shelley Green	Indoor	1995	6th -- 4X400 Relay
	Outdoor	1995	7th – 4 X 400 Relay
Tamara Johnson	Outdoor	1999	8th – 4 X 100 Relay
Jennifer Jordan	Indoor	1995	3rd – 400m
		1997	6th – 4 X 400 Relay
	Outdoor	1995	7th – 4 X 400 Relay
		1996	5th – 4 X 400 Relay
		1997	6th – 4 X 400 Relay
		1998	2nd – 4 X 400 Relay
Nzingah Karmani	Outdoor	1999	8th – 4 X 100 Relay
Stacy Milligan	Indoor	1995	8th -- 400m
		1995	6th -- 4X400 Relay
	Outdoor	1994	4th – 4 X 100 Relay
		1995	7th – 4 X 400 Relay
		1996	5th – 4 X 400 Relay
Kristin Mulliner	Indoor	1991	4th – 4X800 Medley Relay
Natalie Nalepa	Cross Country	1990	*8th NCAA
		1991	5th NCAA
	Indoor	1991	7th – 3,000m
		1991	4th – 4X800 Medley Relay
	Outdoor	1991	3rd – 5,000m

Yulanda Nelson	Indoor	1997	6th – 4 X 400 Relay
		1999	2nd – 400m
	Outdoor	1998	2nd – 400m
			2nd – 4 X 400 Relay
		1999	5th – 400m
			8th – 4 X 100 Relay
			7th – 4 X 400 Relay
Barbara Petrahn	Indoor	1999	6th – 4 X 400 Relay
	Outdoor	1999	7th – 4 X 400 Relay
Melissa Roland	Indoor	1995	6th -- 4X400 Relay
		1997	6th – 4 X 400 Relay
	Outdoor	1994	6th – 4 X 400 Relay
		1995	7th – 4 X 400 Relay
		1996	5th – 4 X 400 Relay
		1997	6th – 4 X 400 Relay
Donna Smith	Outdoor	1994	4th – 4 X 100 Relay
		1994	6th – 4 X 400 Relay
Sherri Smith	Cross Country Championships	1998	20th
	Indoor	1999	8th – 5,000m
	Outdoor	1999	6th – 10,000m
Lisa Stone	Outdoor	1989	8th – 5,000m
		1990	2nd – 10,000m
		1991	3rd – 10,000m
Heather Van Dyke	Indoor	1991	4th – 4X800 Medley Relay

Table III: Women's All-American Track and Field, 1990–1999[8, 28]

28 Top 40 individual finishers are All-Americans

VOLLEYBALL

1993 VB team

Front: Tom Sonnichsen, Head Coach, Jenny DeLue, Erin
McElwain, Laura Welton, Heather Saari, D'Ann Arthur
Back: Brenda King, Brandi Cantrell, Cory Sivertson, Nicole DeNault, Amy
Green, Joanne Nielson, Asst. Coach, Sharon Pratt, Evelyn Tidwell, Trainer

Baylor University, Round Up 1994 Yearbook, (Waco, TX:[Baylor
University], 1994), The Texas Collection, Baylor University, p. 117.

Tom Sonnichsen became head coach of the volleyball team in 1989 and coached the women to three winning seasons in 1991, 1992, and 1993. He was named Coach of the Year in the Southwest Conference in 1991. The 1993 team appeared in the first NCAA-era post season tournament (NIVC) and defeated Butler University, Hartford University, Northern Iowa University, the University of Central Florida, and Oregon State University, before losing to Louisiana State University in the finals.

Both Mitch Casteel in the eighties and Sonnichsen in the early nineties produced winning teams and outstanding individual players in spite of their struggles for financial support in the way of scholarships, coaching staffs, and travel and recruiting budgets. Outstanding players who came through Baylor's system during this time were Corey Sivertson and D'Ann Arthur. Sivertson was named SWC Freshman of the Year in 1991, made the SWC second team as a sophomore, and was named three times to the Amercian Volleyball Coaches

Association All-Region team for the South/District V/Central region. D'Ann Arthur was named to the All-Conference (SWC) in 1995.[9]

Corey Sivertson

Baylor University, Round Up 1993 Yearbook, (Waco, TX:[Baylor University], 1993), The Texas Collection, Baylor University, p. 138.

Brian Hosfield became the first fulltime volleyball coach at Baylor University in 1996. He coached the team from 1996 to 2003, posting four winning seasons in 1996, and 1999 – 2001. Hosfield's 1999 team was the first Lady Bear team to play in the NCAA post-season tournament. Traveling to Penn State University, the team won their first round game but lost in the second round to Penn State University, 0-3. The 2001 team traveled to the NCAA post-season tournament in Fort Collins, CO. before losing to Colorado State 3-1 in the first round. Many other volleyball team members brought numerous honors to Baylor University during their playing years. Perhaps most notable are the academic honors they accumulated.[29]

---

29 These individuals and their honors can be found in the archived media guides for the Lady Bear Volleyball team on the Baylor Athletic Department website.

Brian Hosfeld, 1996–2003

Baylor University, Round Up 2003 Yearbook, (Waco, TX:[Baylor University], 2003), The Texas Collection, Baylor University, p. 119.

Traditionally, the women athletes at Baylor University have been outstanding students, truly epitomizing the student-athlete. Their honors for academic accomplishment are seen at the conference and national level. In the 1995 Athletic Department Self-Study, the observation was made that it was important to have a strong women's athletic program for a lot of reasons, none the least of which was the elevation of student-athlete grade point averages as well as the elevation of student-athlete graduation rates with the presence of the women's programs.

NOTES ON CHAPTER 10

WINNING TRADITIONS BEGIN: LADY BEARS, 1990–2012

1. "2012-2013 Women's Basketball Media Almanac," *Fourth Edition, Baylor Athletic Communications*, 89.

2. "2011-12 Baylor Women's Golf Media Almanac," *Third Edition, Baylor Athletic Communications*, 22.

3. "2011 Baylor Soccer Media Almanac," *Third Edition, Baylor Athletic communications*, 27.

4. Ibid.

5. 2013 Baylor Softball Media Almanac, *Fourth Edition, Baylor Athletic Communications*, 48.

6. "2011-12 Baylor Women's Tennis Media Almanac," *Third Edition, Baylor Athletic Communications*, 31.

7. "2011-12 Baylor Cross Country/Track and Field Media Almanac, *Third Edition, Baylor Athletic Communications*, 29.

8. "2011-12 Baylor Cross Country/Track and Field Media Almanac, *Third Edition, Baylor Athletic Communications*, 29.

9. "2010 Baylor Volleyball Media Almanac, *Baylor Athletic Communications*, 43.

CHAPTER 11

FINANCIAL CHAMPIONS FOR BAYLOR WOMEN'S ATHLETICS

As discussed in Chapter 9, it took a lot of champions to turn women's athletics in a winning direction at Baylor University. There were significant events and leadership champions that provided the right amount of pressure at the right time in the right places to start the money flowing to the athletic department, much of which went to the women's athletic teams. Once this began, the movement toward compliance with Title IX was fast and efficient. While it is impossible to put a date on when the University actually came into compliance with Title IX, an understanding of the requirements for Title IX compliance would suggest that the University was close, if not in compliance, in 2000. Many financial champions had stepped forward to kick start a long range plan for athletic facilities on the campus, i.e., donors to the Riverfront Complex.

Three things that provided support for Baylor's compliance were (1) the turnaround in winning seasons for the women's teams from 1995-2000, (2) the influx of money for the women's programs to conform to Title IX requirements, and (3) the evidence presented as a result of a second Title IX lawsuit against the University in 2003.

Per the Athletic Department Self-Study in 1995, a plan was in place so that all of the women's teams had the requisite number of scholarships and fulltime coaches allowed by the NCAA by 1999. Additionally, the women's program budgets had grown exponentially during this decade, in some cases at a faster pace than that of the men's. As well as requisite coaching staffs and scholarship allotments, the budgets for items such as recruiting, travel, and equipment had grown to satisfactory levels. There was support staff in place for the women's programs, including a sports information director for women, a fulltime female athletic trainer on the staff, a female conditioning coach, and an Assistant Athletic Director for Women. Additionally, two sports had been added to the women's athletic program – softball and soccer.

Nevertheless, in 2003 another Title IX lawsuit was filed against the University. Seven members of the women's crew team, a club sport at the time, alleged discrimination against the team because the University failed to recognize the team as a varsity sport. Obviously, these students, their families and financial supporters did not believe Baylor was in compliance with Title IX at this time. By the letter of the law, that might have been true. In 2003, Baylor needed to add a woman's sport by virtue of the proportionality rule of Title IX. However, I believe the key factor for Baylor at this time is that officials had a plan in place to stay in compliance with Title IX. As part of that plan, Baylor was conducting student body surveys on a regular basis to identify the sport interests of their females. According to a university spokesperson women's crew was not among those sports that surfaced in this survey.

The lawsuit was settled out of court. In response to the litigation, Baylor legal counsel, Charlie Beckenhauer, issued a statement that read:

> "I can state that Baylor University successfully closed an inquiry with the U.S. Department of Education in 1999, and accordingly, Baylor was indisputably in full compliance as late as the closure of that inquiry. Since that time Baylor has monitored the interests and abilities of the Baylor students. Even before the filing of this lawsuit, Baylor has been conscious of its obligations under Title IX and has been striving to maintain compliance"[1]

On September 8, 2003, Ian McCaw, the current athletic director at Baylor, began his work with the University. Under McCaw's leadership, athletic

A Legacy of Champions

programs at Baylor maintained their competitiveness through the 2012 season. One of McCaw's first endeavors was to launch a five-year strategic plan. Released in 2004, the plan contained strategies and plans in five goal areas:

Provide students with the highest quality academic, athletic, social and spiritual experience.

Achieve competitive success in every program.

Develop and maintain a strong Christian environment that promotes equity, sportsmanship, compliance, and diversity.

Enhance revenue streams and increase operating efficiencies in order to fund excellence.

Provide high quality leadership and management.[2]

An outgrowth of that plan was a $95 million development plan titled Victory with Integrity. This fundraising campaign dominated the efforts in the first decade of the twenty-first century to continue Baylor's tradition of excellence in athletics. Numerous new athletic facilities appeared on the campus as a result of this planning effort. The number of Baylor financial champions that made these dreams come true were numerous. Below are a few of the contributors that were identified with these projects. The author extends her apologies to anyone who may have been omitted in this discussion.

Ian McCaw's leadership philosophy, like Tom Stanton's, valued every program and every coach and endeavored to meet the needs of all of the teams in each budget cycle. The size and structure of the athletic department staff grew during this time as did the budget and fundraising efforts begun in the late nineties.

WILLIS EQUESTRIAN CENTER

In 2004, Ian McCaw announced that Women's Equestrian, would be added as the eighteenth athletic sport at Baylor University. Nancy Post, Senior Women's Administrator, confirmed that Baylor added this sport to meet both the interest of female students as well as the proportionality rule for Title IX compliance. Equestrian teams have very large rosters (+80 team members) and help the university offset the large number of football scholarship athletes. According to Post, the Athletic Department conducted its regularly scheduled interest survey to determine the best selection for this addition. Post indicated that the results of the interest survey played a large role in the decision. Knowing that women's equestrian was one of the fastest growing sports in the Big 12 and across the nation also played a role in the decision.[3] Additionally, this was Texas where young women grew up riding and participating in horsemanship contests at very early ages.

While there was a lot of excitement about adding this sport to the women's athletic program, there were no facilities on the campus, facilities that met the needs of the animals as well as the athletes and coaches. Fortunately for Baylor, newly hired equestrian coach, Ellen White, had developed the Willow Spring Equestrian Center. She had taught riding classes and coached equestrian athletes for twenty-five years before coming to Baylor. Her facility was home to Baylor Equestrian for two years. In April 2006 a tornado blew through Central Texas, destroying White's home and wiping out the Willow Creek Farm facility. Baylor equestrian had no home. All was not lost, however, as just a week prior to the weather event, the Board of Regents had approved the construction of the Willis Family Equestrian Center on the campus. Construction began quickly.

The Center was dedicated in October 2006. Funding was provided by Richard and Karen Willis, Baylor alumni with a long history of providing financial support to the University. Beginning in the eighties, the family began regular donations that have resulted in the establishment of need-based scholarship funds in the Hankamer School of Business, in Baylor Athletics specifically for the Equestrian team, in the School of Social Work, the School of Engineering and Computer Science, and the George W. Truett Seminary. The Willis' viewed their support of Baylor as "planting seeds" to help Baylor students make it through school and impact their world through the same spirit of philanthropy demonstrated by this family.[4] Pictures of this facility are available on the Baylor Athletic Department website, www.baylorbears.com.

The Center, a 45,000 square foot facility, was considered Phase I of a three-phase project. It specifically addressed the needs of the four-legged athletes that make up this team. The first phase of the project provided a covered riding arena with spectator seating, a Western arena with spectator seating, restroom facilities, and a paddock area for the horses.

Willis Equestrian Facility

Used with Permission, Baylor University Athletic Department, 2013

In November 2011 Baylor University announced funding for Phase II of the equestrian project. Baylor Regent Ken Carlile provided the financial gift to honor his wife, Celia, their daughter-in-laws, Regan and Leslie, their grand-daughter, Virginia, and the Baylor equestrian student-athletes. In similar fashion as the Willis family, the Carlisle family had made significant contributions to Baylor University over the years, extending support to such projects as the Carlile Geology research building, the Packard Lecture Hall in Physics, the Carlile Geology Renovation, the Student Life Center, and the Law School Capital Endowed Campaign.

The Carlile Equestrian Building is fully-equipped with meeting spaces, a training and treatment lockers, a locker room for student-athletes and administrative offices for the coaches. The facility opened in the fall 2012 and was dedicated in February 2013. With this dedication, the Baylor Equestrian team finally had a home for all of their athletes and their coaches.[5]

SOFTBALL

In 2001 Ted and Sue Getterman, Baylor alumna, provided a generous gift to Baylor University (the largest gift in history to Baylor women's athletics) to support the Jim and Julie Turner complex. With their generosity, the upgrades to the Ted and Sue Getterman Softball Stadium enabled Baylor University to have one of the premier softball facilities in the country. Like most donors to Baylor athletic projects, the Gettermans had demonstrated their generosity in numerous ways over the years, making financial contributions that supported scholarships, capital projects, academic areas and the arts.[6]

Additionally, in 2010 the Gettermans made another significant contribution to Baylor softball, providing funding for the Getterman Indoor Softball practice facility. Opened in October 2010, the facility enables the Baylor softball team to practice year-round in a comfortable and controlled-climate facility. Featured in the facility are a full-sized infield, six retractable batting cages, and two pitching stations on a realistic artificial playing surface.[7] For a better look at Baylor Women's Softball facilities, go to www.baylorbears.com and follow the link to Inside Athletics.

TENNIS

Jim Hawkins is a Baylor alumna. His wife, Nell, is an Alumna by Choice. Both are life-long donors to the University, contributing to academic and athletic scholarships as well as numerous other projects over the years. Speaking in 2011 after being honored with a Baylor Legacy Award, Hawkins commented:

> The thing that impresses me the most is that Baylor has become a world-class school, known for its athletics and academics. I am very excited to see what has happened, and the last 10 to 15 years seem to have been the most dramatic. With all the new facilities, and of course under the leadership of

(athletic director) Ian McCaw, I never
would have dreamed we'd be competing
at this level across the board. Baylor
is such a well-balanced school, and
it makes you want to give back.[8]

Hawkins Indoor Tennis Facility

Used with permission, Baylor University Athletic Department, 2013.

Hawkins and his wife had demonstrated their support for Baylor athletics with an earlier contribution to the Lt. Jack Whetsel basketball practice facility. Being able to see how this facility contributed to the development of the men and women's basketball teams, the couple made the decision to support the Baylor tennis program by making a major gift to support the Hawkins Indoor Tennis facility on the campus. Dedicated on January 25, 2013, the facility provides a year-round facility for both the men and women's tennis programs at Baylor. Built to competitive specifications, the facility features six courts and has spectator seating.[9]

SIMPSON ACADEMIC ATHLETIC CENTER

The Simpson Academic Athletic Center, built on the banks of the Brazos river and adjacent to the Riverfront Athletic complex, opened its doors in 2008. As part of the $34 million Highers Athletic Complex, the academic center was funded by Baylor alumna, Bob Simpson, a 1970 magna cum laude graduate from the Hankamer Business School. Simpson also earned an MBA from Baylor in 1971. This extraordinary building was 93,000 square feet in size and featured two stories. The first story housed the main athletic training room, a weight room, and the football coaches' offices. The second floor of the building housed the athletic administration suite and an academic center for all student-athletes that is second to none in the Big 12 Conference if not the nation. Contained within this center are twenty-two individual tutoring rooms, a computer lab, a learning center, and two classrooms. The center also contains offices for the staff providing tutoring and learning support for the athletes. This center is a land-mark structure on the campus not only for its beauty but also for the statement it makes that Baylor wants its athletes to be successful in the classroom as well as on the field or court. Up to this point, Baylor had led the Big 12 in gradua-tion rates four times and had a graduation rate of 85%. Representatives at Baylor believed that the addition of the Simpson Academic facility would continue to strengthen that legacy of academic excellence. [10]

OTHER FACILITIES

The funding for the Turner Riverfront Complex in the mid-nineties, started a firestorm of funding streaming into the university for Baylor athletic facilities, both men and women's. Tom Stanton's notion that donors to Baylor would be interested in supporting athletics as well as academics was demonstrated over and over after the turn of the century. Ian McCaw was able to capitalize on this notion with the successful implementation of the $95 million dollar develop-ment campaign after he arrived at Baylor. Additional upgrades to the Ferrell Center, including the Lt. Jack Whetsel Basketball practice facility and the Gray's Gym complex occurred as a result of McCaw's Vision with Integrity plan.

Between 1996 and 2013, hundreds of millions of dollars were dedicated to athletic facility development at Baylor University. Credit should be given to Tom Stanton and Robert Sloan for planning and envisioning many of these facil-ity projects. Credit should be given to the Baylor Regents who bought Stanton's idea of building on the installment plan to finance the facilities. And credit should be given to the current Baylor Athletic Administrative team for capitaliz-ing on this momentum. Resultantly, Baylor now has some of the best and most impressive athletic facilities in the nation for both men and women's programs.

The accomplishments of Baylor women's athletic programs since the beginning of the twenty-first century have produced many champions on the court and in the field. However, the accomplishments of the financial champions for Baylor University women's athletic programs cannot be understated. The facilities that they have put in place are second to none in this country. Not surprisingly, most are Baylor alumni, and their love for both athletics and their university is unmatched. One of the important cornerstones of a successful athletic program is its ability to attract the best athletes to the University. Surely, the facilities provided by these champions for women athletics are a crucial part of that cornerstone at Baylor University.

NOTES ON CHAPTER 11

FINANCIAL CHAMPIONS FOR BAYLOR WOMEN'S ATHLETICs

1. Lori Scott-Fogelman, "Baylor University Releases Statements on Title IX Lawsuit," *Baylor University Media Communications,* March 17, 2004.

2. "Baylor University Athletic Department Five-Year Strategic Plan: Above and Beyond." *Baylor University Athletic Department,* September 15, 2004, Executive Summary..

3. Post, Nancy, interview by the author, Baylor University, June 25, 2012.

4. Baylor University. The President's Scholarship Initiative. Richard and Karen Willis, http://www.baylor.edu/development/scholarships/index.php?id=7718. Accessed May 22, 2013.

5. "Baylor Announces Lead Gift for Carlile Equestrian Building." *Baylor University Media Communications,* November 22, 2011. *http://www.baylor.edu/mediacommunications/news. php?action=story&story=104837.* Accessed May 22, 2013.

6. "Getterman Stadium Indoor Softball Facility Dedication." 254sports.com. http://www.kwtx.com/_254sports/home/headlines/Getterman_Stadium_Indoor_Softball_Facility_Dedication_104521024.html#.UZ5E-oKxPq0, October 7, 2010. Accessed May 22, 2013.

7. Ibid.

8. "2011–12 Baylor University Meritorious Achievement Awards." *Baylor Magazine,* Fall 2011, http://www.baylor.edu/alumni/

magazine/1001/news.php?action=story&story=101319. Accessed May 22, 2013.

9. Ibid.

10. "Baylor University Athletic Department Five-Year Strategic Plan: Above and Beyond." *Baylor University Athletic Department,* September 15, 2004, Executive Summary.

CHAPTER 12

DON'T LOOK BACK: LADY BEARS, 2000-2012

Starting with the 21st century and continuing through 2012, the Baylor women's athletic teams extended their winning ways begun in the 1990s. Indeed, they have not looked back.

BASKETBALL

Women's basketball has garnered the most publicity because of their enormous success under Coach Kim Mulkey. Amassing a won-lost record at Baylor of 164-52, Mulkey led the Lady Bears to twelve winning seasons, three Big 12 Conference titles, and two NCAA Basketball championships between 2000-2012. Along the way they made twelve post-season appearances in the NCAA tournament and one appearance in the Women's National Invitational Tournament.

The 2011-2012 team broke the single season record for wins for any men or women's basketball team in the history of the NCAA. Their 40-0 season came, appropriately enough, during the fortieth anniversary year of the signing of the Education Amendments Act of 1972, Title IX.

2012 Lady Bears, NCAA Division I Champions

Used with Permission, Baylor University Athletic Department, 2013

Under Mulkey's tutelage, three Baylor players were named first team All Americans on nine separate occasions, and nine players were given Honorable Mention on All American teams. A standout player for Mulkey's on her 2005 National Championship team was Sophia Young. Young ranked second in scoring among all Baylor players with a career total of 2,480 points. Young also went on to play in the Women's National Basketball Association (WNBA). A teammate to Young on the 2005 National Championship team was Angela Tisdale, also an All-American. Two additional standout players in Mulkey's first years at Baylor were Steffanie Blackmon and Sheila Lambert. All three players were selected to the Associated Press (AP) All-American team during their Baylor careers, and all three went on to play in the WNBA after graduation. Through the years, numerous other Lady Bears have garnered post-season honors within the Big 12 conference. Information on all of these outstanding athletes can be found at the Baylor University Athletic Department website: www.baylorathletics.com in the media section. Most recently Odyssey Sims was named to the AP All-American second team in 2012 and to the USA team in the 2013 World University Games.[30]

---

30 Baylor Basketball media guides provide additional information on all of Mulkey's players and teams.

Steffanie Blackmon – 2001-2005

State Farm/WBCA honorable mention All-American, 2005 AP All-American (3rd team), and first team All Big 12 selection, 2004 and 2005

Baylor University, The Round-Up 2003 Yearbook, (Waco, TX: [Baylor University], 2003), The Texas Collection, Baylor University, p. 127.

Angela Tisdale

Three-time All Big 12 selection, 2008 AP and WBCA All-American (honorable mention)

2005-2006 Baylor Women's Basketball Media Guide, p. 38.

Sheila Lambert

2001 Big 12 Newcomer of the Year, 2002 Frances Pomeroy
Naismith Award winner, and 2002 WBCA All-American

Baylor University, The Round-Up 2001 Yearbook, (Waco, TX: [Taylor
Publishing Company], 2001), The Texas Collection, Baylor University, p. 249.

Sophia Young

2002-2006, two-time WBCA and AP All-American, No. 6 overall
pick in the WNBA Draft (San Antonio Silver Stars, 2006)

Baylor University, The Round-Up 2005 Yearbook, (Waco, TX: [Baylor
University], 2005), The Texas Collection, Baylor University, p. 115.

Mulkey herself has garnered numerous individual awards including twice being named Big 12 Coach of the Year. After the 2000 season, Mulkey was named National Coach of the Year by Real Sports magazine. She received the prestigious New York Athletic Club's Winged Foot award in 2005. In 2012 Mulkey swept all Coach of the Year awards, winning the Women's Basketball Coaches Association, United States Basketball Writers Association, Associated Press, Naismith, and Big 12. Mulkey is the Big 12's winningest coach in both victories—338— and percentage—.811.[1]

**Kim Mulkey, Coach Baylor University
Lady Bear Basketball Team**

Baylor University, The Round-Up 2009 Yearbook, (Waco, TX: [Baylor University], 2009), The Texas Collection, Baylor University, p. 137.

Brittney Griner, the most decorated women's basketball player in the history of Baylor University, began her career as a Lady Bear in the fall 2009. In her four years at Baylor, she has electrified fans with her incredible ability to score, block shots, rebound the ball, and get up and down the court on a fast break. While a book could be written about her illustrious career at Baylor University, the two-time All-American was the first player (man or woman) in the history of the NCAA to score 2000 points and block 500 shots. At the beginning of the 2012-13 season, she had career marks of 2,425 point, 966 rebounds, and 608 blocked shots.[2] In 2012 she was named the AP National Player of the Year. With her leadership the Lady Bears won the NCAA National Championship in 2012.

Brittney Griner

2012 Wade Trophy, Naismith Trophy, and Wooden Award; 2012 AP Player of the Year; 2012 Ann Meyers Drysdale (USWBA) Player of the Year, 2012 Unanimous AP All-American

Baylor University, Round Up 2011 Yearbook, (Waco, TX:[Baylor University], 2011), The Texas Collection, Baylor University.

Mulkey's teams have ranked in the top 25 in average season attendance and set a new single season attendance record in 2009-10, recording 122,500 fans in attendance over seventeen games.[3] Mulkey and her team have captured the hearts of Waco fans, and their following gets bigger every year. Women's basketball at Baylor University will never be the same, but it's harder to imagine how it could be any better.

EQUESTRIAN

The women's Equestrian team competes in two classifications: Hunter Seat and Western. Within the Hunter Seat competition, five athletes compete in Fences and five athletes compete in Flat. In the Western competition, five athletes compete in Horsemanship and five athletes compete in Reining. Each rider is scored by a panel of judges. The cumulative scores in all categories determine the winner of the competition.

Samantha Schaefer

2012 Most Valuable Rider Over Fences
Anchored a strong Baylor team

Used with permission, Baylor University Athletic Department, 2013

Baylor's first competed in equestrian events in 2005, posting a winning season record in 2009, 2010, and 2011. The entire team, Western and Hunter Seat, combined to win their first Big 12 Championship in 2010. In 2012 with strong rides from all team members. the Hunter Seat team defeated Texas A&M for the National Championship of the National Collegiate Equestrian Association. In that competition, Sam Schaefer anchored the team posting a 173 for her final ride to defeat the Aggies. Schaefer received the prestigious "Most Valuable Rider Over Fences" award for the competition. This award is given by the panel of judges for the event.[4] Under the tutelage of internationally renowned dressage coach, Ellen White, the team is expected to compete well as more teams are added in the Big 12 and nationwide.

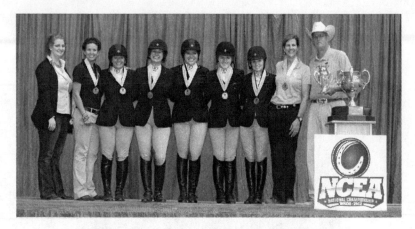

2012 Hunter Seat National Champions

*Second from left, Stacy Sanderson, Assistant Coach, AshleyAnn
McGehee, Lisa Goldman, Kim Woodsum, Samantha
Schaefer, Taylor Brown, Ellen White, Head Coach.*

Used with Permission, Baylor University Athletic Department 2013

GOLF

2004 Women's Golf Team

*19th place finish, NCAA National Championships
Josefin Svenningsson, Meredith Jones, Meg McDaniel, Sherry
Summers, Stephanie Waters, Anna Rehnholm, Sian Reddick*

Used with Permission, Baylor University Athletic Department April 2013

Sylvia Ferdon took the reins of the Baylor Women's Golf team in 1996 and and led the team through the spring 2011. While her teams garnered no Big 12 championships, they averaged an 8th place finish over her twelve-year career, finishing in fourth place in 2001, third in 2005 and 2007.

Sylvia Ferdon, Women's Golf Coach 1996-2011

1999-2000 Media guide, Baylor Women's Golf, p. 2.

Ferdon's teams made eleven NCAA regional appearances and reached the NCAA championships in 2004 where they tied for 19th in the nation.

Melanie Hagewood was an outstanding player for Ferdon in 2001 and 2002, becoming the first Baylor women's golfer and one of six individuals chosen to play in the NCAA Finals in Lansing, Michigan in 2002. Hagewood received the 2001 LPGA Dinah Shore Award recognizing her outstanding achievements in academics, leadership, community service and golf.[5]

Melanie Hagewood 2000-2003

First BU Golfer to compete in an NCAA Championship;
First BU Golfer to Earn Academic All American honors;
2001 LPGA Dinah Shore Award Winner[4]

Baylor University, Round Up 2003 Yearbook, (Waco, TX:[Baylor University], 2003), The Texas Collection, Baylor University, p. 135.

Jay Goble became the head coach of the Women's Golf team in the Fall 2011. Goble was hired away from his assistant coaching position at the University of Florida. In his first season at Baylor, the team finished third in the Big 12, placed fifth in the NCAA West Regional, and advanced to the NCAA championships for the second time in program history. The team finished tied for sixteenth in the nation with Texas A & M University. Freshman Hayley Davis received All-American honors from the National Golf Coaches Association and Golfweek. She was the first Baylor woman golfer ever to be named to an All-American team.

Hayley Davis

2012 All American

Used with permission, Baylor University Athletic Department, 2013

SOCCER

Marci Jobson inherited a losing situation when she took over the Women's Soccer program in 2008. The women had not had a winning season since 2000 and had placed no higher than seventh in the Big 12 standings since 2001. Jobson began to turn the program around, posting winning seasons in 2009, 2010, 2011 and 2012. The 2011 team placed third in the Big 12 Conference and made its first NCAA post-season appearance since 1999, beating Texas State 3-0 in the first round.[6] They lost in the second round and finished the season with a 15-4-3 record.[7]

2012 Soccer Team - Big 12 Champions

#11 in 2012 NSCAA/Continental Tire Postseason Rankings;
NSCAA Team Academic Award winner

Used with permission, Baylor University Athletic Department, 2013

Capitalizing on this momentum, the 2012 team turned in its best season in the history of the program, winning the Big 12 Championship and finishing with a 19-1-5 record, losing to North Carolina in the third round of the NCAA tournament after three overtimes.[8] Baylor finished the season ranked #11 in the nation, the highest ranking for any Big 12 team. Dana Larsen was named the 2012 Big 12 Soccer Scholar-Athlete of the Year and the 2012 Capitol One Academic All-American of the Year for women's soccer, posting a perfect 4.0 grade point average. The team as well as several individual players garnered academic post-season honors. Larsen also became only the third Baylor soccer athlete named to the NSCAA All-America team in the history of the program.[9, 10] Soccer was back at Baylor University, the winning had begun again.

Dana Larsen

2012 NSCAA All-American

Baylor University, Round Up 2011 Yearbook, (Waco, TX:[Baylor University], 2011), The Texas Collection, Baylor University, p..

SOFTBALL

Coach Glenn Moore took the helm of the Lady Bear Softball team in June 2000 and led them to twelve consecutive winning seasons. While no Big 12 Championships were garnered, the team made strong showings in the Conference play and had seven NCAA Tournament appearances. Moore has coached nine National Fastpitch Coaches Association All-Americans.

Glenn Moore, 2000–present

Baylor University, Round Up 2011 Yearbook, (Waco, TX:[Baylor University], 2011), The Texas Collection, Baylor University, p. 163.

The 2007 and 2011 teams appeared in the Women's College World Series, making it through regional and super regional play to the top eight teams in the country.

Whitney Canion

2011 Second Team All American;
2011 WCWS All Tournament Team

Baylor University, Round Up 2011 Yearbook, (Waco, TX:[Baylor University], 2011), The Texas Collection, Baylor University, p. 165.

The 2011 team played in the WCWS semifinals and ended their season ranked fourth in the nation. This was the highest national ranking for any Baylor softball team in its history. Baylor placed two women on the 2011 WCWS All-Tournament team, Whitney Canion and Holly Holl. In addition to numerous Big 12 honors, Whitney Canion was named to the 2011 NFCA All-America second team.

Canion arrived at Baylor in 2009 but dealt with a shoulder injury and an anterior cruciate ligament team in 2010 earning a medical hardship waiver. Her 2011 year was her first year back from her injuries, and she performed well for the Bears, leading the team to an appearance in the Women's College World Series and their fourth placed ranking.

Additionally, Dani Leal, Whitney Canion and Kathy Shelton also received 2011 All-Region honors. Numerous other players over the years and in 2011 have garnered post-season academic awards.[11] The 2012 team earned an at-large bid to the NCAA championships but were eliminated by Stanford in their third game of regional play.

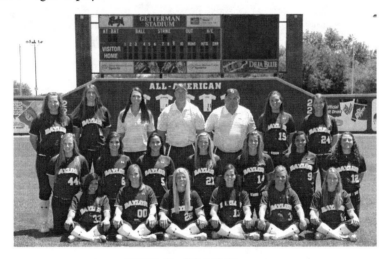

2011 Softball Team

WCWS qualifier; 4th in the nation final ranking

Used with permission, Baylor University Athletic Department, 2013

TENNIS

By the end of the nineties, Dave Luedtke had begun to turn the women's tennis program in a winning direction. Coaching the team through the 2002 season, he led the team to winning seasons 2000-2002 and NCAA Tournament appearances in 2000 and 2001. The 2002 team entered post-season play in the National Indoor Championships.

2003 Women's Tennis Team

First Baylor Tennis Team to Win a Big 12 Tournament Championship
Front: Asst. Coach, Cintia Tortorella, Vida Mulee, Zuzana Krchnakova,
Head Coach, Joey Scrivano
Back: Alison Bradley, Daria Potopova, Barbora Blahuitakova,
Stephanie Balzert, Izabela Mijic

2005 Women's Tennis Media Guide, P. 43.

Luedtke retired and Joey Scrivano replaced him for the 2003 season. Between 2003 and 2012, Scrivano's teams racked up eight regular season Big 12 championships and six Big 12 tournament championships. The team had five NCAA Elite Eight appearances, and two NCAA Final Four appearances. Scrivano coached Zuzana Zemenova to victory in the NCAA Singles Championship in 2005. Zemenova was the first unseeded player in NCAA history to win a national championship, and she did that as a freshman. In so doing she became the only Big 12 women's tennis player to win an individual national title. Among her honors were Big 12 Freshman of the Year, All Big 12 Selection and Big 12 Champion in singles. She was also named the Southwest

Region's Rookie of the Year. In 2006 she received her second consecutive All American ranking from the Intercollegiate Tennis Association (ITA). She reached the NCAA tournament round of 16 before losing to eventual singles' champion, California's Suzie Babos.[12]

Zuzana Zemenova

2005 NCAA Singles Champion,
Big 12 Player of the Year, Big 12 Freshman of the Year

2006 Women's Tennis, p. 15.

Twenty-one Lady Bears have earned All-American honors under Scrivano. Along the way, Scrivano became the most decorated tennis coach in Baylor history garnering Big 12 Coach of the Year honors three times, ITA Texas Region Coach of the Year twice, and TTCA Coach of the Year in 2005. Dominating is the only word that could describe the Lady Bear Tennis team under Scrivano, posting a 75-2 match record against Big 12 opponents 2009 – 2011, and an overall fifty-seven match win streak during his tenure. In 2012 Scrivano's career match record at Baylor was 218-56.[13]

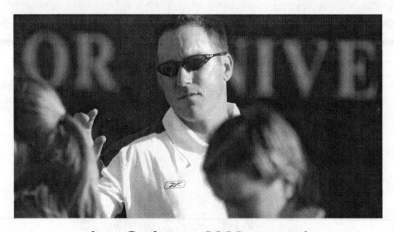

Joey Scrivano, 2003–present

Baylor University Photo Archive, CB 0458, March 13, 2006

TRACK AND FIELD

One could write an entire book about the accomplishments of the Baylor Women tracksters during the first decade of he twenty-first century. For sure, they continued their winning ways, racking up so many individual honors and awards it is impossible to mention all of them here. A few of the standouts are mentioned below, and more information can be found on the Baylor University Athletic Department website: www.baylorbears.com.

The Women's Cross Country Team built a solid winning tradition in the decade of the nineties, and that tradition continued into the twenty-first century. While the team has not won a Big 12 championship, they have consistently placed in the top 10 every year and finished in second place in 2003 and 2008. [14]

Between 2000 and 2011, the Baylor Women's Indoor Track team finished in the top five at the Big 12 Conference meet five times. Their best finish was third place in 2005. Numerous individuals have won Big 12 event titles during this period. Some of those who went on to gain All-American honors are mentioned below.

Erin Bedell, a distance specialist, made outstanding contributions to the Cross Country, Indoor and Outdoor teams during her tenure at Baylor but especially in her junior and senior years, 2008 and 2009. Erin racked up

All-American honors in 2007 Cross Country, finishing 37th overall in the finals. During the indoor and outdoor seasons, Erin competed in the 3,000-meter and the women's 3,000-meter steeplechase in 2008. Erin anchored both the Distance Medley Relay team and anchored the 4 x 1600 meter relay team, both of which won several championships during her career. She was a three-time All-American honoree between 2006 and 2009 and was the Big 12 outdoor 1500-meter champion in 2009, clocking a time of 4.22.03. [15]

In the 2012 Big 12 Indoor Conference Championships, senior Tiffany McReynolds, Baylor sprinter, successfully defended her championship in the 60-meter hurdles and added to her point total with a third place finish in the 60 meter dash. She went on to place fourth in the NCAA 60 meter hurdles, gaining All-American honors for that accomplishment. These two performances duplicated her accomplishments from 2011 when she also won the Big 12 Outdoor 100-meter hurdle event. Tiffani was named to the Academic All-Big 12 (1st team) in 2012 and was a four time Big 12 Commissioner's Honor Roll selection. Only five feet in height, Tiffani was a giant on the track and in the 60-meter hurdles event.[16]

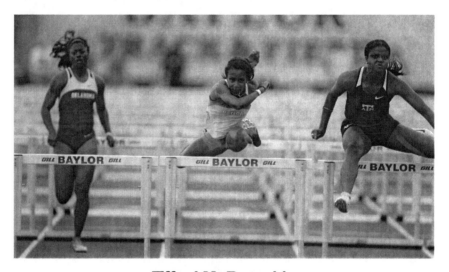

Tiffani McReynolds

All-American
2012 NCAA Indoor 60 meter hurdles, 4th place finish

Used with permission, Baylor University Athletic Department, 2013

Tiffany Townsend, 2008-2010, was also a sprinter for the Lady Bears and made her presence known whenever the 100-meter and 200-meter races were held. Townsend racked up thirteen All-American performances during her Baylor career running the 100-meter and 200-meter in both the indoor and outdoor seasons as well as the 4 x 100–meter relay and the 4 x 400-meter relay teams. Townsend was also the on the winning relay team in the International Amateur Athletic Federation World Junior Championships.[17]

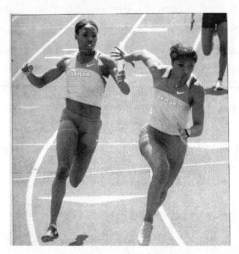

Tiffany Townsend

2008-2011, 5-time NCAA All American 100 and 200 meters

2008-2009 Cross Country/Track and Field, p. 10

Skylar White throws things really well. Specifically, she throws the discus and shot put really well. In her Baylor career she won the shot put and discus events at numerous meets in the state and across the country. She was a two-time Outdoor and Indoor All-American in the discus (2011–2012) and a three-time All-American in the shot put (2011–2012). She was named to several All-Big 12 teams and holds the Baylor school records in the indoor and outdoor shot put and the indoor and outdoor discus. Skylar was a two-time Big 12 Commissioner's Honor Roll selection.[18]

Baylor's 2012 Indoor team placed fourth overall in the Big 12 Conference championship. Fourteen Baylor women managed twenty-one all-conference performances. The team racked up several third, fourth, and fifth place finishes, and placed fourth overall for the championship.[19]

Skylar White

5-Time All American, Shot Put and Discus

Used with permission, Baylor University Athletic Department, 2013.

Women's Outdoor Track continued their strong winning record at the turn of the century, finishing in the top five at the Big 12 Outdoor Championships seven times between 2000 and 2011. The team made thirteen straight NCAA appearances between 2000 and 2012, with its best overall finish coming with a tenth place finish in 2009. There were no NCAA individual or relay team championships during this time but twenty Baylor women earned All-American honors in multiple events during this time period.[20]

April Holiness

*2004 NCAA Midwest Regional Outdoor Long Jump Champion;
5-time All-American Long Jump*

*Baylor University, Round Up 2005 Yearbook, (Waco, TX:[Baylor
University], 2005), The Texas Collection, Baylor University, p. 135.*

VOLLEYBALL

Rebuilding was a good way to describe the Baylor Women's Volleyball during
this decade. Having experienced some coaching stability from the late 1990's
to 2003, the team experienced winning seasons in 1999 and 2001 as well as
NCAA Tournament appearances in those two years. Jim Barnes inherited the
program in December 2003. The team experienced five consecutive winning
seasons, 2004-2008 and posted an overall 155-133 record since Barnes became
coach. Barnes led the team to NCAA Tournament appearances in 2009 and
2011, making it all the way to the sweet sixteen in 2009. Along the way several
Lady Bears have garnered post-season Big 12 athletic and academic honors.
Taylor Barnes and Anna Breyfogle, 2009, became the first Lady Bears to earn
All-American honors in volleyball, both receiving honorable mention on the
American Volleyball Coaches Association (AVCA) 2009 All-America team. In
her junior and senior year, Taylor Barnes broke the Big 12 and Baylor career
record for assists racking up 5,120 during her playing days. More of an offensive
specialist, Barnes was named to the AVCA All-Central Region team in 2008

and 2009 as well as the All-Big 12 First Team in both of those years. Breyfogle showed off her defensive prowess in 2009, and for her efforts was named the Big 12 Defensive Player of the Year in 2009. She also was named to the All-Big 12 First Team in 2008 and 2009 as well as the Academic All-Big 12 team in 2008.

Jim Barnes steadily built the volleyball program, and in 2012 experienced his fifth straight winning season.[21]

Taylor Barnes and Anna Breyfogle on the Block

2009 AVCA All-Americans Honorable Mention

Baylor University, Round Up 2008 Yearbook, (Waco, TX:[Baylor University], 2008), The Texas Collection, Baylor University, p. 109.

ACROBATICS AND TUMBLING – THE NEWEST SPORT FOR WOMEN

2011 Acrobatics and Tumbling Team

Used with Permission, Baylor University Athletic Department, April 2013.

In 2009 Baylor needed another women's sport to again meet the proportionality rule required by Title IX. Resultantly, in July 2009 the Baylor Regents voted to add an eleventh sport to the women's athletic program. Competitive cheer/ acrobatics and tumbling was the recommendation of the athletic department after an overwhelming response to a campus survey conducted earlier in the year. The addition of this sport put Baylor on the map as the only Big 12 school to offer a team in this area and only one of three Bowl Championship Series schools (Baylor, University of Oregon and University of Maryland) to have this program. In presenting the recommendation to the Board, Athletic Director, Ian McCaw indicated that Baylor and its students would be well-served in adding the program because of the strong potential for feeder programs in Texas high schools. In an interview with Nancy Post, Senior Women's Athletic director at Baylor, she acknowledged that competitive cheer/athletics and tumbling was not a sport recognized by the NCAA but that a great deal of support was in place nationally for this to become a reality in the future. Since Title IX compliance does not require that the sports offered at a university be recognized by the NCAA, the addition of Competitive Cheer strengthened Baylor's Title IX compliance status, currently ranked fourth in the Big 12 conference behind Texas A & M, the University of Kansas and Iowa State University.[22]

At the time of its addition to the Baylor program, Competitive Cheer had no competitive structure under which the few existing teams in the country could compete. In January 2010, representatives from the University of Oregon, University of Maryland, Baylor University, Quinnipiac University, Fairmont University, Azusa Pacific, Fort Valley State, and Ohio State University met and formed the National Competitive Stunts and Tumbling Association to serve as both the governing body and coaches association for the sport. One of the first acts of the new organization was to structure its events. Individuals would compete in four individual events and on team event.

According to Deborah Yow, University of Maryland Athletics Director, "competitive cheer is a passion for young women across our nation."[23] Mike Belotti echoed this sentiment by stating "Creating this sport at the varsity collegiate level has always been about meeting the interests and needs of hundreds of thousands of young women that participate in the sport nationally at the high school and club levels."[24] Belotti indicated he believed the sport had tremendous potential for growth.

The inaugural season was held in 2009 with the first national championships being held at the University of Georgia. The University of Maryland won that meet. The second national competition was held at the University of Oregon in 2010 where the Baylor team, competing for the first time and seeded fourth, defeated Fairmont State in the quarterfinals but lost to Oregon in the semifinals of that meet. Oregon won that national championship.

In its inaugural season, the Baylor team had fifty-one athletes on its roster and was coached by Karry Forsythe who came to Baylor from Blinn College in Houston. Forsythe led that team to six national appearances in the National Cheerleaders Association Collegiate Cheer and Dance Championships, finishing second in 2009. The team practiced in Marrs McLean Gym on the campus and hosted meets in the Ferrell Special Events Center.

In 2011 the organizing schools officially adopted the name of the National Acrobatics and Tumbling Association (NCATA). Baylor's team made steady improvement from its inaugural season in 2009 and in 2012 placed second in nationals, losing for the second time to the University of Oregon.[25]

THE YEAR OF THE BEAR

The academic year 2011-2012 came to be known in the media as the Year of the Bear because of the incredible success of all of the athletic programs at Baylor University. Indeed all nineteen sports advanced their teams to post-season play. The women's teams won two national championships – one in basketball and one in Hunter Seat. Brittney Griner was the National Player of the Year in women's basketball and Coach Kim Mulkey was named the National Coach of the Year.

The Baylor softball team made it all the way to the Women's College World Series and finished its season ranked fourth in the nation.

The golf team advanced to the NCAA championships and finished tied for 16th in the nation out of the twenty-four schools represented in the tournament.

The women's soccer team won the Big 12 and advanced to the second round of the NCAA tournament for the first time in school history.

The tennis team qualified both singles and doubles to the NCAA Final Four and finished ranked 6th in the nation.

The 2011 volleyball team advanced to the NCAA post-season tournament, and the 2012 team completed its second twenty-win season in program history.

The acrobatics and tumbling team, competing in only its second season, advanced to the national quarterfinals.

The women's Indoor track team qualified three athletes to the NCAA Indoor meet, all three gained All-American honors, and earned the team a tenth place finish nationally.

The Women's Outdoor Track and Field team finished fifth at the Big 12 Conference meet and qualified five athletes to the NCAA championships.

Perhaps Marci Jobson, soccer coach, summed it best in 2012 when she said "This season isn't the end of something special, it's the beginning. We just have to keep getting better every single day and continue the hard work."[26] My guess is this has been and is the mantra for all of the women's teams and coaches at Baylor University.

From humble beginnings in 1904 to the undefeated National Championship Lady Bear Basketball Team of 2012, Baylor University has always had women's athletic champions, and champions that support women's athletics. Baylor's athletic house was built on a strong foundation of love for athletics, determination to succeed, leadership excellence, and pride in the Bear tradition. Fans of Baylor women's athletic teams can rest assured that Baylor will always have women's athletic champions. The house continues to get stronger and bigger, brick by brick, day by day, year by year.[31]

Sic 'Em, Bears!

NOTES ON CHAPTER 12

DON'T LOOK BACK: LADY BEARS, 2000-2012

1. "Kim Mulkey", *Baylorbears.com,* Accessed May 22, 2013, http://www.baylorbears.com/sports/w-baskbl/mtt/mulkey_kim01.html

2. "2012-13 Baylor Women's Basketball Media Almanac," Fourth Edition, Baylor Athletic Communications, http://grfx.cstv.com/photos/schools/bay/sports/w-

3. "2010-2011 Baylor Women's Basketball Media Almanac," *Baylor Athletic Communications,* http://grfx.cstv.com/photos/schools/bay/sports/w-baskbl/auto_pdf/1011-ma-full.pdf, accessed May 8, 2013, 38.

4. "Hunter Seat Takes Down Aggies For National Title," *Baylor Women's Equestrian Archive,* http://www.baylorbears.com/sports/w-equest/recaps/041412aae.html, April 14, 2012.

5. "2012-13 Baylor Women's Golf Media Almanac, *Fourth Edition, Baylor Athletic Communications,* http://grfx.cstv.com/photos/schools/bay/sports/w-golf/auto_pdf/2012-13/misc_non_event/12-13MediaAlmanac.pdf, Accessed May 8, 2013, 22.

6. "History in the Making: Soccer Wins 3-0," *Baylor Women's Soccer Archive,* http://www.baylorbears.com/sports/w-soccer/recaps/111211aaa.html, November 12, 2011.

7. "Soccer Ends Historic Season with 5-0 Loss," *Baylor Women's Soccer Archive,* http://www.baylorbears.com/sports/w-soccer/recaps/111811aaa.html, November 18, 2011.

8. "Soccer Ends Historic Season with 1-1 Draw vs. UNC," *Baylor Women's Soccer Archive*, http://www.baylorbears.com/sports/w-soccer/recaps/111812aab.html, November 18, 2012.

9. "Larsen Named Big 12 Soccer Scholar-Athlete of the Year," Press Release, *Baylor Athletic Communications*, http://www.baylorbears.com/sports/w-soccer/spec-rel/120712aaa.html, December 7, 2012.

10. "Larsen Adds NSCAA Scholar All-America Honor," Press Release, *Baylor Athletic Communications*, http://www.baylorbears.com/sports/w-soccer/spec-rel/121712aab.html, December 17, 2012.

11. "2013 Baylor Softball Media Almanac," *Fourth Edition, Baylor Athletic Communications, http://grfx.cstv.com/photos/schools/bay/sports/w-softbl/auto_pdf/2012-13/misc_non_event/13-media-almanac.pdf, 24, 48.*

12. College Tennis Online, "Zuzana Zemenova's profile," http://www.collegetennisonline.com/BaylorUniversity-W-Tennis/Player.aspx?plId=43724, Accessed May 21, 2013.

13. "2012-13 Baylor Women's Tennis Media Almanac," *Fourth Edition, Baylor Athletic Communications,* http://grfx.cstv.com/photos/schools/bay/sports/w-tennis/auto_pdf/2012-13/misc_non_event/12-13-wt-almanac.pdf, *13, 32.*

14. "2011-12 Baylor Cross Country/Track and Field Media Almanac," *Third Edition, Baylor Athletic Communications,* http://grfx.cstv.com/photos/schools/bay/sports/c-track/auto_pdf/2011-12/misc_non_event/12-TF-Almanac.pdf, 29.

15. Cross Country, Erin Bedell Profile, http://www.baylorbears.com/sports/c-xc/mtt/bedell_erin00.html, Accessed May 22, 2013.

16. Track and Field, Tiffani McReynolds Profile, http://www.baylorbears.com/sports/c-track/mtt/tiffani_mcreynolds_734663.html, Accessed May 22, 2013.

17. Track and Field, Tiffany Townsend Profile, http://www.baylorbears.com/sports/c-track/mtt/townsend_tiffany00.html, Accessed May 22, 2013.

18. Track and Field, Skylar White Profile, http://www.baylorbears.com/sports/c-track/mtt/skylar_white_511086.html, Accessed May 22, 2013.

19. "TF Women 4th, Men 5th at Big 12 Indoors," Press Release, *Baylor Athletic Communications*, http://www.baylorbears.com/sports/c-track/recaps/022512aad.html, January 25, 2012.

20. "2011-12 Baylor Track and Field/Cross Country Media Almanac," *Third Edition, Baylor Athletic Communications*, 29.

21. "2011 Baylor Volleyball Media Almanac," *Third Edition, Baylor Athletic Communications*, http://grfx.cstv.com/photos/schools/bay/sports/w-volley/auto_pdf/2011-12/misc_non_event/11-ma-full.pdf, 22.

22. "Competitive Cheer to Become 19th Sports Team," Press Release, *Baylor Athletic Communications*, http://www.baylorbears.com/sports/comp-cheer/spec-rel/012010aaa.html, July 24, 2009.

23. "Universities Form Stunts and Tumbling Association," *Press Release, Baylor Athletic Communications*, http://www.baylorbears.com/sports/comp-cheer/spec-rel/012810aab.html, January 28, 2010.

24. See note 22 above.

25. "Bears eliminated in semifinals after dropping all six events," *Press Release, Baylor Athletic Communications*, http://www.baylorbears.com/sports/w-acro/recaps/042812aab.html, April 27, 2012.

26. "2012 Baylor Soccer Media Almanac," *Fourth Edition, Baylor Athletic Communications,* http://grfx.cstv.com/photos/schools/bay/sports/w-soccer/auto_pdf/2012-13/misc_non_event/12-media-almanac.pdf, 16.

APPENDIX I

NATIONAL EFFORTS TO GOVERN WOMEN'S INTERCOLLEGIATE SPORT AND ATHLETICS IN THE UNITED STATES, 1899 – 1982

Date	Event
1899	American Association for the Advancement of Physical Education (AAAPE) forms the Women's Basketball Rules Committee
1903	AAAPE becomes the American Physical Education Association
*1905	The Women's Basketball Rules Committee becomes the National Women's Basketball Committee. (1957), then to the American Association for Health, Physical Education, Recreation and Dance (1975) and is known today as the American Alliance for Health, Physical Education, Recreation and Dance (AAHPERD). The organization maintains is relationship to women's athletic governance efforts and becomes the underpinning organization for the Association for Intercollegiate Athletics for Women until 1982.
*1917	National Women's Basketball Committee becomes the National Committee on Women's Sports

1917	Blanche M. Trilling and student members of the Women's Athletic Association conduct a regional meeting of leaders in women's athletics and organize as the Athletic Conference of American College Women (ACACW), which creates local Women's Athletic Associations to advance strong intramural programs in their universities.
1918	Trilling's meeting meets annually and spreads to a national representation.
1924	National Association of Directors of Physical Education for College Women forms (NADPECW). Membership consists of women who direct physical education programs for women in colleges and universities. Eventually becomes the NAPECW.
*1927	National Committee on Women's Sports of the AAHPERD becomes the Women's Athletic Section (WAS).
*1931	WAS becomes the National Section on Women's Athletics (NSWA).
1933	Trilling's organization, ACACW, becomes the Athletic and Recreation Federation of College Women (ARFCW) whose purpose is to advance the standards established by the NSWA. ARFCW subsequently becomes the American Federation of College Women.
1936	Gladys Palmer at the Ohio State University approaches NSWA to create a national governing body to regulate competitive intercollegiate athletics for women. NSWA does not support a competitive national structure for women.
1938	APEA becomes the American Association for Health, Physical Education and Recreation
1941	Gladys Palmer, Ohio State University, requests that NADPECW and NSWA form a national governing body for women's sport. Both organizations decline the request. NADPECW issues a resolution not to form a national governing body for women's athletics.

1941	Palmer moves forward without national support and launches the first National Collegiate Golf Tournament, July 1941. The event resumes in 1946 after WWII and continues until 1966.
1953	NSWA becomes the National Section for Girls' and Women's Sports (NSGWS). Its purpose expands to all of women's sports, high school and college, still under the APEA umbrella.
*1957	National Section for Girls' and Women's Sports (NSGWS) becomes the Division of Girls and Women's Sports (DGWS). APEA becomes the American Association for Health, Physical Education and Recreation (AAHPER).
1957	DGWS takes the lead to establish the National Joint Committee on Extramural Sports for College Women (NJCESW) is formed. Its purpose is to streamline jurisdictional issues over women's sports. Continues to rebuff the idea of intercollegiate athletics for women.
1965	NJCESW disbands and transfers function to DGWS. New leaders in DGWS change its long-standing position against intercollegiate athletics for women.
1967	DGWS establishes the Commission on Intercollegiate Athletics for Women (CIAW) specifically to create and govern national intercollegiate championships for women.
1972	CIAW becomes a membership organization and transforms into the Association for Intercollegiate Athletics for Women (AIAW).
1974	AAHPER becomes the American Association for Health, Physical Education, Recreation and Dance (AAHPERD).
1979	American Association for Health, Physical Education, Recreation and Dance becomes the American Alliance for Health, Physical Education, Recreation and Dance.
1982	NCAA offers intercollegiate championship for women's basketball and expresses its intent to expand to all of women's sports.

1982   AIAW does not have the financial structure to compete with the NCAA; it disbands. NCAA becomes the governing body for women's intercollegiate sports.

*Mabel Lee, pgs. 246-259

APPENDIX II

PERSONAL INTERVIEWS CONDUCTED BY THE AUTHOR FOR THIS BOOK

1. Betty Ruth Baker, Draper Academic Building, Baylor University, Waco, Texas, June 21, 2012, in her office.

2. Dr. Ted Powers, Professor, June 21, 2012, Marrs McLean Gymnasium, Baylor University, Waco, Texas, in his office.

3. Jody Conradt, Special Assistant, University of Texas Intercollegiate Athletics Offices, Austin, Texas, June 22, 2012, in her office.

4. Sherry Castello, June 24, 2012, Waco, Texas, in her home.

5. Nancy Post, Senior Women's Administrator, Baylor University Athletic Department, June 25, 2012 at the Simpson Building on the Baylor Campus.

6. Mary Tindle, Retired Professor, Baylor University, Waco, Texas, June 25, 2012, in her home.

7. Elizabeth Bianchi, Retired Professor and Swim Coach 1960s through 1979, Baylor University, Waco, Texas, June 25, 2012, in her home.

8. Tom Stanton, Rappoport Foundation, 5400 Bosque Blvd., Suite 245, Waco, Texas, June 2013.

9. David Taylor, Retired, Rappoport Foundation, 5400 Bosque Blvd., Suite 245, Waco, Texas, June 26, 2012.

10. Jeanne Nowlin, Rappoport Foundation, 5400 Bosque Blvd., Suite 245, Waco, Texas, June 26, 2012.

11. Julie Bennett, Director of Athletic Communications, Baylor University Athletic Department, Waco, Texas, June 28, 2012.

12. Paula Young, Director of Game Operations, Ferrell Center, Baylor University, in her office, June 28, 2012.

13. LaRuth Kendrick Gates, telephone Interview, July 2, 2012.

14. Dave Leudtke, Waco Montessori School, Waco, Texas, July 2, 2012.

15. Sonja Hogg, Senior Director, Special Constituencies, Baylor University Development Office, July 2, 2012, Baylor University Student Union.

16. Pam Bowers, telephone interview, July 9, 2012.

17. Dr. Dick Ellis, telephone interview, October 10, 2012.

18. Clyde Hart, Director, Baylor University Track and Field/Cross Country, Ferrell Special Events Center, October 29, 2012.

19. Shirley Poteet, telephone interview, May 17, 2012.

20. Dutch Schroeder, telephone interview, May 21, 2013.

21. Joan Hult, September 22, 2012, Lake Chelan, Washington.

22. Sherry Castello, October 28, 2012, Waco, Texas.

23. Betty Rogers Bryant, June 20, 2012, Floyd Casey Stadium.

24. Al Myers, November 9, 2013, Ft. Worth, Texas.

APPENDIX III

CHARTER MEMBERS—BEARETTE EMBLEM CLUB 1975-1976

BASKETBALL	TRACK AND FIELD
Karen Aulenbacher	Loretta Buxkemper
Leah Box	Kathleen Matusik
Sarah Davis	Becky McClenny
Cathy Hart	Joan Rogers
Judy Kafer	Suzie Snider
Lynnell Pyron	Marsha Talley
Suzie Snider	Christa Womack
Connie Freeman, Mgr.	Cyndi Lyles, Mgr.
SOFTBALL	**VOLLEYBALL**
Marsha Adams	Marsha Adams
Karen Aulenbacher	Cindy Bartlett
Judy Blalock	Barbara Bloomer
Leah Box	Karen Conrads
Sarah Davis	Diane Johnson
Cathy Hart	Charlotte White
Cathy Lee	Cynthia Williams
Karen Moon	Chrissy Kessler, Mgr.
Penny Peschel	
Lynnell Pyron	
Kim Rothfus	
Debbie Watson, Mgr.	

Olga Fallen personal letter to Athletic Director, Jack Patterson, May 6, 1976, The Olga Fallen Collection, Accession 3797, Box 13 or 14, The Texas Collection, Baylor University, Waco, Texas.

THE AUTHOR

DR. NANCY R. GOODLOE

Dr. Nancy Goodloe is a Lady Bear sports fan. Her love of the Baylor women's sports program runs deep and spans five decades.

Goodloe received her bachelor's and master's degree from Baylor University, 1968—1969 and became a member of the Baylor University faculty in the fall 1969. She received her doctorate degree from the University of Oregon in 1978 and returned to the Baylor faculty. She retired from Baylor University as an Emeritus Professor of Health Education in 2000.

As an undergraduate, she was a Baylor Bearette, participating on the basketball, track and field, badminton, and golf teams. From 1969—1976 she split her time between coaching Bearettes in volleyball, track and field, and badminton, assisting Olga Fallen, Women's Athletic Coordinator, and teaching in the Department of Health, Physical Education and Recreation. In the mid-seventies, she brought athletic training services to Baylor's female athletes and trained the first two female athletic trainers at Baylor University.

During her 31-year tenure on the Baylor faculty, Nancy also served as a member of the Women's Athletic Cabinet and the Faculty Athletic Council.

Dr. Goodloe lives in Ellensburg, Washington where she is active as a community volunteer.

CPSIA information can be obtained at www.ICGtesting.com
Printed in the USA
LVOW11s1815040314

376007LV00005B/1130/P